DALTON McGUINTY

DALTON McGUINTY

Making a Difference

DUNDURN
A J. PATRICK BOYER BOOK

TORONTO

Project editor: Dominic Farrell
Copy editor: Jonathan Schmidt
Cover designer: Sarah Beaudin
Interior design: Courtney Horner
Front cover photo: Jenna Muirhead
Back cover photo: Office of the Premier
Printer: Marquis

Library and Archives Canada Cataloguing in Publication

McGuinty, Dalton, 1955-, author
    Dalton McGuinty : making a difference / Dalton McGuinty.

Includes index.
Issued in print and electronic formats.
ISBN 978-1-4597-2957-5 (bound).--ISBN 978-1-4597-2958-2 (pdf).--
ISBN 978-1-4597-2959-9 (epub)

    1. McGuinty, Dalton, 1955-. 2. Ontario--Politics and government--
2003-. 3. Premiers (Canada)--Ontario--Biography. I. Title.

FC3077.1.M44A3 2015   971.3'05092   C2015-900557-4
                                        C2015-900558-2

1 2 3 4 5   19 18 17 16 15

We acknowledge the support of the **Canada Council for the Arts** and the **Ontario Arts Council** for our publishing program. We also acknowledge the financial support of the **Government of Canada** through the **Canada Book Fund** and **Livres Canada Books**, and the **Government of Ontario** through the **Ontario Book Publishing Tax Credit** and the **Ontario Media Development Corporation**.

Care has been taken to trace the ownership of copyright material used in this book. The author and the publisher welcome any information enabling them to rectify any references or credits in subsequent editions.

— *J. Kirk Howard, President*

The publisher is not responsible for websites or their content unless they are owned by the publisher.

Printed and bound in Canada.

VISIT US AT
Dundurn.com | @dundurnpress | Facebook.com/dundurnpress | Pinterest.com/dundurnpress

Dundurn
3 Church Street, Suite 500
Toronto, Ontario, Canada
M5E 1M2

To Terri, Carleen, Dalton Jr., Liam, Connor, and all the McGuintys. And to those everywhere striving to make a difference in the noble enterprise of politics.

The Bullfight Poem

Bullfight critics ranked in rows
Crowd the enormous Plaza full
But only one is there who knows
And he's the man who fights the bull.

— Domingo Ortega
(translation by Robert Graves)

CONTENTS

PROLOGUE
A Rite of Passage

The wedding took place outdoors, in the Gatineau Hills of Quebec, on a crisp and sunny fall day in 2012. It was a simple, elegant ceremony, and as my wife, Terri, and I looked on, I was moved much more than I had expected to be.

It was an event that the whole family had looked forward to for some time. After all, my daughter, Carleen, and her soon-to-be husband, Eric Mysak, had dated for thirteen years. But seeing your first child marry is a powerful rite of passage in the life of any family. It marked the official end of my favourite role in life: provider and caregiver to my children. Our younger children had not yet reached Carleen's stage, of course, but I realized with some paternal sadness that they weren't far behind.

I was learning that the hardest part about raising your kids is that they leave you.

For the first time, I took a long, hard look at my life post-children and discovered a new reference point: its end. I began to consider what to do with the rest of my years. My father had died at sixty-three years of age, only five years older than I was then. I was gripped by a new sobriety, inspired by my realization of how really and truly finite life is. My heart was telling me it was time for a change. That was what I needed. And as I thought about it, my head was telling me change was what my party needed too. I had been my party's leader for sixteen years and premier for over nine. We each needed renewal.

At first, I told very few people of my plans to retire. Of course, Terri could tell something had changed the moment we came home from the wedding. We had been married for thirty-two years and we had dated for seven years before that, so of course she knew. When I told her I was getting out, she threw her arms around me and kissed me. It was the end of an exciting, incredibly rewarding, often demanding, and sometimes painful adventure.

When I broke the news to our children, they were relieved and happy for me. Connor, my youngest, said, "I was starting to wonder when you were going to get out."

My brother Brendan was the next to know. As my closest political confidant, he, too, had noticed a change in me. "I could tell you were thinking about it. You seemed to be somewhere else these days."

Six days after the wedding, I attended the Ontario Liberal Party's annual convention — held that year in my hometown of Ottawa. Party rules required that my leadership be judged. I was overwhelmed when I received the endorsement of 86 percent of the delegates, but it felt strange that weekend, speaking to my Liberal family, one I had gotten to know so well since I had first been elected as the Ottawa South Liberal riding association president twenty-six years earlier, in 1986. As I moved around the hall, shaking hands, making small talk, and, above all, thanking party members for their hard work, I was intent on quietly soaking up as much joy as I could out of the last party function I would attend as leader.

Outside of my family, no group inspired me and sustained me in politics as much as the members of my party. It was the men, women, and youth of the Ontario Liberal Party who had taken a chance on me back in 1996 and made me their leader. After I lost my first election, they stuck with me as I grew into the job, sometimes stumbling but always determined to grow stronger for my party and, eventually, my province. There were many there with whom I wanted to share my decision, but I knew I couldn't. I knew my departure would cause disruption and anxiety, and I was resolved to manage this in the best way possible for my party and Ontarians.

After the party's annual general meeting, I widened the circle of those who knew I was going to step down as party leader and premier, informing my very senior staff, including my chief of staff, David Livingston, and my long-time director and executive assistant, Tracey Sobers, who, more than anybody except Terri, had put up with me for years. My staff were, to a person, relieved and supportive. It had been a long haul for us. Starting from the hard years in Opposition, I had been blessed with hard-working, devoted staff who believed in me and the work we were doing. Together, we quickly began to consider how I might put into place an orderly transition plan.

I decided I would make my decision public on Monday, October 15, by announcing it to my caucus in the presence of the media. I felt I owed it to my colleagues to tell them directly and not through an announcement made only to media. It had been my great honour to work beside my fellow Liberal MPPs since my first election in 1990. They, too, had been supportive of me for over two decades. I had stood on their shoulders as premier. On a number of occasions, including at the time of Ontario's adoption of the harmonized sales tax (HST), they had followed me on policy positions they did not at first welcome. I was grateful for their loyalty to me and their devotion to public service. I received much advice as premier, but the advice I trusted most was the collective wisdom of my caucus. And what I admired most in my colleagues was their decision to get into the arena of politics. Many hoot and holler while others quietly pontificate from the comfort and convenience of the stands, but my colleagues had stepped into the arena and personally confronted the risks found there. I remain inspired by their courage and commitment to public service.

Terri and Brendan joined me in my Queen's Park office late in the afternoon of October 15 as I went over the remarks I had prepared for caucus. I had met earlier with my party president, Yasir Naqvi, to give him the heads-up. I had also communicated with two of my closest colleagues Greg Sorbara and Dwight Duncan. My plan was to keep the circle of those in the know as tight as I could. I didn't want word to get out — not an easy thing to do where this kind of news is concerned. I wanted my caucus colleagues to be the first to hear and I was pleased, for their sake, that I was successful.

As I sat at my desk readying myself for what was to come, Brendan said, "Here, put this on."

It was my father's watch. I was proud to wear it on this occasion. My father, the former MPP for Ottawa South, had never lived to see my political career. And yet it was he, more than anyone else, who shaped it.

Terri and I walked from my second-floor corner office toward the caucus room, located on the same floor. Along the way I looked once more at the many pictures and paintings of former Ontario politicians who, over the past 120 years, had been active participants in the exercise of our democracy. We passed the impressive entrance to the legislative chamber, now quiet. I recalled the excitement and honour I felt on that first day in 1990 when I had taken my seat on the Opposition benches — the last seat in the last row. I would move to the front row as the newly elected leader of my party in 1996. It would take me seven more years to travel the twenty feet separating the leader of the Opposition's chair from the premier's.

As we approached the caucus room, I could see a few members of the Queen's Park press gallery hurriedly making their way ahead of us. The reporters gathered there would be wondering why I had asked them to be present.

When I walked into the caucus room, Terri left my side and took a seat in the front row. Although she left my side then, on neither this occasion nor any of the thousands of others, big and small, was Terri ever just an observer. Politics was never her first choice, which made Terri's unfailing support for me as I relentlessly pursued my passion to make a difference all the more astounding. And humbling. We had achieved much together in politics, but our life's most important work was our family. As you can guess, Terri did the lion's share of this work. She is the biggest reason why our four children, Carleen, Dalton Jr., Liam, and Connor lead happy, fulfilled lives. I am proud of my political achievements but my pride in those will always be eclipsed by the pride I feel for my children.

My colleagues were seated in the neat rows of chairs that had been arranged for my announcement. They could tell something was up. For one thing, the meeting had been called on short notice, and the time of the meeting, six o'clock, was very unusual. For another, the media were present inside our caucus room sanctuary, also an unusual occurrence.

I had delivered remarks to my colleagues on hundreds of occasions in the past. This time, while the subject was very different, I felt calm. I had no misgivings. It was time. I felt confident I had made a difference. Ontarians were benefitting from demonstrably better health care and education, a healthier environment, and a growing, prosperous economy. I had laid a solid foundation of progress upon which my successor could build. I began my remarks:

> Sixteen years ago, when I was elected leader of our party, the Ontario Liberals had won exactly one election in fifty years. We couldn't do anything to help Ontarians because we couldn't win an election. That's changed. We've won three elections in a row. But more important is what those election wins have allowed us to do.
>
> In every area that matters most to families — their schools, their health care, their environment, and their economy — we've made huge progress. We've gone from struggling schools to the best schools in the English-speaking world, from Canada's longest health-care wait times to the shortest, from dirty air to clean air, and we now have the toughest drinking water standards anywhere.
>
> When it comes to the economy, we've made our workforce one of the world's strongest and our taxes very competitive. We're renewing our infrastructure and we keep creating jobs. We've positioned Ontario for decades of success.
>
> Our government hasn't been perfect. But when it comes to the big things that families count on us to get right — schools, health care, the environment, and the economy — we've gotten it right every time.... As the party and government of relentless progress, we're always looking for new ideas and ways to renew ourselves. And I've concluded this is the right time for Ontario's next Liberal premier and our next set of ideas to lead our province forward.... I thank you for the honour of serving as your leader and your premier ... in Ontario, the greatest province in the best country in the world.

As I spoke, I could see shock and disbelief in the eyes of my colleagues. They hadn't seen it coming. But they are pros, and they quickly adjusted to their new reality and steeled themselves for the flurry of party activity I had just unleashed. They kindly gave me a standing ovation and several took turns saying nice things about me. I may have been reading too much into their expressions, but I thought I could already see the wheels turning in some aspiring leadership candidates. I felt comforted by that. It confirmed for me that it was time for me to go, and I had confidence in the pool of talent from which my successor would be chosen.

CHAPTER ONE
Sticking Together

I was born in Ottawa in 1955, the third child and first son in the family. I was named Dalton James Patrick McGuinty but I would be known as Jamie to my family. There were seven more children to follow. Both my parents worked — my mother, Elizabeth (friends and family call her Betty), was a nurse, and my father, Dalton Sr., was a professor of English. My parents had so much on their hands, with all those kids to be looked after, that I have often joked I had to change my own diapers.

I grew up fast, having to take on some of the responsibility for my younger siblings. I was expected to help my parents at an early age, doing everything from cleaning the bathroom to hanging up clothes, from vacuuming the floor to washing the dishes and making school lunches. As one of the oldest — and especially as the oldest of the six boys — my parents expected me to set a good example, which I usually managed to do. I began to take it upon myself to make sure that homework was done, that lunches were made, and that everyone's teeth had been brushed. In winter, there was the driveway to be shovelled; in summer, the grass to be cut. But I never felt put upon. I thoroughly enjoyed my childhood and began to crave responsibility, although my siblings were a little less enthusiastic about the role I embraced. I'm sure they sometimes saw me as bossy. Little did I know that dealing with all their personalities and finding a way to get the work done was great training for my political responsibilities to come.

I do recall feeling some resentment as a teenager when I realized that I had less freedom than most of my friends. And it seemed to me I was forever "breaking in" my parents for the benefit of my younger siblings. If I had to be home by eight o'clock, they were allowed to be home by nine. Later on, if I came home with beer on my breath, there was hell to pay. My brothers got away with "Get to bed and sleep it off." And as for discipline, over time and with each successive child, my parents transitioned from occasional spankings and scoldings to gentle reprimands and reasoning. I kid my younger brothers and sisters that they owe me much for the way I trained our parents to their benefit.

One real perk that I enjoyed as the oldest boy was new clothes, although sometimes an older male cousin's castoffs inconveniently worked their way into our household. My brothers had little choice but to wear my hand-me-downs. This led to my mother chastising me for "putting holes in your brothers' pants." My mother taught us how to wash, iron, sew, and take good care of our clothes. To this day, Terri laughs at me for the great care I give them, and she won't even try to hang up my pants for me.

Although a lot was expected of me growing up, our lives were so busy I didn't have much time to feel sorry for myself. And as I got older, I began to thoroughly enjoy all the challenges we took on as a big family and the role I played in that.

———————

When I was first brought home from the hospital as a newborn, we moved in with my dad's mother in the west end of Ottawa for several months until my parents were able to afford their first home. Living with my grandmother during those first few months of my life sowed the seeds of my very special relationship with her. My grandmother, Honorah Foley, was married at sixteen to my grandfather, Charles McGuinty, who was thirty-two. From all accounts, Charlie never knew what hit him. My grandmother was a force to be reckoned with and she called the shots. My grandfather worked as a night watchman and my grandmother held a variety of jobs to help make ends meet, including as a baker at Ottawa's Murphy-Gamble department store and a housekeeper in the Immaculate Heart of Mary Church rectory. She also turned their home into a rooming house for many years.

My grandmother had a short fuse and a hot temper. She enjoyed her grandchildren in small doses — with one exception: me. I was her favourite, the first-born son of her youngest son, who was the apple of her eye. My father was the only one of her children who went on to university. And I was the only grandson that spent his earliest days with her. That sealed the deal.

As I grew up in the busy McGuinty household, I looked forward to the occasional weekend spent alone with my grandmother. My dad would ask, "How about it, Mick?" (That was my parents' nickname for me.) "Do you want to spend the weekend at Granny's?" I always jumped at these opportunities to be spoiled and doted on, or to experience "unconditional love," as I would say, following the weekends, to tease my mother. I would quickly pack my things — a toothbrush and one pair each of clean underwear and socks — in a brown paper grocery bag.

One evening, unbeknownst to me, I was being taken to my grandmother's by my dad as a peace offering. I was seven or eight years old. The two of them had had an argument of some kind and I wouldn't be at all surprised if my dad had started it because he enjoyed teasing his mother just to get a rise out of her. As I stood outside the screen door beside my father, there was a rapid-fire exchange of heated words between him and my grandmother, who more than stood her ground on the other side of the door. My father brought things to a head by saying, "So, you don't want him?"

My grandmother shot back, "No, I don't!"

I was crushed. I made my way to the car only to hear my grandmother shout, "Get over here, Jim!" (Her name for me.) She took me in her arms, fired a few more unpleasantries at my father, and slammed the door shut. Once again, I had my loving grandmother all to myself.

When I was a few months old, my parents bought a two-storey fixer-upper in Kirk's Ferry, a tiny community on the Quebec side of the Ottawa River, where we lived until I was four. Unfortunately, the house had rats in the basement. Years later, my mother told me how, in a creative effort to rid our home of the rats, my dad hooked up a hose to the exhaust of the car and fed it into the house. The only problem was that I was asleep in my bed at the time. That was the end of the rats, but fortunately not of me; luckily my father remembered I was in my bed and came to my rescue.

My dad was an English professor at the University of Ottawa. Raising ten kids meant there was pressure for extra income, so in addition to the usual course load, he taught night school and summer school in places near Ottawa like Hawkesbury and Pembroke. So he was away a lot. Which again meant I had to step up and pitch in. When I was very young in our Quebec home, we had a big dog, mostly German shepherd, called Skip, who was supposed to protect us during my dad's absence. We got rid of Skip after he bit me. So much for protection.

My mom had trained as a registered nurse, and whenever she could she would go back to work, including during our days in Kirk's Ferry. In Ottawa, she worked at the old Civic and Riverside hospitals, but for most of her nursing career, she was at the Children's Hospital of Eastern Ontario.

In 1959, when I was four, we moved into a two-storey, four-bedroom house in Alta Vista, an Ottawa suburb (where Terri and I later made our own home). It turned out our Latvian-Canadian neighbour was a carpenter. My parents soon put Mr. Krumbergs to work building us another bedroom and bathroom. We kids were fascinated by the inscrutable Mr. Krumbergs, with his heavy accent and shiny tools. He took a shine to my brother David ("the Davis," he called him) and allowed him to use his best tools while I, "the Jeemmy," was relegated to cleanup duty.

Even with the extra space added to our home, I always shared a room with at least one of my brothers. On two occasions, in two separate homes, we were four boys in a room. (In speeches later on I always got a good laugh by joking that I never slept alone until I was married.) I didn't mind the crowd. It made for more horsing around. Sometimes, being cooped up and getting on each other's nerves led to a fight. Disagreements with my brothers and sisters were my first introduction to politics. Often, we would settle our differences with a vote. Being the older or stronger carried only so much weight. You had to woo your supporters, and bribery was strongly encouraged. A reward for supporting my position could even include a choice of some prize piece of junk from my junk drawer, which included whatever interesting paraphernalia I could get my hands on that my mother would allow into our home. My all-time favourite was an old electric razor that was just waiting to be dismantled to see what its insides looked like. My treasures also included old wallets, colourful tin containers, and some old coins. I didn't bother to wash the coins but I did discover a way to get them really clean.

One day when I was about ten years old I was upset to discover that three old coins I had left on the dresser in my bedroom had disappeared. My mother, wise as always, quickly concluded that my little brother, whose crib was beside the dresser, had swallowed the coins. She said we had to wait for them to show up in Michael's diaper. I was unhappy with the unbidden journey my coins were on but delighted when they emerged shiny as new! Who knew? I thought about repeating this process with other old coins, but one look from my mother convinced me otherwise.

While we kids had developed our own form of democracy at home, it was a different story when it came to my dad. He liked to say "a family is not a democracy but a benevolent dictatorship." And he was very good at making us toe the line. My dad was a big man at six feet, four inches, 230 pounds, and when he let out a roar, we quickly fell into line. Neighbouring parents marvelled at how well behaved the McGuinty brood was. What they didn't know was that my mother had eyes in the back of her head, that her wooden spoon wasn't just for cooking, and that my father could drive our station wagon on a busy highway and comfortably locate a child in the third seat at the same time.

And speaking of the perils of station-wagon life for a big family, on a few occasions my dad trapped a child in the rear window when he raised the automatic window while driving. The imprisoned child would let out a howl and my father would lower the window while offering his usual words of sympathy: "I told you to keep your arms and legs inside the car."

My dad was larger than life, gregarious, and warm. He was a complicated guy. He was as comfortable reciting Romantic poetry as he was wielding a chainsaw. Dad could be impetuous and he was always creative. He painted his shoes white (with house paint) and called them his "Pat Boone shoes." When the pressurized can of Quick Start he sprayed into our frozen car-engine carburetor ran out, he opened up the bottom with a can opener to get out the last few drops while I scurried for cover from an explosion that never came.

When I asked him why he always threw out the assembly instructions for new appliances or toys, his stock response was, "Makes it more of a challenge." That meant I later had to take up the task of reassembly in order to make use of the leftover pieces. And Dad loved Johnny Cash, whom he saw as a cowboy-poet best heard blasting at an embarrassingly high volume from his truck, which was equipped with an eight-track tape player boosted by extra speakers. When he played his beloved Johnny Cash near my school or in our driveway, I immediately made myself scarce. Johnny Cash was just not cool. Of course, now that my dad has passed away, I love Johnny Cash. He really was a poet … and he reminds me of my father.

My dad didn't have much of a father figure in his own life. He rarely talked about his father, who died before I was born. But, clearly, his mother ran the show. This meant my own dad was figuring out how to be a father on the fly. Lucky for us, he was motivated by an overwhelming desire and energy to keep giving of himself to us. This meant forever teaching, motivating, and loving us. Sometimes in his own gruff way.

If he became angry, though, he would let out a roar. After dinner, which we always had together as a family, he liked to rest, and anything that disturbed that rest inspired an animated response. He would recline in his La-Z-Boy chair, put a newspaper over his face, and take a nap before going off to teach a night course. Meanwhile, we kids would all be on our sugar highs from dessert — usually vanilla ice cream by the bucket — and would be running around like idiots. At some point, if the sound level rose too high, Dad would shout and scare the bejesus out of all of us.

My father was a great raconteur. He enjoyed an audience and it enjoyed him. He was entertaining and, when he wanted to be, profound. My mother was more relaxed socially. While my dad felt the need to hold forth, my mom was at ease and a better listener. My dad was more of a hard-liner on the positions he took and the issues he confronted in life. He taught me the power and purpose of principle. My mom was more accommodating and patient in her way. She taught me how to understand people. You could say my dad taught me what to do and my mom taught me how to do it. And there is no doubt I caught the political bug from my dad.

My father was very interested in politics and he later became an MPP, but he had a special interest in American politics. He was a big fan of John

F. Kennedy. In 1960, when Kennedy became the first Catholic president of the United States — a president of Irish descent, to boot — his portrait quickly joined the revered St. Thomas More's on our living room wall.

My father had record albums of Kennedy's speeches and he would play them on our hi-fi. I recall how we would clamber over our giant of a dad like Lilliputians as he lay on the rug, lost in the words and thoughts of JFK. I marvelled at how words could so move him. My dad often talked about how powerful language can be. When I was nine, he bought me two books about Kennedy (*PT 109* and *JFK: From Boyhood to Whitehouse*). He encouraged all of us to read. Thanks to my father, I was reading Dickens and Melville before I was twelve. And he took me to university productions of Shakespeare.

My dad loved to sermonize on the issues of the day at the dinner table. He had lots of opinions on lots of people and policies. It was interesting but not that exciting … until we joined a campaign team in 1967 in support of a local Liberal candidate, Joe McDonald. The McGuinty brood was a welcome sight as we showed up at the campaign office on a weekend morning. We were polite and hard-working and enjoyed putting up signs or delivering pamphlets. Front-line politics was a lot more exciting for me than listening to my dad pontificate. And besides, there was free food.

While my dad's earliest days were spent in the Ottawa Valley, my mom grew up in a single-parent francophone family in Timmins, a northern Ontario community. She moved to Ottawa to complete her nursing studies and became a flight attendant for Trans-Canada Air Lines, the predecessor to Air Canada. My dad would joke that my mom's career at TCA was brought to an abrupt halt when she showed a passenger looking for the washroom to the wrong door. The truth is, she met my dad, he was instantly smitten, he pursued her, and they fell in love.

My mom was the rock on which our family was built. She had the final say on all child-rearing issues. When we were looking for permission for something, it was well understood that we would try Dad out first. If it involved anything controversial, he was quick to deflect us with a "check with your mother." My mother was the one who laid down the law, a law that was rarely broken by any of us, including my father. My dad had lots of what we kids thought were great ideas (he once wanted to buy a hovercraft), but my mom wisely cut him off at the pass. We went to French schools because my mother insisted, just as she insisted we get part-time jobs in high school, when we were expected to start paying "rent" (twenty dollars a month).

If my dad used a broad brush in life, my mom was more of a detail person. She made sure that any work we did in life, and certainly in her domain, was not only done but done well. This included using a toothbrush to scrub the floor at the base of the toilet as part and parcel of any genuine effort to clean a bathroom.

If my parents differed in their temperaments, one thing they had in common was the fact that they were both strong Catholics. My father, in particular, was quite devout. He would not drive by a church without making the sign of the cross. And because the Church then demanded it, we would not eat meat on Fridays or eat three hours before communion. We observed Lent, which usually meant forgoing dessert. My experience with my own faith has been tempered over time by what I have learned from Ontario's rich diversity of cultures and faiths. This has developed in me a great appreciation for the value of all the great faiths, which, at their core, teach love and compassion.

My parents had high expectations for their children — not so much in terms of what we accomplished as in terms of how we got there. They expected us to work hard, be true to ourselves, and do the right thing. Neither was effusive with praise for their children, preferring instead a quiet pride.

At the twentieth-anniversary celebration of my time in politics, a reporter said to my mother, "You must be proud of your son." My mother replied matter-of-factly, "I'm proud of all my children." She meant that while politics and a public life were what her eldest son had chosen, what really counted was doing your best at whatever you did. My mom was always good at keeping me grounded. As premier, I phoned her a few times every week. This was not satisfactory. On one call she noted that Pierre Trudeau phoned his mother every day. "And he was a prime minister!" I took the hint and, ever since, I have tried to call my mother every day.

Years later, after my dad had passed away and my mother was living alone, she fell down some stairs and broke her hip. Fortunately, my sister was with her at the time. My mother had her get me on the phone. As she lay in pain on her back on the floor, she asked me if I could arrange to have an unmarked ambulance pick her up because she didn't want the neighbours to know she had fallen and hurt herself. She didn't want them to think she was old. I told my mom that was something I couldn't do for her, that she would have to use a regular ambulance like everybody else. She was silent for a moment. Then she asked my sister Anne-Marie for some lipstick. It was that quiet pride again, but this time it had to do with her own sense of dignity too.

It goes without saying that our parents shape us. But so do our siblings. And it would be hard to exaggerate the influence for good my brothers and sisters had on me during our early years together. While still young, they each taught me something different, something I have tried to incorporate into my own character.

Joyce taught me patience.

Liseanne taught me independence.

Dylan taught me hard work.

Patrick taught me good humour.

David taught me leadership.

Michael taught me adventure.

Anne-Marie taught me perseverance.

Brendan taught me to go for it.

Noralyn taught me courage.

My oldest sister, Joyce, was a special gift to us. She came to live with us as a young teenager. I cannot remember a time when she was not part of our family. She had been given up by her own parents and had been introduced to mine by my maternal grandmother. My parents immediately decided Joyce was wonderful and invited her to live with us. Lucky for us, Joyce agreed. She came into our home and supplied us with much love, patience, understanding, and good example. Many years later, when I was articling after law school, I asked my parents if I could bring an application in court to have them formally adopt Joyce, who was by then in her thirties. They immediately agreed. I could not have been more proud to play a role in finally officially recognizing what needed no recognition at home: Joyce was our sister.

I believe that life's most important lessons are learned at home, while we are still young. I can always recall my father looking into our faces at the dinner table and telling us that we had to stand up for each other, that "none of us is as smart or as strong as all of us together." I heard my dad's voice many times in my head later on when I led my party and my province, and that expression found its way into many of my speeches.

The importance of sticking together was brought home to us as a family on a very rare (in fact, only) trip to Florida. There were nine of us at the time (the two youngest hadn't been born yet) and we all piled into a Ford station wagon — unconstrained by today's seat belt laws — for the long trip. My oldest sister, Joyce, flew down.

My parents told us we were going to Florida for Christmas instead of Santa coming. You can tell this was never put to a vote. (As soon as we got to a beach in Florida, after our fifteen-hundred-mile car ride, my brother Patrick complained, "It's too hot!") By the time we got to Georgia, we had tired of my mother's monotonous head counts, so at the next stop we all just rushed out of the gas-station washroom back into the car. It was about fifty miles later that my mother asked, "Where's your brother Michael?" We all thought Michael was in the front of the car with our parents. But he wasn't. So my dad hit the brakes and we drove back to the gas station.

We found our four-year-old brother, no worse for wear, chatting up two big gas-station attendants who, upon seeing us, said, "We knew you would come back for him."

After that experience we laughed a lot about losing Michael, but we never forgot the wisdom in my dad's advice to stick together and look out for each other. As premier, I've told this story in the United States to impress upon our American cousins that the strength of our relationship is built not so much upon our two leaders as upon the relationships forged between ordinary Canadians and Americans. Whenever I think of my personal relationship with the United States, I cannot help but think of the kindness of the two strangers who watched over my little brother until we returned for him.

———————

As if we didn't have enough frenetic activity in our household with all those people (in the summer my dad would say, "It's not the heat, it's the humanity"), we also had two dogs. Gulliver had befriended us at our Quebec cottage. We took him home with us, but we never really owned him. He ran away on several occasions, always in search of a better standard of living. He slept in the garage with Shane, our Irish setter. My mom was never a big fan of dogs, but she especially disliked Shane. "He's big, Irish, and doesn't listen," she said in a thinly veiled reference to her husband. She liked to call my dad, *tête de pioche*, which, loosely translated, means pigheaded in Quebecois French. My dad, on the other hand, delighted in calling my mother "the barracuda."

We thought our dogs were goners when, one Christmas Eve while we were all in church, Gulliver and Shane got into the two dozen *tourtières* ("tortures" as my father called them because of their effect on his digestive tract), that my mother had carefully prepared and placed on top of the garage freezer. But the dogs survived both the tourtières and my mother.

With ten kids to feed, my mother worked when she could, often the evening or night shift, and my father supplemented his professor's salary by teaching evening courses in communities outside of Ottawa, an hour or more from our home.

Given our family's limited budget, my mother was a miracle worker. Lunches were invariably peanut butter on dry brown bread, which made us McGuinty kids cast our envious eyes over other school lunches that were not only moist but that might even contain meat. One of our regular trips with my dad when we were young was to the Morrison Lamothe bakery, an Ottawa institution. We would load up on day-old bread, buying five dozen loaves headed for one of our two big freezers. Meals at home were simple and hearty, with lots of meat and potatoes, spaghetti, and bread. In the early years, my mom would serve liver ("Eat it! It's good for you!"), or, on occasion, a complete chub of baloney, nicely scored, decorated with pineapple and cloves, and baked in the oven. Breakfast, made by my father, was usually porridge — something we escaped on weekends when we had puffed wheat from pillow-sized plastic bags. My mother kept the Corn

Flakes under her bed to ration out as a treat. Desserts after dinner often consisted of ice cream from a two-gallon plastic container. After my little brother Patrick repeatedly volunteered to return the container of leftover ice cream to our industrial-sized freezer in the basement, we began to suspect him of foul play. Sure enough, when we frisked him, we found a spoon in his back pocket.

To help the family finances, my father not only worked extra jobs, he also fostered a sense of entrepreneurship in the family, something unusual for an academic. In addition to his studies at Colgate University and the University of Ottawa, he had been enrolled in the Harvard Business School before deciding literature and teaching were his true passion. He may have quit his business studies, but he never quit his lifelong interest in entrepreneurship. He was the teacher and we, his children, had become his students. Our family's entrepreneurship began modestly with enterprises like babysitting, grass-cutting, and selling firewood and manure. (Terri jokes that my involvement in sales of the latter was her first inkling that I was headed for politics.) We also sold fruits and vegetables from a boat on a lake.

As we built up a head of steam, my dad bought houses that were fixer-uppers. My brothers and I did our part by helping with the renovations, tearing stuff down, patching, painting, and cleaning. Next, we learned how to manage some income properties as my father bought a few duplexes. The family enterprises combined with my parents' hard work outside the home, paid real dividends. We were able to buy a nice new home for ourselves. Of course, it needed more bedrooms, and the brilliant Mr. Krumbergs was called upon once again and he built us another bedroom and bathroom in the basement. That's when the McGuinty enterprise made a big jump by starting up a summer camp.

In 1971 my father bought a cottage for us in the Gatineau Hills of Quebec. I loved the time I spent there. Apart from the huge amount of time and effort required to cut grass on the five-acre property, it was a great place to relax, with lots of space to run around. But that relaxation was not to last long. Relaxation was not the McGuinty family way. In short order, my dad borrowed money to buy two adjoining properties, including forty acres of white pine forest, to start a summer camp. My parents were forever intent on keeping us close and teaching us responsibility, and Erindale Acres, the name of the summer camp we started from scratch and ran for eight years, was our biggest family commitment outside of politics.

I'll never forget being gathered around the dinner table when our parents broke the news. I was informed that I would be teaching sailing.

"I have never sailed anything in my life," I protested.

"Take a lesson," my dad said. (It was yet another piece of practical wisdom I learned from my father that I would embrace in my own career: we can always accomplish so much more than we think.)

According to my father, Dylan would be teaching canoeing. His reaction, the same as mine, produced the same response: "Take a lesson." And so it went around the table.

I did take several sailing lessons. In the end, I taught sailing and waterskiing; my siblings taught horseback riding, canoeing, archery, arts and crafts, swimming, out-tripping, and a host of other activities to fifty children (at our peak) in each of four two-week sessions. One of the things I learned from my father through our summer camp experience and so many other family adventures was that just because you have never done something before doesn't mean you can't learn how to do it and do it well.

Working under the direction of Mr. Krumbergs, we began by digging outhouse holes and then building the outhouses. From this we graduated to building picnic tables. Then we built three sleeping cabins, two tent platforms, several docks, and, eventually, a house.

There was some trial and error involved in the minor projects where Mr. Krumbergs gave us a free hand. My brothers and I built an outdoor riding ring, digging the many holes needed for the posts, to which we nailed wooden rails. Our activity was the subject of some bemusement by a local farmer who stopped to observe us from a distance. It was only when our mounted campers were knocking their knees against the posts on the inside of the ring did it occur to us that we had installed the rails on the wrong side of the posts. So we took the rails down and hammered them to the inside of the riding ring. Live and learn. I would do lots of living and learning in politics, an environment where there were many more observers than one good-natured farmer.

One time, when my father and I were alone at the camp, he decided we were going to build horse trails through our densely wooded forest. This meant chopping the lower limbs off individual trees to a height of eight feet with an axe. As I braced myself, axe in hand, facing what I considered an impossibly huge undertaking, I grumbled that there were thousands of trees, each with dozens of branches to be limbed. My father just took a swing with his axe and chopped off one limb.

"The best way to begin is to begin," he said.

And so we began. And we got the job done. It took a lot of time and a lot of work. But we got it done. This lesson would serve me very well later on when many around me were of the view that we were taking on challenges that were too big and too risky.

Besides building the camp, my siblings and I worked there as counsellors for eight summers. At its peak, the camp had a staff of twenty, including my future wife, Terri, and my cousin, Mark Kennedy, renowned in my family today as a great journalist and back then as someone with a high-tolerance level for crazy McGuinty work schemes. My father was the groundskeeper, my mother was the nurse, and by the age of twenty I had grown into the job of camp director. We ran the camp the way we did things at home. With a dozen people at home, it would have been madness if everyone just did their own thing. So we were each given some responsibilities — responsibilities that challenged us. The same was true for campers at our camp. Their parents really enjoyed that aspect of it.

I remember a young camper who complained to his father at the end of a two-week session costing $250 (a lot of money back in the 1970s) that, despite the cost, every morning he and his fellow campers were expected to ready their bunks and sleeping cabins for inspection. Worse, after meals campers were required to wash their own dishes. Swimming lessons were mandatory, rain or shine. No exceptions. The father — a military man with a stern manner — asked me if this was true. Sheepishly, I admitted it was. I thought I would be reprimanded. "I see," he said, and immediately signed his son up for a second two-week session.

———————

The more I look back on my childhood, the more amazed I am by my parents. In politics, people often ask you about your greatest influences. They expect you will rattle off the names of great figures in history or even more recent times. I always say my greatest influences and my greatest source of inspiration were my parents. They brought energy, resourcefulness, and good humour to everything they took on. They taught me the importance of family and community service. They impressed upon me the value of hard work, honesty, and the joy of finding ways to make a difference for others. Most important in terms of my political career, my parents taught me responsibility and that I should be eager to take things on. The energy they poured into raising us, the sacrifices they made for us, and the love and support they gave to us were nothing short of astonishing. Knowing first-hand how hard my parents worked while always managing to put family first has made an indelible mark on me. Raising my own family with Terri, and watching devoted parents everywhere dedicate themselves to their children, has impressed upon me the power of this intergenerational commitment. I believe this has been the foundation for human progress since the dawn of humanity. It is a timeless narrative: the older generation commits to building a safer, happier world for the next generation; that generation, in turn, commits to the next. We all participate in this important work by loving our kids and giving them our best.

CHAPTER TWO
My Own Way

While I learned many valuable lessons at home, I also benefitted from a strong public education. I attended a French Catholic elementary school in Ottawa. My mother came from a francophone family, and my father was a big proponent of bilingualism. Since I had spent my early years speaking mostly English at home, I found French a little difficult at first. I can recall not knowing how to ask to go to the washroom in kindergarten and wetting my grey flannel shorts as we sat in a circle on the floor. I insisted the liquid was water, but an unhelpful school chum put his nose to the floor and grandly announced to the class, "Ce n'est pas l'eau. C'est pipi!" But I soon became immersed in the French language and came to love the Franco-Ontarian culture. In the schoolyard, it was always a mix of French and English, which was a constant source of consternation for the principal and teachers. Their challenge was to create a preserve of francophone learning in a threatening jungle of anglophone culture. I have come to greatly admire the relentless efforts of francophone parents, educators, and others in the community to preserve their language and culture. And I believe the reason Ontario's French-language schools consistently outperform their English counterparts is because the former take on a greater responsibility than teaching the regular subjects one finds in school curricula. They are also entrusted with the defence and preservation of the francophone culture, a powerful organizing mission. Attending a French school and getting to know my classmates in their homes gave me a taste of what it is like to belong to a minority. Our school's shop classroom was shared with a nearby English school, and some of the anglophone kids would call us names — "frogs" and that kind of stuff. It was an important formative experience that has made me sympathetic to the challenges faced by Franco-Ontarians. It also taught me about minorities generally and the challenges they face in preserving their sense of identity.

After elementary school, I attended St. Patrick's, an English Catholic school on Heron Road in the Alta Vista neighbourhood. It was an all-boys school and a lot of the teachers were priests. By today's standards, it was quite strict; ties and jackets were mandatory. But it was also a lot of fun.

I knew very few of the other students in grade nine. Most of my francophone pals from elementary school had gone to French high schools. But I soon made new friends.

I was a low-key guy in high school. I did not stand out in any way, either academically or athletically. I was a B-plus student. My best subjects were English, biology, chemistry, and physics.

I played volleyball and basketball for the school teams, but only for one year, as I then took on a part-time job after school cleaning the wooden butcher blocks and the meat locker at the local A&P. It was a messy job, but it gave me the opportunity to tip off my mom and dad when bread or other stuff was put on sale.

There were the usual coming-of-age events. I had my first beer in a field near St. Pat's after a school dance. I became very interested in cars, because all the cool guys seemed to have them and I was envious of the freedom their cars gave them. Instead of a car and freedom, I had nine siblings and our summer camp. I called it the "work camp." As soon as the snow melted, we were up there every weekend. My parents considered it one of their responsibilities to exhaust their children so that we didn't have any energy left to get into mischief. They were very successful in that regard.

Outwardly, at least, I appeared confident to others. I wasn't easily pulled off task. I made sure to get my homework done. I kept pretty quiet but I very much enjoyed the antics of my classmates. My most rebellious act consisted of going out one evening for my prom and not coming back for two days. When I finally came home very late that second night and rang the doorbell to get into the house, my dad was awake, waiting up for me. He drew back the curtain on the side window by the door, assured himself that it was me and that I was no worse for the wear, and then promptly turned off the outside light and went upstairs to bed. I was out in the cold, literally. I tried the other doors and windows, but everything was locked up "tighter than a cow's ass in fly time" — one of my dad's favourite Ottawa Valley expressions.

Not even the car was unlocked.

So I walked the streets for six hours. By this time the sun was up and I figured one of the little ones would be awake. Fortunately, Brendan was up and allowed me access to my home and bed.

After my grade twelve year, St. Patrick's closed its doors. This was in the days before Premier Bill Davis extended full funding to Catholic high schools. Parents of students in grades ten to thirteen had to pay tuition fees. But those fees were insufficient to keep the school doors open. So for grade thirteen, I had to transfer to another school, St. Thomas More, which was co-ed. It was there that I met Terri Taylor.

I was dating other girls, but Terri had caught my eye. She was beautiful and kind, an irresistible combination. On one occasion as our class was walking outside, returning from an off-campus visit, I caught her looking back at me. Just for an instant. But that was enough for me. It was the signal. At least that's how I chose to interpret it.

A few days later, I approached Terri in the lunchroom. The best I could come up with was, "Can you lend me a nickel for the vending machine?" Lame, I know. But it worked. We struck up a conversation.

At her surprise birthday party a few days later, I gave her the latest Elton John album, *Goodbye Yellow Brick Road*. It was very hot in 1973. (Thirty-five years later we would both be thrilled to meet Elton John when he came to Toronto as an investor in a film production studio. Later that evening we were lucky enough to meet up with him backstage before his concert.)

We began dating steadily after that, and we have never looked back. I recall our first date very well. I picked Terri up in the family station wagon. Definitely not cool. Her dad gave me the once-over and told me to have his daughter home by midnight. It was a very cold Saturday evening in January in Ottawa. I wore my Converse basketball shoes, jeans, a light shirt, and a jean jacket. *Very* cool. Literally. Terri was more sensibly attired in a ski jacket. We went to a pub downtown, ordered drinks, and made small talk while local jazz pianist Gloves McGinty (different spelling; no relation) serenaded the room. The crowd was older and we didn't really fit in. It was hardly the most romantic environment but we didn't care. We were both smitten.

We enjoyed outdoor activities. In winter we skated on the Rideau Canal and skied in the Gatineau Hills. In summer, we worked together at my family's summer camp. In the fall, we worked as bike patrols on the Ottawa bike paths.

Terri was an instant hit with my family, which was important to me. Her sunny ways, kindness, and love of children made her a natural in my home. People sometimes ask about the secret to our relationship, which has been going strong for more than forty years now. My stock answer used to be that: a relationship takes a lot of work and you have to keep investing in it. And that is true enough. Over time, however, I have come to adopt Terri's much wiser response: we've always been in love.

John Boyd, a long-time friend and the president of my political riding association, once told a reporter, "Dalton would be lost without Terri." That took me by surprise. I had always thought of myself as determined, disciplined, and well-suited to meeting life's challenges. But the truth is more complicated. I have self-doubts and misgivings; on occasion I lose perspective or lack insight. It's Terri who keeps me balanced, self-aware, and happy. In or out of politics, I have never wrestled with any tough issue without seeking — and benefitting from — Terri's insight. She knows me better than I know myself. When I think of all the personal sacrifices she made for my political career — all the time she spent alone raising our children, all the events she attended with me, all the Canadian and overseas travel she did with me, all the energy and attention she devoted to me when I needed support or constructive criticism, all the time I stole from her own career, and on and on — I am humbled. I have been thanked by many along the way, and I can never adequately acknowledge just how absolutely essential Terri has been in building whatever successes I have achieved for Ontarians. I really *would* be lost without her. And, as we shall see, not having Terri by my side in my first campaign for the leadership of my party would prove to be a big mistake.

While dating, I discovered Terri's household was a treasure trove of foods, including steak superbly barbecued by her dad on Saturday evenings, and lemon pie, my favourite, exquisitely crafted by her mom. And the beer was cheap. We would stuff Terri's big purse with bottles of her dad's beer and take it with us when we went out to a bar. Once there, I would order one beer, the same brand as her dad's, and then keep replacing the empty one with a full one from her purse. Our waitress was always amazed at how I could nurse one beer for an entire evening.

I am very grateful for all the love and support I have received over the years from Terri's parents, Ed and Marion Taylor; her three brothers, Tim, Ted, and Tony; and their respective families. It was one thing to welcome a son-in-law into the family. It was quite another to keep the welcome warm when I became premier and they had to endure all the associated ribbing and criticism.

After graduating from high school in 1974, I entered the pre-med program at the University of Ottawa. I liked the program because half the courses were arts and the other sciences, so I didn't have to specialize in one area or the other. However, after a couple of years in Ottawa, I decided to transfer to McMaster University in Hamilton. One of my motives for transferring out of town was just to get away. I was still living at home and playing the role of responsible big brother. It was time to move out.

McMaster had a medical program that was way ahead of its time. Founded by the late John Evans, a man I later learned first-hand was as kind as he was brilliant, the program was grounded in problem-based learning. This approach has since been adopted by many schools around the world.

When I transferred to McMaster, however, it did not have a pre-med program as such, so I had to transfer into a science program, biology.

I spent two years at McMaster, worked very hard, volunteered at the local hospital, and emerged with a bachelor of science degree. I did not get into medical school. The application process was very competitive then, as it is now. I was pretty disappointed. That left me with two options: do some graduate work to boost my marks and apply again to medical school, or move on to something else. In the end I decided I didn't want to spend any more time looking through a microscope. Instead, I took the exam for entrance into law school and was accepted at the University of Ottawa for the term commencing September 1978.

My mother had very practical destinies in mind for us: she used to tell us she wanted one son to become a priest to look after her eternal soul, another to become a doctor to tend to her physical ailments, another to become a dentist to care for her teeth, and, finally, one to be a lawyer to look after her worldly goods.

Instead, she ended up with four lawyers, leading her to ask, "What am I supposed to do with four lawyers?"

I found law pretty dry. But looking back now, I can say that my legal training was indispensable in developing my critical thinking. There were mounds of material to get through and the only way to survive was to become adept at separating the wheat from the chaff and formulating a cogent argument, skills that would serve me well in politics. In some ways, attending law school was like going back to high school. The classes were much smaller than in my undergraduate years at university, and you could get to know everybody in the school. We were all in it together. I made some very good friends there — friendships I have maintained.

I got my first taste of politics when I ran for the law school seat on the university senate. I visited classes, gave my speech, and asked for support. I lost, and discovered one of life's most valuable lessons: there is much to be learned from losing. Including how to win next time, another lesson that would serve me well in the future.

The most compelling feature of law for me was its human dimension. I was never really that keen on commercial contracts, real estate, taxation issues, and other aspects of solicitor's work. Civil litigation was more interesting, and criminal law was fascinating. It is very people-focused.

The legal aid program where I volunteered at university helped to flesh out my education. I met directly with clients about landlord/tenant disputes, workplace injuries, family law issues, and so on. I found it rewarding to try to help people overcome their legal challenges.

One of the biggest challenges in a legal education is that it all takes place in a classroom. In medical school, you are thrust into a hospital setting in your very first year. That gives medical students a feel for what it is really like to be a doctor. But you don't do that in law school. In one of my last efforts as a sitting MPP, I was proud to help local legal legend and friend David Scott build a courtroom at the University of Ottawa law school with one-way mirrors so that students could observe court proceedings and comment on them in real time. It was like an operating theatre at a hospital.

David is brother to the late, and also great, attorney general Ian Scott. I once asked Ian, at the time my MPP colleague, how the Scotts — an Ottawa family — ended up with Ian in Toronto while David remained behind. Ian's response: "Toronto had first pick."

One of my law school professors was Ed Ratushny, a leading expert on the judiciary and on criminal evidence; as premier I would call upon his expertise often. He taught a Monday evening class on criminal justice administration. Successful completion of the course required students to write and present a paper and attend every class. If you were absent from even one class, you failed. Luckily, Professor Ratushny made an exception for me on the Monday after Terri and I were married, in October of 1980.

It was important to Terri that we be married before she turned twenty-five, and so we were. Before we got married, however, there were times — during my early years at university, for example — when I asked myself where our relationship was headed. But our fates had been determined. We were meant for each other. And Terri, always the wiser in matters of love, knew this long before me.

We had no money for a honeymoon so we went to my neighbour's cottage for three days. By then, Terri had just begun work as a teacher, and I moved into her apartment as a happily married second-year law student

I had considered going to Calgary to article after law school and to start up a new life out West. I went to a number of interviews there. But I just didn't like the thought of being a million miles away from home. So, with Professor Ratushny's help, I got an articling position at McCann and Bayne, the top criminal law firm in Ottawa at that time. The lawyers I worked with there, including Don Bayne (who would later represent Mike Duffy at his trial) and Pat McCann, were consummate professionals, from whom I learned much, including the importance of preparation. Putting this into practice in politics taught me, for example, that my very best extemporaneous speeches were the ones I had best prepared. As an articling student, I was soon immersed in criminal law and thoroughly enjoyed it. I was able to assist on some murder trials, and I handled less serious matters entirely on my own.

I remember one case in particular. We lost. Our client, a man in his early twenties, was convicted of murder. In a drunken rage, he had beaten his victim to death with a baseball bat in the market area in Ottawa. He was sentenced to life in prison, and while serving his sentence he was murdered. I also assisted on a case involving a client who stomped another man to death with his construction boots. And there were some sexual assault cases. For someone who grew up in a quiet suburban neighbourhood, this was a powerful first acquaintance with the other side of life.

What I learned from that experience was that, as a society, we were not doing nearly enough to prevent crime from happening in the first place. There are too many depressed neighbourhoods in too many communities where the odds are heavily stacked against the families living there — places where parents, often single moms, have a hard time keeping their kids on the straight and narrow. And where, if nothing changes, there is a good chance the kids are going to get into trouble. The predictable downward spiral for young people with time on their hands and too few positive role models and constructive opportunities might begin with yelling obscenities and defacing property, then move on to shoplifting, auto theft, drug offences, break and enter, assault, and finally jail for an extended period of time. All this costs taxpayers a lot of money. This is something I would remember in government and attempt to address by investing in community crime prevention. Some politicians choose to exploit our fear of crime, but the truth is, crime is down in Ontario and Canada. Instead of looking for more ways to put more people in jail, we should be doing more to prevent crime where we can and more to prepare those who are rightly incarcerated for their release into society.

McCann and Bayne had made it clear at the outset that there were no jobs to be had there at the end of my articling. They just weren't hiring. So I started my own law practice. In hindsight, this was a risky move. After all, I had a young family and no guarantees that when I hung up my shingle clients would walk in the door. It would have been safer to join a firm. But I can see now that all those entrepreneurship lessons I had learned at home gave me the confidence to start from scratch. It was this same confidence that would later lead me to run for office, become party leader, rebuild my party, and win elections.

I rented space from an existing firm in downtown Ottawa, Grant and Wake, and at first focused on criminal law. That was a hard go, and I wasn't making much money. On the inside cover of my court binder were the stickers I had been given in the delivery room at the birth of each of my three youngest children, stickers showing their time of birth and birth weight. I used this as motivation to keep plugging away to earn a decent living for our family. (Terri stayed home with the kids after our second child and ran a daycare out of our home. She returned to teaching once our youngest child, Connor, was in school.) This led me to later expand my practice into other areas such as real estate and wills. I did some legal aid work as well, although it didn't pay well.

I worked hard for my clients and, especially in a court setting, tried to be calm, thoughtful, and respectful of the other side and the process. But I do recall embarrassing myself on one particular occasion. I was defending a repeat client, a young professional woman, against a shoplifting charge. I put forward what I believed to be a very strong defence against the Crown's case. I firmly believed in my client's innocence, and when she was convicted, I was dumbfounded.

The judge must have noticed my state of shock. "Come now, Mr. McGuinty, surely this is not the first time you have had a client convicted."

Unthinkingly, I responded. "No," I said, "but this is the first time I have had an innocent one convicted."

Immediately, I regretted my rude outburst. The judge, however, ignored my show of disrespect and was gentle in his reprimand. I learned a valuable lesson about staying cool in the heat of the moment.

Our first child, Carleen, was born in August 1981. I was thrilled to be a dad and crazy about my baby girl. At the time, I was enrolled in my bar admission course and Terri was the sole breadwinner. My course was mornings only, so I was home in the afternoons to care for Carleen. We lived on the upper floor of an older home in Ottawa's Glebe neighbourhood; essentially it was a one-bedroom apartment with a tiny second room we used as Carleen's nursery. With so little space we learned quickly how to improvise. Terri had the kitchen table covered with her classroom lesson prep, and I used our ironing board as my desk.

Our first son, Dalton Jr., was born in 1983, and our accommodating Italian-Canadian landlord generously built us a tiny laundry room to make life easier for our growing family. Our landlord and his wife, Eugenio and Rosa Pino, had no children of their own and they took a real shine to ours. As babysitters, their avowed objective was to fatten up our kids and never let them cry. They were wonderful.

When my law practice was up and running, we had a decent living. So with a third baby on the way, and much to the disappointment of our landlord, we bought a bungalow in Alta Vista, the Ottawa suburb where I had grown up. My father gave me a second mortgage and we used the money to convert the basement into an apartment we rented to generate some revenue. Terri was staying at home in those days, and she brought in a little extra income for us by running a daycare out of the house.

Our next two children, Liam and Connor, were born in 1984 and 1986, respectively. Our family was now complete, and nothing was, or ever has been, as important to me. When I look back on our early days as a family, when we had so little by way of things but so much by way of fun and hope, I consider them some of the happiest days of our lives.

———————

My brother Dylan joined me in the law practice in 1985. I was proud to have him join me because he's a very hard worker with great people skills. In an effort to keep in closer touch with our clients, Dylan suggested that we set up a satellite office in a shopping mall in the Alta Vista neighbourhood. That second office quickly became the busier and more lucrative part of our practice, so we closed the downtown office and expanded our space in the suburbs.

I enjoyed client work. Most of it, of course, was of a technical nature. But I really liked the personal connections: helping people. Legal work can be a rich and rewarding crash course in human nature. I remember a father who wanted to cut his son out of his will because his son hadn't spoken to him in a long time. I talked him out of it by pointing out that a will is an opportunity to forgive and forget, instead of trying to get even. I also recall a couple that wanted to sign an unusual pre-nuptial agreement before they got married. They were thinking of an agreement that would stipulate who was going to do the dishes on which days, who was going to take the garbage out on alternate weeks, et cetera. I told them they needed to take a step back for a moment before going any further.

––––––––––

While I enjoyed helping people, the law practice lacked something. I had been helping my mom and dad and my brothers and sisters almost since the day I was born. I wanted to help in a bigger way, to make a difference. I saw politics as an exciting avenue worthy of exploration. And I had been inspired by my brother Dylan's 1985 run for city council. This was an exciting race, immersing the McGuinty family in our first full political campaign. Dylan lost by a mere 202 votes. We had a lot of fun and learned a lot along the way, including the downsides of using cardboard lawn signs in the fall when it rains a lot. My father would say you don't run for the fun or the experience, you run to win. This is true. But sometimes you need to lose before you can win. I had lost my bid for a university senate seat. Dylan lost his race for city council. Later, I would lose my first race for the premiership. These losses would serve as the foundation for my subsequent successes.

I began my career as a lifelong Liberal by becoming president of my local provincial Liberal riding association in 1986. I was following in my father's footsteps. He had been president of John Turner's federal riding association. They had known each other since high school, but they had a big falling out when Turner, Pierre Trudeau's justice minister at the time, brought in a bill liberalizing Canada's abortion law. My father, a devout Catholic, decided that he could not in good conscience support the government's bill and he resigned as riding president in protest. The two men never spoke again.

Despite this falling out, my father remained a Liberal. It was perhaps natural, therefore, that my brothers and I would become Liberals too. This is what happened, and years later, long after my father's death, I organized a tribute dinner for Turner to thank him for his public service. I had observed the former prime minister sometimes sitting alone on a park bench at the end of my street and it occurred to me that we don't do a very good job as

Canadians to honour those who have given so much of themselves to public service. So I decided we should do just that. In preparation for that celebratory event, I had John into the premier's office for lunch. We were joined by my son Liam, who was impressed by John's achievements both as a sprinter and as a politician. "You were the fastest man in Canada *and* you were prime minister."

John replied, "Yes, and I was fast at that, too," a reference to his short time in office as prime minister.

Abandoning federal politics, my father sat as a Catholic school trustee on Ottawa's public board for sixteen years. In 1987 he decided to run for the provincial legislature in Ottawa South, where I was the riding president. It was a seat that had been held continuously by the Progressive Conservatives since it had been formed in 1926. The political tides were shifting, however, and the seat appeared to be up for grabs.

The Ontario Liberal hierarchy did not want my father to win the nomination, though; they favoured Albert Roy, a former MPP trying to make a comeback. Both sides furiously signed up more than 2,500 new members, and the nomination meeting had to be moved to the Ottawa Civic Centre to accommodate the crowd.

The rules had been changed (at our insistence) to prevent alcohol from being served at the meeting. Alcohol was a traditional enticement served up to supporters to keep them from leaving before the voting was over. We served ice cream instead — something that had huge appeal for our young supporters, drafted from local high schools by the McGuinty children, who had worked hard together in the nomination fight. (The minimum age for party membership was sixteen.)

My father had worked long and hard on his speech, and as he was being invited to the podium he turned to me and asked for his copy. To my horror, I realized I didn't have the speech. I shouted to Dylan, "Get Dad's speech!" and then witnessed my brother clambering over chairs and people all the way to the rear of the hall and back. He finally put the speech in my father's hands. One more lesson learned: check and then double-check that you're ready to go.

In the end, we won the nomination because we brought out the most supporters and kept them there. We had followed my dad's advice: "You don't win a nomination, you take it." We had taken the Liberal nomination in Ottawa South for Dalton McGuinty Sr. My father proved to be a popular candidate and we had no shortage of volunteers. The whole family worked on the ensuing 1987 election campaign, which my father won by more than six thousand votes, part of a province-wide Liberal landslide.

On election night, we gathered at the campaign headquarters on Bank Street to celebrate my father's victory. To say the least, we were jubilant. We were waiting for the winning candidate to address us, but he was nowhere to be found. I found my father in the parking lot next door. For a guy who had just won, he looked like he had lost his best friend.

"You've got to come in and say a few words, Dad," I said.

He appeared overwhelmed. He stayed silent for a while, then replied, "This is a big responsibility, you know." After another brief pause, he walked inside and gave a great speech.

Looking back now, I can see that my father felt tremendously honoured to have been chosen to serve in office. In his eyes, though, it was much more a serious matter than a cause for celebration. It's been said that what's bred in the bone will out in the flesh. Maybe this is why I would not only seek political office, but I would always find my victories more sobering than joyful.

Despite having strong credentials, my father remained a backbench MPP at Queen's Park. Having been overlooked for Cabinet, he became a bit of a thorn in the side of Premier David Peterson and his government. It was an activist government, but my father saw that many of its measures were unpopular with Ontarians. He coined a phrase for it — "operation alienation" — which he used frequently in caucus. It turned out that he was prescient.

Observing my father's disappointment with his Queen's Park experience did much to turn me off politics. In addition to seeing his frustrations at being on the outs with the centre, I could see that my father was working long hours away from home, working weekends when he was home and, for the first time, I could see the thankless side of politics, where hard work and sincere efforts are too often met with easy criticism and cynicism. Who needs it? I asked myself. Better to stay out of politics and find a more gratifying way to make a difference. I may have put politics out of my mind but fate had politics in mind for me.

CHAPTER THREE
What's Bred in the Bone

It was a foggy evening on Friday, March 16, 1990. I was in the middle of my usual Friday night routine, horsing around with the kids while their mother took a break. It was a tradition started by my father. We called it "chuckle night." It was my chance to blow off some steam and for some father-child bonding. But this particular Friday evening would end up being anything but routine.

Our playtime was interrupted by a phone call from my mother. She said I should come over to her house as soon as I could. My mother is a pretty calm person, so she didn't say it with any sense of urgency. I thought I had time to get changed and spend a bit more time with the kids before getting in my car to drive the kilometre or so to my parents' house. Then I got a call from my brother Michael, who was staying with my parents. He yelled into the phone, "Jamie, get the hell over here!" It was then I knew something wasn't right.

I drove over as quickly as I could. On my arrival I discovered a scene on the back deck I will never forget: my father was lying on his back and my mother was giving him mouth-to-mouth resuscitation. My brother Michael was ashen and down on bended knee beside the two of them. I eased my mother away and took over the artificial respiration while she applied chest compressions. We kept this up while we waited for the ambulance to arrive. When it finally did and the attendants took my father away on a stretcher, we got in my car and followed on behind to the hospital, which was only a five-minute drive away. I waited with my mother and brother in a holding room until the doctor informed us that my father had passed away from a heart attack. He was just sixty-three years old and had been in good health. Active to the end, my father had been shovelling snow on the deck. My mother had discovered him there hours later.

We were in shock. I remembered something that my dad had said about a friend who had also died relatively young. "It wasn't the years that caught up to him. It was the mileage."

My brother, mother, and I were ushered into the room where my dad lay on a hospital table. I ran my fingers through his hair, something I would never have done when he was alive. His curly, silver hair was a lot softer than I had thought it would be. I suddenly longed for a closeness with my dad that we had never achieved when he was alive. He had given me so much. Still, I wanted more. I wanted to know more about him. About his own hopes and dreams and fears for himself — about his relationship with his own father, for example. But he was more comfortable keeping a certain distance, something more typical of his generation than mine. And now it was too late. I led my mother and brother in a prayer and then we drove my mother home. It hit me on the drive: the rest of us would get on with our busy lives, but my mother was left with a huge hole in her life.

I got on the phone and called all my siblings to break the bad news. These were tough calls. When we got around to talking about funeral arrangements, I told my family that, just about a month earlier, my father had dropped by my law office to let me know that he had bought a burial plot and that he wanted his funeral to be at St. Patrick's Basilica in downtown Ottawa. I said that was an awfully big church, with a capacity of about a thousand. "Trust me," he said. "I can fill it." He was right. There was an overflow crowd at the cathedral for the funeral mass just as there was at the wake at Kelly's Funeral Home. For our grieving family, it was heartwarming to see the large number of people showing their admiration for our father and their sympathies for us.

At the family's request, Premier David Peterson spoke at our father's funeral. He spoke well and movingly. He was on crutches at the time, having broken his leg in a skiing accident. After the mass, family and close friends gathered in the family home. A few of my brothers and I had gathered around the premier for a conversation. He asked, "Have you guys given any thought to running in your dad's riding?"

We looked at each other. Finally, one of us replied, "We'll have to see."

After my father's passing, my mother proved she is nothing if not strong. She carried on by herself for ten years, then one day she phoned me at Queen's Park, something she almost never did. "I was married today, " she said. Fortunately, I was sitting down. Her new husband, Dr. Don McCunn, was a much-loved ophthalmologist and a neighbour of ours when we were growing up. Don was a widower and the father of six children. Getting his six and the McGuinty ten together for a wedding would have been a long and complicated exercise, and the bride and groom wisely tied the knot largely under the radar. Sadly, Don passed away in 2014 after being married to my mother for fourteen years.

Following my father's funeral, the family was forced to deal with the big question raised by Premier Peterson. Looking back on it now, the question was never *whether* a McGuinty should run for my father's seat in the legislature, but rather *which* one of us would. Throughout our lives at home and long after, my dad had preached the gospel of working hard to support each other and finding a way to help build something better for our community. We all felt a responsibility to carry on. My father had built the foundation. Now we had to build something on top.

My head was telling me not to do it. I had a second mortgage on my home, four small children, and a law practice to maintain. And I had an enviable lifestyle, with my office just an eight-minute walk from my home. Why would I want to mess that up by going into politics, with all the associated uncertainty? But my heart was telling me to run. That's always been the thing about politics and me. It's been much more an affair of the heart than the head. I would later understand that getting out is even more difficult than getting in. In both cases, I was guided by my heart.

Terri could tell by the look in my eyes that I was beginning to consider the possibility of running. And she was absolutely opposed. Not because of the rough and tumble side of politics, something we would not really learn about until I later became leader of my party, but simply because politics would take me away from our family. Terri knew my father had been away in Toronto four days a week and that, even on weekends, there were political obligations to attend to in the riding. Terri's dream had been for us to lead a nice, quiet family life, one where we were always there for our children, helping with their homework (the kids were in French schools and I was the one who spoke French), taking them to ballet practice, hockey, soccer, and baseball games, and skiing as well as the usual medical and dental appointments. For Terri, when the kids were young, family meant being together as a family, all the time. Politics just didn't fit into her vision of our future. And she made it perfectly clear. "There's no way you are going to run. We have four kids under eight. Let one of your brothers run. I don't see why you have to do this!"

When I look back on it now, I can see that Terri understood far better than I just how heavy a load she would have to carry when I was away from our young family. But at the time, I was too duty-bound (or selfish, depending on whether you side with me or Terri) to notice. Lucky for me, I have a supportive and perceptive life partner. Terri could see how much running meant to me. She didn't say anything to encourage me. But I could tell she understood. And I felt I could eventually get her onside.

The more I thought about it, the more I felt a sense of obligation to run. It would not be easy — for me, or more especially for my family — but I had spent my entire childhood and youth taking on responsibility and enjoying the challenge. And there's no doubt I was influenced by the thought that my father would have been proud to know I was following in his footsteps. One of my few regrets arising from twenty-three years in politics was that my father was not around for those days. Not even one.

I think he would have been proud.

My brothers and I met conspiratorially downstairs at my house in Terri's absence. They were all younger than me, and each had better reasons than me not to run. However, my brother David (later an MP) also expressed an interest in running. This didn't surprise me. He was naturally inclined to public service and well-suited to the enterprise of politics. At first I was prepared to defer to him, but ultimately I decided I had to do it myself.

My dad, Dalton McGuinty Sr., graduating from St. Patrick's College, Ottawa (1947).

My mom, Elizabeth (Betty) McGuinty, a proud nursing graduate (1952).

My mom and dad on their wedding day (1953).

On my dad's knee in Kirk's Ferry, Quebec (1956).

At two years old, in my father's boots (1957). A sign of things to come.

First communion (1961).

Eight years old and looking spiffy (1963).

Grade nine class photo, St. Patrick's High School, Ottawa (1969).

Me as a teenager — proud of that hair!

High school graduation with my high school sweetheart, Terri Taylor (1974).

Early days — me and Terri.

Cottage weekend with my law school buddies (1979).

Me with my parents and siblings. (Left to right): David, Liseanne, Michael, Dad, Patrick, Mom, Noralyn, me, Brendan, Joyce, Anne-Marie, Dylan (1988).

Dalton McGuinty, Sr., MPP (1988).

Being a dad with Carleen — my favourite job (1982).

Reading time with Carleen, Liam, and Dalton Jr.

Horsing around with Dalton Jr., Carleen, Liam, and Connor.

Skiing with the kids in the Gatineau Hills, Quebec.

Camping in northern Ontario with my boys (2010) — a family tradition. (Left to right): Liam, Connor, me, Dalton Jr.

The McGuinty clan in the nineties. (Left to right): Anne-Marie, Michael, Liseanne, Brendan, Mom, Dylan, Joyce, David, Noralyn, Patrick, and me.

Our family and Premier David Peterson during the 1990 election.

Brother Brendan working the phones for the 1990 election.

*The newly elected MPP for
Ottawa South (1990).*

My backbench — the kids visiting Queen's Park.

Getting ready for the 1996 Liberal leadership convention. The McGuinty brothers are looking out for me.

The 1996 leadership convention — behind the scenes at Maple Leaf Gardens with (left to right) Doug Lauriault, Murray Elston, and Dave Pryce.

The 1996 leadership convention — momentum building.

New leader and a warm caucus welcome (1996). (Left to right): Gerard Kennedy, me, Jim Bradley, and Bruce Crozier.

Leader of the Opposition and senior staff, the early years. (Left to right): Kelly Legris, Matt Maychak, me, and Monique Smith.

Dalton Jr., legislative page at Queen's Park, with proud father.

David agreed the timing was a lot better for me than it was for him since his family was even younger than mine. Thus the decision, at least among my brothers, was made for me to run. We would later joke that since the election signs in the garage already had the name "Dalton McGuinty" on them, I had no choice but to be the candidate.

I approached Terri gingerly. We had all agreed that I was the guy to do it, I explained. I was the McGuinty who should run.

Terri gave me the cold shoulder for at least a week afterward. And then she put question after question to me. "Doesn't this mean we will take a pay cut? What's going to happen to your law practice when you are away in politics? What happens if you don't get elected? What happens if you do win this time but lose next time? What happens if you don't like the job? What about all the terrible things people say about politicians? Do you really want to do that to yourself? To us and the kids?"

These were all good questions. Terri instinctively knew, way back then, how stressful our life in politics would become. She was making excellent arguments. The truth is, it *is* so much more comfortable to avoid the arena. So much easier to remain a spectator. Why risk public disapproval? Why not safeguard our quiet, happy lives?

While in my head I was somewhat torn, in my heart there was no doubt. I had to run. Terri could tell.

Eventually, she came around and she has been my single greatest political asset throughout my career. Not that she ever really came to enjoy politics and the demands it placed on our family. But nobody knew me better and, battling the strong winds of politics, nobody was of greater help to me in ensuring I stayed on course by being true to myself.

Unlike my father, I faced no opposition to my nomination from within the Liberal ranks. I benefitted from a quiet courtesy in politics: if a politician dies in office and a member of the family seeks the nomination, no one will contest it.

I asked the late Herb Gray, then Leader of the Opposition in Ottawa, a man as affable as he was distinguished, if he would nominate me at my nomination meeting. Herb said yes without hesitation. (Over twenty years later, I would be honoured to name the Herb Gray Parkway after one of Canada's greatest parliamentarians.) Terri and our children joined me on stage as I gave my acceptance speech in the Ridgemont High School auditorium. I began my remarks with the standard McGuinty event joke. "I want to thank all those sitting in the first ten rows, my family." I talked about how my father had inspired me, how politics is a noble undertaking, how proud I was of the Peterson government's achievements, and how much I looked forward to making a contribution. I closed by promising to give my very best.

"I know a lot of people are down on politics," I said, "but I am a fan."

> I see politics as a means to a higher end, a way to keep building on the rich inheritance we have all received from those who worked so hard before us. Our quality of life, our standard of living, our schools, our hospitals, our supports for those of us who fall on hard times … these are extraordinary gifts and our shared responsibility is to do more than prize them. We must enhance them for our times and prepare them for our children's times, always informing our work with the timeless values that inspired the work of our parents and grandparents. And in my own work that I do for you, I promise to give you my best.

After being nominated, I went to a gathering of candidates in Toronto where I spoke privately to Peterson. The occasion was the mandatory photograph with the party leader, one to be used in my campaign materials. The premier was kind and warm toward me. But I could tell he was troubled. "What do you think?" he asked. "Should I call an election?"

I didn't pretend to know. So I just said, "I'm ready to go."

When Peterson opted for an election in the summer of 1990, just three years after he had received an overwhelming mandate from the voters, it soon became pretty clear that it was an unpopular decision. I recall coming back to my headquarters in Ottawa South on the third or fourth day of the campaign and saying we had to take down all the Peterson posters. He had become unpopular. I wondered whether I was being disloyal, but I told myself the best thing I could do for my leader was to win my seat.

As I knocked on doors, I came to understand that the early election call was a symbol of how the activist Peterson government had come to alienate many of our original supporters. We were seen to be out of touch and, as voters decided, out of time. I was proud of all the Peterson government had accomplished. Proud of the change it had ushered in. But Ontario voters saw it differently. In politics, you can be the toast of the town one day and toast the very next, and it is sometimes hard to see it coming.

I learned a lot knocking on doors in the 1990 election. It's different when your name is on the sign and your reputation on the line. If I met five hundred people in a day and three of them swore at me, those three were the only ones I thought about when I lay in bed at night. There was a lot of anger and I was the messenger. And in politics, voters will happily shoot the messenger. One man chased me off his property with a stick. Many laid into me verbally. They had been itching for an opportunity to tell the government off. Others turned their backs on me. I tried hard not to take things personally. I began to develop a thick skin. Even twenty-five years later, however, I can still feel the painful sting of those critical barbs directed at me over the years. And that's a good thing. Better to retain some sensitivity to what your critics are saying than to be completely impervious. Because the truth is they are never as wrong and we are never as right as we would like to think.

On one memorable occasion in the 1990 campaign, the inimitable Ian Scott — attorney general at the time — volunteered to canvass with me. Ian was a ball of fire as we jogged through the Billings Bridge Shopping Centre together, shaking voters' hands, offering warm smiles, and leaving a strong impression of energy and goodwill. I was amazed at how much enthusiasm Ian brought to the task. He taught me much that day about perseverance in times of strong political headwinds. Put your head down and keep moving. And keep smiling.

That's something former premier Bill Davis was to teach me as well. I came to treasure the occasional pearls of wisdom offered to me by Premier Davis, even as I served as premier. He would phone sometimes or I would see him at events, where he would inevitably receive more applause than me. When he was at the podium, I had to endure his good-natured ribbing. But up close and personal, Bill Davis, though a lifelong Progressive Conservative, was sincere, non-partisan, and always helpful. His advice to keep smiling seems trite. But it is profoundly important to show voters that you are enjoying every minute of the job and that nothing gets you down. Who wants to be led by a leader who doesn't enjoy the job?

In the 1990 Ontario election, won by Bob Rae and the New Democrats, I was the only new Liberal candidate to succeed. Dozens of incumbent Liberal MPPs went down to defeat. In 1987 we had won ninety-five seats compared to the NDP's nineteen seats and the Conservatives' sixteen. In 1990 we were reduced to thirty-six seats, while the NDP won seventy-four (a comfortable majority), and the Conservatives trailed with twenty. For the Peterson Liberals, it was an old-fashioned shellacking.

The first Liberal caucus meeting after the election felt like a wake, with the defeated candidates as well as the three dozen survivors in attendance. David Peterson sat behind a desk at the front of the caucus room and gave every impression of being a mere shell of the man I had come to know and admire. His political demise had been swift and harsh. He even lost his own seat. He was physically exhausted and emotionally drained. Many caucus members never saw it coming, either.

Maybe the Peterson government had moved too quickly on too many fronts. (My father's phrase, "operation alienation," came to mind). Or maybe it had just plain moved in the wrong direction. Now, in the languor of Opposition, we would have time to consider these and other questions. It was a painful loss and it would shake our confidence for a long time to come. The 1987 victory had been our first in fifty years, and three short years later we found ourselves again banished to Opposition. It would be another thirteen years before our next win. The road back was to be a hard one and, as I learned, it would start with strengthening the foundation: getting Ontario Liberals to believe in themselves.

I owe a lot to David Peterson. He was the first person to lead the post-war Liberals out of the wilderness. He showed us that we could win. And he taught me that government is like a wonderful set of tools for building a bright future. If you get into government and have no appetite for change, than why the hell are you there? If you are not a builder, make room for someone who is.

I will never forget David's trademark question to me and my party colleagues: "Are you having fun?" Implicit in that question was the sound advice that you need to find a way to enjoy the ride, no matter how rough it gets.

David told me something else I never forgot and that came in handy when I became Leader of the Opposition (a job he accurately describes as the toughest in politics). I was feeling dejected because no matter how hard I tried I couldn't seem to get a message out to Ontarians. David observed, "Just when you think you are going to be sick if you say it again, that's when people are hearing it for the very first time." His advice would serve me well in my long climb to the premiership.

Terri and I also owe a lot to Shelley Peterson, David's gracious wife. The Petersons were there for us as we sailed the choppy waters of opposition for seven years and then the more exciting seas of government for a decade. They offered sound advice on how to protect our family and how to endure the inevitable blows. In 2011 I was proud to host a sold-out evening in Toronto to celebrate the Peterson family and all they have given to our province.

How did I feel at being elected for the first time back in 1990? I was absolutely elated. Becoming a member of provincial parliament is a great honour, and I was eager to find ways to serve my constituents and Ontarians. I promised myself that no matter how long I was in politics, I would never lose my tremendous sense of gratitude for the privilege of public service. Whereas some of my colleagues languished in Opposition at Queen's Park, I was happy to play whatever modest role I could and eager to get to it. I got to know the community leaders in my riding, I developed a better understanding of the local issues, and I had my own community cable show. Lucky for me, I had inherited my father's Queen's Park and constituency office executive assistants, Frank Rioux and Carol White, respectively. They expertly guided me through my initiation as a rookie MPP.

I recall my first few days roaming the halls of Queen's Park. I especially enjoyed walking there in the evenings when the place was empty, the lights were dim, and the faces of previous generations of politicians stared down at me from their pictures and paintings on the walls. The architecture of the Ontario legislature is not particularly warm. You might even call it austere. Nonetheless, there is a quiet majesty to the place that spoke to me of the rich history in which I was now a modest participant. I quickly fell in love with the place. In truth, I fell in love with the idea and the promise of the place just as much as I did with the place itself. It was a place where Ontarians could come together and, at our best, do great things for ourselves and our children.

As much as I enjoyed sitting as an MPP, I found it difficult to adjust to the atmosphere in the legislature — especially its lack of decorum. I was startled and frankly offended by the constant and often quite rancorous heckling; I thought it disrespected members and dishonoured our calling. One day, I made this very argument to my more experienced colleagues in caucus.

"Why are we heckling so much?" I asked. "Doesn't this make all of us look bad?"

My earnest appeal was met with a painful silence. I realized I was barking up the wrong tree. That was simply the way things were in the legislature. I have since come to appreciate the value of a good interjection in the legislature. But I still believe there is far too much gratuitous heckling that adds nothing and, indeed, subtracts from the debate. Too often it is unacceptably personal, and that demeans all of us. When I became premier, I tried to use my influence to change this, through my own conduct, or, when I had the floor, my choice of words. But sadly, heckling lives on. It bothers me still that conduct a parent or teacher would find unacceptable coming from a child is accepted as the norm among our elected officials.

As a rookie MPP, I discovered that there is no better place to begin a political career than in Opposition. I had the last seat in the last row in the legislature. On a clear day, I could see the Speaker. It was a great vantage point from which to watch, listen, and learn. It didn't take me long to understand that the one-hour Question Period was the focal point of the legislative day and that the one and only objective of players in that theatre was to get on TV. Given the choice between a calm, thoughtful, and balanced critique of the government and an over-the-top attack embellished with a reddened face and fist pounding, we all knew which the media preferred.

Throw in the ubiquitous heckling and you have the maelstrom that so often defines Question Period. In this respect, we are far from our best. As premier, I would come to long for the Westminster-style Question Period, where the questions are provided to the government in advance, eliminating the "gotcha" aspect of our Question Period and forcing both sides to make substantive arguments rather than shallow ripostes.

There was one aspect of my first few years in politics that I particularly enjoyed, something that seemed to elude me as time went on: camaraderie with members of other parties. Being the only rookie in my party, I sought out counterparts in the other parties to get their sense of the experience we were all sharing. I particularly enjoyed getting to know my Conservative colleagues Ted Arnott, Jim Wilson, and Gary Carr, people for whom I still feel the bonds of friendship. This relationship building was facilitated by our work together on committees travelling Ontario, something that has been all but shut down today. It was then that I really got to know and enjoy the company of members in the other two parties. I know that initiatives like investing taxpayer dollars in travelling committees or in social activities that bring all sides together are frowned upon, but experience has taught me that these can go a long way to check the spread of the poisonous partisanship that thrives when opposing parties are always at odds and when members never really get to know each other.

Of course, one of the players I observed closely in the legislature in those years was the premier. Bob Rae was a surprise victor in the 1990 election. He would not have had the opportunity to ready himself psychologically for his win. I'm sure it came as a shock to him. And then there was the matter of his ambitious reform plan and how it was so badly out of sync with Ontario's bleak economic reality. At the time, we struggled with a deep recession affecting our province and much of the world.

I felt for Premier Rae. He carried the weight of huge expectations. This was the first NDP government in Ontario. After waiting so long for their proverbial ship to come in, the party's supporters would discover the government's hold was largely empty. To his credit, Premier Rae soon came to terms with Ontario's dire economic reality; bringing his supporters off the clouds and back to planet Earth, however, was another story. He would have to scale back the NDP agenda *dramatically*. When Rae broke the news to them, public-sector unions and other partisan groups dug in and accused him of betrayal. In fact, he was honouring his higher responsibility to all Ontarians to grapple with the recession by, among other things, imposing pay restraint on government workers.

Observing Rae battling one faction or interest group after another taught me how challenging it can be to change course when that change is dictated by circumstances beyond your control. His fiscal reality made a run-in with teachers over increased pay inevitable. Twenty years later, I would face the same problem and would battle the same entrenched positions. I believe beyond a shadow of a doubt that I bent over backwards as premier to support teachers and the teaching profession. Still, many would oppose my policies of fiscal restraint and bitterly accuse me of betrayal.

Plus ça change …

———————

I worked hard on my maiden speech, which I delivered in the legislature on November 28, 1990. In it, I paid tribute to my father. "He spared no efforts," I said, "with the resources at his command — his intellect, his eloquence, his wit, his courage — to lead his constituents, his fellow Liberals, and this House along a path which he felt deeply to be the right path." I also laid out my political philosophy:

> Over the years this chamber has witnessed the contributions made to this province by our predecessors. I am proud to follow in this tradition. There can be no doubt that politics has its problems, but these are problems inherent in the players, not in the play. Politics remains, for me, an honourable profession.
>
> We would do well to keep in mind that this Parliament, like all parliaments before it, will settle nothing finally.
>
> Our successes will only be temporary successes when examined under the light of history. Today's solutions will not

solve all of tomorrow's problems. But this does not mean that we struggle here in vain to improve the lot of the people of Ontario. On the contrary, we in our turn are laying a foundation upon which our successors and their successors will build. The strength of the foundation we construct will be directly related to the breadth and depth of the vision shown by the members of this Parliament. This relationship dictates that in all of our work here we must look to the next generation, not merely the next election....

I believe there is, implicit in each member's election to this Parliament, a mandate for leadership. I believe also that if we sit in this House merely as human barometers of public opinion, that is not leadership. Leadership requires that we enlist the people of Ontario to our causes, causes espoused by us because of their unremitting merit.

In the words of that great parliamentarian Edmund Burke, "Your representative owes you, not his industry alone, but his judgment; and he betrays, instead of serving you, if he sacrifices it to your opinion."

In exercising that judgment, we must beware of influences which would divorce us from our conscience.... A conscience is a good thing in this House. To my mind, there is no better anchor than a conscience when we are buffeted by the winds of political expediency.

When I read these words today, a quarter century later, I can see how much I was inspired by a rich idealism, but I can also see that I had yet to nail that idealism down to the bedrock of political reality. Those encounters with *realpolitik* were still to come. What I see as most important is that from the outset of my political career, I *had* ideals. Sadly, it's been my observation that many don't. They see politics as just a game, or a way to be somebody. For me, politics is fundamentally about public service. And public service isn't about being somebody. It's about making a difference for others. Looking back on my time in politics, I can see how my ideals guided me. They still do today. I didn't always stay on course. But I had a compass that showed me when I was off track — and how to find my way back. Politics is not a good place to discover your values. There is too much expediency. Better to bring your values compass with you into politics. And, as for the ideas shaped by our values, we would do well to abide by the Latin inscription found carved in the legislative chamber: *Audi alterem partem* (hear the other side). I can think of one particular instance where, as a rookie MPP, I lived up to my ideals, and another where I failed.

I am very proud of my private member's bill, the Donation of Food Act, 1994. Back in the early 1990s, it was apparent that food banks were becoming a permanent feature of the Ontario landscape. As someone who used to work in a grocery store, I knew that cans with dents and turkeys with a bit of freezer burn were regularly thrown in the garbage. The fast food restaurants were also tossing out lots of meat and buns. I asked representatives of the restaurants and grocery stores why they weren't turning wholesome foods over to the food banks instead of the waste bin. They said they were afraid they might get sued by a disgruntled recipient of donated food. I learned that the United States had what was known as Good Samaritan legislation, which protected would-be donors from lawsuits so long as they took the usual precautions in preparing and handling the food. I adopted the idea in a private member's bill. The operators of the food banks were solidly behind it ... with one exception: an impressive young man named Gerard Kennedy, head of Toronto's Daily Bread Food Bank. As fate would have it, it would not be the last time Gerard and I would oppose each other along the way to becoming friends. Happily, my bill was passed by the legislature, and I am still very proud of it. It felt great to be able to make a difference for families in need. I had followed my compass, leading change and doing what I thought was the right thing.

On another occasion, however, I lost my bearings.

In 1994 the Bob Rae government introduced Bill 167, a proposal to amend the definition of "spouse" in provincial statutes to recognize same-sex couples as being equal to opposite-sex couples in terms of their rights and obligations (but not granting the right to marriage, a federal matter). Debate was heated. In the end, the bill was defeated, with a dozen NDP members joining Liberals and Conservatives to oppose passage. In hindsight, this initiative seems eminently sensible and fair, if not innocuous.

But at the time it was very controversial. Scaremongers had a field day assert-
ing that this initiative would fundamentally change society for the worse.
It made for great talk-radio fodder and my constituents were incensed.
Our caucus was badly split over the issue. I could see that our leader, Lyn
McLeod, was struggling with it. Rural members pushed her hard to oppose
the bill and, in the end, she did. (We had lost a by-election in rural Ontario
and many interpreted our loss as the result of Lyn's support for gay rights.) I
always had the sense my leader was going against her conscience on that one.
I knew all about that because that is what I did. It was the roar of the crowd
on one side and my conscience on the other. And I went with the crowd. I
opposed the bill even though leadership demanded that I support it.

Unlike my Donation of Food Act, I didn't get this one right. I ignored
my compass. Do-overs in life are few and far between, but had I a chance
for a do-over I wouldn't hesitate. I would support the initiative to bring
respect and fairness to Ontario's gay community. And in retrospect, I am
confident the good people of Ottawa South would have re-elected me had I
voted my conscience. It was a lesson I would not forget. I am grateful for the
opportunities I later had as premier to champion fairness for all Ontarians,
including our gay community.

Years later as premier, I faced a similar dilemma over our own proposed
changes to the sex-education curriculum. While the proposal had been in
the works for three years and subjected to extensive consultation among
teachers, for parents it came out of nowhere when it finally hit the media in
2010. I myself had no idea our government was even considering changes
to sex ed until a reporter asked me about it in a press scrum. Instinctively,
I defended it. I believe that, in the Internet era, children have to be better
equipped to deal with the sexual realities they are encountering at an earlier
age than ever before.

Over the ensuing weeks, however, our MPPs began receiving negative
feedback on the proposal from their constituents. As the curriculum details
emerged, Ontarians learned that it suggested teachers broach some controversial subjects. For example, grade seven students were to learn that sexually

transmitted diseases could be spread through anal intercourse and oral sex. All the pushback made me understand that we had put the cart before the horse. We needed to slow down and get it right. First, we needed to make the case for a stronger sex-ed curriculum with parents. Then we needed to get parents' input. And then, and only then, could we get parents' support for what would be broadly seen as sensible changes to modernize how and what we teach our kids about sex.

At the time, some said I had buckled under pressure from Christian fundamentalists. In fact, I chose to ignore that extreme position. Rather, we changed our approach in response to the legitimate concerns of Ontario parents who were blindsided by their government on a very sensitive matter affecting their children. "What's this you want to teach my kids? And at what age?" they demanded to know. The issue became very difficult to manage. Our government had lost control of the debate. Talk radio and the Twitterverse were buzzing with rumours and fundamental inaccuracies about our policy. So I did the responsible thing: I put our proposal on ice with the intention of sending it out for consultation with parents. Unfortunately, my resignation as premier put that process on hold, and all I could do was hope my successor would find a way to move the proposals ahead.

I have learned that successful, accepted, and enduring change requires, as a prerequisite, thoughtful debate. I have also learned that in a world where information competes every day on an equal footing with misinformation and disinformation, it's getting harder and harder to have that thoughtful debate. In this respect, social media has not been our saviour. Rather than open people's eyes to the other side, social media seems often to have facilitated the gathering of the like-minded, reinforcing our biases rather than dismantling them.

In addition to my job as a rookie legislator at Queen's Park, I also had my riding responsibilities. The importance of the latter was reinforced by my late father's oft-spoken words: "There are no votes for you at Queen's Park. They're all back home in the riding." The first Ottawa South issue to test me as a rookie MPP concerned the noise made by air ambulance helicopters visiting the Children's Hospital of Eastern Ontario, a beloved Ottawa institution gracing my riding. Neighbours of the hospital complained to me that the helicopters were extremely noisy. At first, I was taken aback by any argument against the life-saving efforts being made by airborne paramedics to speed their young patients to hospital care. But my constituents were irate and demanded action. It was only when I personally visited their homes and saw how low the helicopters were coming in and felt the engine vibrations causing their houses to shake that I truly understood their concerns. I decided to organize some meetings between hospital officials, air ambulance representatives, and the affected neighbours. In the end, I brokered a compromise. The helicopters would use two flight paths over vacant land, alternating paths every day, but the pilots would always have the discretion to come in on the shortest route possible in cases of genuine emergency (but not for purposes of transporting stabilized patients). It was a small victory in the grand scheme of things, but I felt good about finding a way to bring opposing sides together to broker a mutually acceptable solution. This experience whetted my appetite to do more to help my constituents. And it taught me to keep an open mind in the face of a complaint I might otherwise be quick to dismiss.

Another local issue I embraced was the effort to bring paramedics to Ottawa. Our city had one of the lowest heart-attack survival rates in North America. Experience in other communities told us paramedics make a big difference. The province was already funding paramedics in other Ontario communities and I knew it would be difficult for the government to say no to a request to do the same in Ottawa. But governments tend to resist expanding programs on an ad hoc basis and I knew it would take a strong community effort to make a winning case at Queen's Park. Working with community leaders like Dr. Justin Maloney, his brother and city councillor, Mark Maloney, and Sandra Clarke, we formed Action Paramedic. Together, we hosted various community activities around Ottawa and collected over fifty-five thousand signatures petitioning the government. I delivered the petitions to Queen's Park on a stretcher. We got attention, and in 1994 we got our paramedics. This whole exercise taught me much about grassroots politics and how to organize a winning community movement.

———————

Throughout my time as MPP for Ottawa South, I was blessed with a team of devoted staff, which over the years was led by such talented individuals as Carol White, Ginette Brennan, and John Fraser, the last of whom I was delighted to see win the riding as my successor. There is no better feeling for a campaigning incumbent than knocking on a door and hearing "Your staff were very helpful to me, so you can count on my vote." Because of the hard work of my staff, I heard those words many times.

Shortly after the 1990 election, I was on a bus headed for a caucus retreat, sitting beside fellow MPP Greg Sorbara. I liked Greg from the moment I met him. He has a big heart, tons of energy, lots of ideas, and he's absolutely devoted to his family. Over time, Greg would become a good friend, a fearless ally, and a strong champion of both me and our party. But back then, I barely knew him. We were on our way to a caucus retreat in Niagara-on-the-Lake, and Greg, who had been a minister in the Peterson government, shared some of his memories of my father. Suddenly, in the middle of the conversation, he turned to me and said, "You know, you could be leader of this party one day." I was flattered but rebuffed the suggestion. The truth, though, is that it was not an idea that I dismissed entirely. Of course, that could probably be said of most of my caucus colleagues. A political caucus is like a football team consisting entirely of quarterbacks. We all want to call the plays. We are all leaders in our own right, having been elected by our own constituents to lead. So we all feel we have the potential to lead all of us.

In the wake of the 1990 defeat, the provincial Liberals needed to elect a new party leader. In the meantime, the party would be led by the old warhorse Bob Nixon, a man I greatly admired. His father, Harry Nixon, had briefly served as Ontario premier. More important for me, Bob had succeeded his father in politics when the older Nixon passed away. I felt some real kinship with Bob. For all his years in politics, he was still rough around the edges. I very much enjoyed that about him. He was the last of the unvarnished leaders. He did not work on his presentation skills or dress for effect. He was there to work hard and get the job done.

He brought a wonderfully grounded approach to his responsibilities and garnered much respect from all sides of the House. I considered it a great honour to be invited to sit beside him in the front row of the Opposition benches as he gave a speech.

But now it was time to choose a new leader. I was only peripherally involved in the race which, when I look back, is a bit surprising given how I would pour my heart and soul into the next one as a candidate. My first choice for leader was Murray Elston, minister of health under Peterson, and a very able politician. I had invited Murray to speak to my riding association back in 1988, and he had been kind enough to oblige me. I visited Murray in his office in early 1991 and pressed him to run for the leadership. He said he was very grateful for my support but that he had decided not to be a candidate. I then decided to throw my support behind Lyn McLeod, Peterson's minister of energy. Lyn had always impressed me. She was principled, intelligent, and hard-working. Apart from my colleague Gerry Phillips, I can think of no one who better prepared for any speech or project, whether in the caucus or the House.

Three or four weeks later, however, Elston reversed course and entered the race. I sought him out again, only this time to inform him of my decision to back Lyn McLeod. He understood. At a hotly contested convention in 1992, McLeod won on the fifth ballot, defeating Elston by just nine votes. She became the first woman ever to lead a major party in Ontario. I was proud to stand behind Lyn and looked forward to the future of our party.

As an interesting footnote to the 1992 leadership race, it was the only time Terri and I were ever on different sides in politics. Never having committed to Lyn, she backed Murray.

Lyn had a quick mind and a voracious appetite for policy. This had much appeal to me, for what was politics really all about if not good ideas? As it turned out, Lyn (and I) had much to learn in this regard. It takes a lot more than good ideas to win. It takes good ideas that resonate with voters. And it takes strong presentation skills to drive those ideas to electoral victory. Lyn never had an easy time with our push-me pull-you caucus, split as we often were between rural conservatives and urban liberals. I learned much by observing her as she worked hard to connect with our caucus, our party, and

Ontarians. She grew stronger and more sure-footed as time passed but, as it turned out, an election would get in the way before she was able to really find her footing. That would happen in my case, as well. Only I would demand a second chance. I remain astonished and grateful for Lyn's loyalty to our party and me when she stayed on as a caucus member for seven years after my election as leader. That is something I never could have done.

———

Being an MPP can be hard on family life, especially if you are an out-of-towner. During the thirteen years that I served in Opposition, Terri and our children stayed in Ottawa while I was living in an apartment in Toronto, although I managed to make it home every weekend. (Until I became leader of our party, I also maintained my law practice back in Ottawa on a half-day-a-week basis; prudence — who goes by the name of Terri in our household — dictated that I have something to fall back on in case I lost the next election.) As Leader of the Opposition, my routine would see me return home on Thursday or Friday evening unless there were weekend events elsewhere that required my attendance. And there were many of those, including party gatherings sprinkled around the province, and the countless Ontario fairs, festivals, and celebrations that populate the schedule of someone on the hunt for recognition and votes.

I called home every night to talk to everyone and listen to the stories of their day. I knew it was going to be a rough call when Terri started out by saying, "Let me tell you what your son did today." They were always *my* children when they misbehaved. And then she would put the errant child on the phone, expecting me to chastise him or her. This was an impossible task. I could only offer a weak "You have to listen to your mother" admonition.

Whenever I was home, I tried to cram one week's worth of fathering into the little time I had with the kids. It wasn't easy, but Terri and I made it work. And truth be told, she had the tougher job. I remember very well that while I was away carrying out my political responsibilities, Terri was juggling a complex schedule that involved — among a million other things — twice-a-week hockey practice for three boys and ballet for our daughter, Carleen. This was in addition to her job as a teacher.

You can't raise a child over the phone, and I thank God Terri was there on the front lines.

During school holidays, Terri and the kids would occasionally join me in Toronto. The kids loved visiting attractions like the zoo, the Hockey Hall of Fame, Blue Jays games, and the Royal Ontario Museum (they were enthralled by the bat cave). Terri and I worked hard to bring some balance to our divided lives, always keeping the kids in the centre.

As for me, I kept busy both on the job and after work. The lessons I learned from my mother about cleaning, laundry, and cooking served me well. I scrubbed my apartment regularly and used a toothbrush around the base of the toilet. In order to prolong the life of my dress shirts, I washed them by hand in the bathtub, where I hung them to dry before ironing them. I sewed on missing buttons and fixed drooping pant hems. I had promised myself that I would keep my out-of-town living costs (those not covered by the member's allowance) to an absolute minimum. I knew how to perform these small tasks and I had the time. So I did them.

Later, when recruiting prospective candidates, I found many of them were concerned about the impact of political life on their families. I told them that if they wanted to make it work, they could. I told my own staff that I had entered politics with my family intact and I was planning to leave the same way. That meant I needed family time built into my schedule. My family is my foundation, and if it is disturbed I just can't perform well in my job. My staff came to understand it was in everyone's interest that I get my family time and, for the most part, they accommodated me. Anybody who knows me well knows I consider it my greatest responsibility in life to be a good father. Being premier is important, but being a good father is really important. So maybe it wasn't that surprising (and, for me, a bit flattering) when the media began calling me "Premier Dad."

When the 1995 election came round, we Liberals were feeling very good about our prospects. The polls predicted we would win province-wide. Premier Bob Rae and the New Democrats were clearly on the way out, and the Conservatives, under Mike Harris, seemed too extreme. But we underestimated Harris and his appeal, just as we misjudged the public mood. Ontarians had grown tired of the recession and frustrated with the missteps of the Rae government; many NDP supporters had turned against Rae and the party as it tried to walk a precarious balance between more government and less debt. The attitude among voters reminded me of the frustrated hero in Paddy Chayefsky's 1976 film *Network*: "I'm mad as hell and I'm not going to take it anymore!" Well, Ontario voters were mad as hell. As an alternative to Rae and the NDP, the Conservatives offered straightforward simplicity; their program ran to less than twenty-five pages. Ours weighed in at a chubby eighty-two pages. We offered a comprehensive plan. They offered a revolution.

In fact, they named their platform the Common Sense Revolution — a great title. Who could be against common sense? Harris promised sweeping cuts to taxes and public services. He appealed to a sense in the province that government had become part of the problem, not the solution. He made it clear he was on the side of "ordinary Ontarians" and not "special interests." Even people on welfare told reporters they were planning to vote for the Conservatives notwithstanding their promise to cut benefits by 22 percent. In short, the Conservatives were much better judges of the public mood than we were. This made the Liberals and our plan ripe for attack.

For instance, in a media scrum Lyn McLeod was pressed for details on a policy the Liberals supported that would allow judges more leeway in evicting a spouse accused of abuse from the home. Reporters wanted to know exactly what would trigger such a court order.

"What about verbal abuse?"

Yes, she admitted, verbal abuse could be included as a reason for eviction. Well, that was all they needed.

"YELL AT YOUR SPOUSE AND LOSE YOUR HOUSE!" screamed the headline in the *Toronto Sun* the next day. We did not think anyone would actually believe that, but a lot of people did. Maybe they were just looking for an excuse to get mad. Ironically, five years later, the Harris government would pass the Domestic Violence Protection Act, which empowered judges to evict spouses for verbal abuse.

While there was a lot of pent-up anger and frustration in the 1995 campaign and Harris tapped into it very effectively, it must also be said, however, that the rise of Harris was due in part to our failure to deliver a strong, focused, and determined Liberal message that resonated with voters. That election also drove home to me a fundamental rule of politics, which I have never forgotten but which too many, media included, do: campaigns count. According to the polls, the Liberals were destined to win that election. We lost. We didn't run the campaign we needed to win. This truism would later help guide my actions as premier. I wouldn't feel the need to be popular every day, a sentiment that would have paralyzed my leadership. But I had damn well better be popular on election day, which meant my team and I had better be good at campaigning.

Harris and the Conservatives won a sweeping majority in 1995 and collected eighty-two seats. The Liberal total actually fell to thirty seats (down from thirty-six in 1990), but we remained in second place; the New Democrats crashed to just seventeen seats. I held on in Ottawa South and faced another term in Opposition, and another change in Liberal leadership as Lyn McLeod resigned two months after the election. My life was about to change dramatically.

CHAPTER FOUR
Never Too High, Never Too Low

After the 1995 provincial election, it quickly became obvious that there was going to be another leadership vacancy in my party. I thought long and hard about whether to enter the race. I have learned that in deciding to run for public office, and even more so in deciding whether to seek the leadership of your party, you have to be able to answer yes to two questions.

First question: Are you prepared to win? Put another way: Are you prepared to assume the burden that comes with winning — all the hours, all the responsibility, all the scrutiny, and all the impositions on your family?

Second question: Are you prepared to lose? If losing is going to deal you a blow from which you will have real difficulty recovering, then you shouldn't run.

I struggled with these questions. I felt it was something I should do, but when I mused about it with Terri, she was, at first blush, completely opposed — and for all the right reasons. We both had a sense of how hard running for the leadership could be on our family in terms of the time commitment and the travel. And what about the costs? Who was going to cover those? We had both heard of losing leadership candidates saddled with big personal debts after the race was over. And it wasn't as if I was being swept up by an Ontario-wide "Draft Dalton" movement. We both knew I was a long shot.

On the other hand, what if I *did* win? Terri and I are parents before anything else, and we were concerned about how the kids would react to the shots that would be taken at me, politics being a blood sport. How would we deal with that?

Then there was the scale of the challenge facing a new leader. Back in 1995, people didn't talk about the "Big Red Machine." And with good reason: it didn't exist. But they did talk about the "Big Blue Machine," because that was a team that knew how to win. This meant a long-term commitment for me and Terri. I figured if I was really lucky, I could win the election, likely scheduled for 1999. And once you win one, of course you run in the next one. And, assuming I was lucky again and won that second one, tradition dictated a leader step aside for a successor two years or so before the next election. That meant I was considering a ten-year commitment. If I was lucky! Being honest with myself, I knew I would likely spend more time in Opposition than I wanted. And that could be abbreviated by a party that decided not to stick with me if I lost an election. Realistically, assuming my party didn't dump me after I lost my first election and I could then manage to win the next two, I was looking at something closer to a fifteen-year commitment.

When I added it all up — the time commitment, the financial risk, the imposition on Terri and the kids — running for the leadership just didn't make sense. But as usual for me when it came to politics, I went with my heart and not my head. I *felt* that running for the leadership was something I had to do. Something I should do. I could have justified my run by telling myself that I was running to make an impression, to get noticed, and to position myself for more opportunity down the road. But that wasn't my objective. My objective was to win, not to impress. And it didn't matter to me if at the outset very few believed I could get there. Nor did it much matter that I had almost no experience in leadership races. Like so much I had already taken on in life, I was prepared to dive in to new experience and learn and grow along the way. In this regard, I have a personal mantra which has kept me on task and resolute: "Never too high. Never too low. Just relentless."

I wanted to run because I felt it was time for a new generation of ideas in the Ontario Liberal Party: new ideas to grow our party, new ideas to win votes — and new ideas on how to govern. I loved ideas. For me, the best part of politics has always been the ideas. I far prefer policy to politics. In 1996 I didn't pretend to have all the new ideas we needed, or even most of them, but I believed I could convince Liberals they could count on me to lead our intellectual renewal and win an election. I understood turning our party around was a long-term project and I also knew I was suited to the task. I play the long game. I am very disciplined. And I am absolutely determined to keep growing. My job would be to convince Liberals I could get them to the promised land. But first I had to convince Terri to let me out the door.

Terri had grown to quietly accept and support my MPP responsibilities, notwithstanding the burden this placed on our family. We had adjusted to our new norm. To say that she was disappointed when I raised the possibility of running for leader would be an understatement. Again, she raised all the intelligent questions. "Why do you have to do this? Who is going to support you? How much does it cost to run? How much more are you going to be away? We don't have any money for this so how are you going to pay for it? And if you do win, where would we live?"

The only solid reassurance I could give her was that, should I win, our family would not move to Toronto. Moving would be necessary only should I become premier. In the end, Terri said, "You know I believe in you and I think you would make a great leader, but I'm afraid of what this means for our family." She had always been intent on protecting our family from the vicissitudes of politics. More and more I would develop an ability to roll with the punches, but she would take things personally and she didn't want the kids to get hurt. As it turned out, our children would grow resilient over the years and come to enjoy the fun side of politics. Yes, there were dark times when I was under attack. We would miss each other, too, when I was on the road, but we enjoyed campaigning together and, if nothing else, politics always brought excitement into our lives. I knew the kids were embracing their future when Terri was saddened to report to me that she had overheard them in the sandbox "playing campaign."

"Why can't they just be normal?" she asked.

Two things here go without saying. Terri eventually gave me her blessing in my quest for the leadership. And I never could have done it without her.

I spoke to my brothers and sisters about running for party leader — in particular, David, Dylan, and Brendan, who were all living in Ottawa. They were my "kitchen Cabinet." All of them urged me to run, and I knew I would be able to count on all my family getting behind me in a real way. That was significant. In a bid for the leadership, you are lucky if you have even a few hardcore supporters you trust implicitly to go to the wall for you and make the personal sacrifices needed to help you win. I had ten such volunteers in my mother and my siblings. But I knew family alone wouldn't do it. I would need more help. Lots more. I recruited many outstanding supporters along the way, people who took on leadership roles in the campaign, including our future party president, Ross Lamont, future MP Judi Longfield, Dave Pryce, and Doug Lauriault. I was also very grateful for the support given to me by Murray Elston, who had barely lost to Lyn McLeod at our last leadership convention.

There were six other candidates, most with a higher profile than me, including Dwight Duncan, Annamarie Castrilli, John Gerretsen, Joe Cordiano, and Gerard Kennedy. I was a dark horse, with little support in caucus or the party hierarchy. At the outset, only one other MPP backed my candidacy: Tony Ruprecht. (Seven years later, when I was first elected premier, Tony sent me a handwritten note: "My dear Premier: Some of us did predict the future. Congratulations. Tony.") The other Ottawa-area Liberal MPPs eventually came around to supporting me, but only out of a sense of obligation to support the local guy. I understood this and was grateful for their support. When I kicked off my campaign, Jim Coyle, the *Ottawa Citizen*'s Queen's Park columnist and a gifted writer, wrote a column laying odds on the leadership contenders. Of me he wrote:

> Dalton McGuinty (Ottawa South): Many attributes. No baggage, part of new Grit generation. Thoughtful, earnest, bilingual, ideologically suited to the times on party's right wing. Lovely family. One big problem: a charisma deficit bigger than Ontario's fiscal one. (Odds against winning: 150-to-1.)

The kids and I thought this was hilarious and we proudly hung the newspaper column on the kitchen fridge for the duration of the campaign.

After all, it was true. I was a long shot, and nobody was complaining I was causing them to swoon in my presence. It has been said that success in life depends on having both a sense of perspective and a sense of humour. I tried to bring both to the campaign.

It never hurts to be endorsed by senior members of the party — provincial or federal — and I was pleased to get the support of John Manley, my federal riding mate. I also called on Senator Allan MacEachen, someone who had run unsuccessfully for the 1968 federal Liberal Party leadership and for whom my father had written campaign speeches. I asked the distinguished senator for his advice about running. He offered a one-word response: "Don't." I thanked the senator for his time and kept moving.

It was going to be a year-long campaign, culminating in a convention at Maple Leaf Gardens in November of 1996. While campaigning, I confirmed what I had suspected. Our party was in a deep funk in the wake of the 1995 election, an election many of us thought we had in the bag. One of the first pieces of literature I put out was a brochure that asked, "Have you heard the good news?" Inside, the brochure supplied the answer: "We get to try again." I'm a golfer (a lousy one), and golf (like my father's motto for our family: *Ne umquam respexerit* — never, ever look back) has taught me that the most important hole is the next one. You have to block the previous hole out of your mind.

I was a very optimistic campaigner, very idealistic, very energetic, and very eager to meet Liberals and Ontarians to learn from them and to debate the issues. I travelled as far and wide as I could in my minivan. My only companion was Doug Lauriault, candidate aide extraordinaire, speech writer, and policy wonk. Doug had volunteered for my 1990 campaign in Ottawa South. Back then, he just showed up at my campaign headquarters one day and offered to accompany me to the doors. I figured I would try him out. He was high energy, good-humoured, and perfectly bilingual. I wanted him at every door with me after his first shift.

My brother David used his considerable powers of persuasion to secure a Ford Windstar minivan as a contribution from Ottawa's Donnelly family car dealership. I had no idea how many miles I would be logging but David informed the dealership we would return the car in good working condition after the leadership race was over. Little did Doug and I know we would drive over sixty thousand kilometres in just over ten months, starting in the brutal cold during the first week of January and going non-stop until the end of November. My stock joke on the road became: "I have driven thousands and thousands of kilometres to meet thousands of Liberals and I have come to one overwhelming conclusion: I should have run in Prince Edward Island!" I visited pretty well every community where Liberals were to be found. And many places, I visited several times over. One thing I knew for sure, my opponents would never outwork me.

When not crafting speeches or fine-tuning policy ideas from the passenger seat, I spent hundreds of hours on the phone. Our van was equipped with an old-school Motorola phone the size of a shoebox that had to be plugged into the lighter socket for power. It would take another six years before the first BlackBerry appeared and eleven years before the first iPhone. Back then cellphone towers were few and far between, often making the call experience incredibly frustrating. In a typical week, I would leave Queen's Park at the end of afternoon Question Period. As I settled into the van, Doug would hand me a call list that Dave Pryce and Judi Longfield had carefully curated and prepared that day, each being experts at warming up potential supporters and delegates. I would settle in and start dialling. My job as candidate was to "seal the deal" over the car phone while driving en route to meet with Liberals. Unfortunately, I would regularly lose the signal and get cut off mid-conversation. On the other end, delegates would sometimes get upset, thinking either I had hung up on them or was not paying attention. Either way it was bad. They had no idea I was using a car phone and had little understanding of the technical challenges it created. Necessity being the mother of invention, it didn't take long for my campaign team to adjust their daily message. Each morning call with potential delegates thereafter would begin with Judi or Dave saying, "Dalton will be calling you from his car phone later today, and sometimes the call cuts out because this is a very new, cutting edge technology he is using to reach out to you." It doesn't seem like much, but it was so important. Remember the cliché about never having a second chance to make a first impression? It's true.

At the end of the campaign when we turned the van over to the dealership, my high-school friend Tom Donnelly was delighted with my victory, but somewhat less enthusiastic about the odometer reading!

A leadership race is far from glamorous. To save money, we would spend the night at a supporter's home whenever we could. I remember one night at the home of a supporter, where my sleep was interrupted by his parrot, which swore like a trooper, and his cat, which kept pounding on my bedroom door in a futile quest to be allowed in. On the road, I would get changed in gas station washrooms and eat at fast-food joints. It was all very energizing but at the end of a long day, we were dead tired. Once I stopped off at a hamburger joint, came back out, and got into the van only to find a woman sitting behind the wheel. I had gotten into the wrong van.

One evening, I recall phoning Terri. I was dog-tired and mistakenly dialled the wrong number. A woman answered and I asked her how things were going.

"Just fine," she said.

I asked if she had put all the kids to bed.

"Yes," she said, "they're all in bed."

Then something clicked. I said, "You're not my wife."

"You're not my husband!" she said and hung up.

We met Liberals in every corner of the province. At one gathering in Kenora, in northwestern Ontario, a guy was eager to remind me I was not from around there. "So, you're from the south, eh?" he said.

I replied that I was from Ottawa, believing this distinguished my home from the real south in our province. "That's the south," he insisted.

Eager to ingratiate myself with my audience, I proudly pointed out that I had family in North Bay, Timmins, and Kapuskasing: all three indisputably northern locales.

"That's the east!" he declared.

I learned that all politics truly is local. I couldn't go into a community and just talk about regional or provincial or national issues; I also had to address very local concerns.

There were half a dozen leadership debates organized in various parts of the province for us. These were mostly tame affairs but they gave us a chance to try out our stuff in front of friendly audiences. Differences began to emerge, not so much in terms of our policies but in terms of our leanings. I found myself in the centre-right camp, along with Dwight Duncan and Joe Cordiano. Others, including Gerard Kennedy and John Gerretsen, were more centre-left. I'm not sure non-party members would have been able to see a clear distinction, but party members certainly did. The latter could also be divided between those who were from Toronto and those who were not. I was concerned about playing to that division because I knew one thing for sure: if we were to become winners, we needed to be united. We could not enjoy the luxury of sowing seeds of division in our own ranks.

Back home in my law office in Ottawa, we set up phone banks, and once the voting delegates had been selected by the party, we began calling every single one of them. It became a family undertaking. If your last name was McGuinty, you were conscripted. If it wasn't me on the phone, it was my mother or one of my siblings, and they could say with authority that they knew me and what I stood for. That was important. This made for a powerful connection between me and the delegates.

In approaching delegates who were already committed to other candidates, we took the high road. My own script went like this:

> Thanks for getting involved in the process. I think the future is bright for our party. I fully respect your decision to support another candidate. I've gotten to know your candidate over the course of the campaign, and I can see they've got a lot of great qualities. But should your candidate fall off the ballot, I just want you to know I would be honoured to have your support.

It was a soft sell, with a positive spin. I insisted there be no negativity. My goal was to be everybody's favourite *second choice*. Nobody was going to win this on the first ballot. There were too many candidates for that to happen, and none of us was eclipsing all the others. I made a point of personally calling every voting delegate. I wanted them to hear from me directly. I reached more than two thousand of them.

I have always been very idealistic and positive in my approach to politics. Some may find that hard to believe, given the expediency and self-interest cynics would have us believe characterize all politics today. But I worked very hard to avoid those traps. I recall a newspaper cartoon showing me and two other politicians reacting to a statement about how beautiful a day it was. A thought bubble over the other politicians' heads revealed them to be attacking each other and me. But in my thought bubble I was saying, "It really is a beautiful day." I don't know who the cartoonist was, but he or she certainly had me pegged. That positive approach is what has sustained me. The alternative is to become a cynic. And voters aren't looking for cynicism from their leaders. They are looking for inspiration. In a life that can get you down, they want leaders and ideas to lift them up.

On the leadership trail we didn't do any polling because we just couldn't afford it. But I could sense that I was being well received by the other leadership camps. My phone calls and meetings with voting delegates were confirming this for me. This quiet momentum helped sustain me through the daily grind as we got closer to the convention. And there were noteworthy outward signs of my team's progress too. I was especially pleased when former federal finance minister Donald Macdonald kindly offered to host a fundraiser for me at the Toronto Club. We raised more than $10,000, our biggest haul outside of my hometown of Ottawa.

The 1996 Liberal leadership convention was the old-fashioned kind with all the hullabaloo, excitement, and uncertainty associated with an election where party faithful crowd into a room to vote instead of clicking on a computer back home. It makes for good TV, which is just what an attention-starved opposition party needs in an effort to try to excite the public.

My strategy at the convention was to keep positive and stay loose. Or, to use a baseball analogy that coach Greg Sorbara (one of my leadership supporters) would later teach me: relax at the plate. Batters have no idea what kind of pitch is coming until the last second, so they mustn't grip the bat too hard and seize up.

We weren't sure how the convention was going to unfold. But we knew the most precious commodity on a convention floor is momentum, and we were determined to find ways to generate that.

The good news was that I came into the weekend with no political debts. I had made no deals with any of my fellow candidates. The bad news was that, because I had made no deals, I had no alliances. I was on my own. Which meant I was going to have to rely on the relationships my team and I had worked hard to forge with individual voting delegates. I had tremendous faith in my team and our ability to grow support on the floor. We had assembled a great team of volunteers who had been trained in how to work the floor and recruit delegates. Their instructions were to stay positive and take the high road. Their best weapons in the hand-to-hand combat for support would be a firm handshake, a warm smile, and a sincere but irresistible invitation to join Team McGuinty. The media and pundits, of course, didn't think I had much of a chance. And I can understand why they held this view. They just weren't privy to all the groundwork we had done to cultivate secondary support among the other candidates' delegates. This wasn't the last time in politics I would enjoy the advantage of being underestimated.

Delegate voting began on the afternoon of November 30, a Saturday, but equipment problems delayed proceedings and the first ballot results were not announced until 7:30 in the evening. No surprise, Kennedy, the acknowledged front-runner and favourite to win, was in first place. But he had just 770 votes. In other words, just *30 percent* of the 2,558 delegates who had cast ballots. That left him a long way from victory, which meant I had a chance. But I had a lot of climbing to do. Ahead of me were Cordiano in second place, and Duncan in third. I was in fourth place with 464 votes, or 18 percent. After that came Gerretsen, Castrilli, and Greg Kells, a party outsider. With every successive ballot, the candidate with the fewest votes was removed from the list. Our plan (and everybody else's) was to attract the delegates of the fallen candidate.

Kells freed up his delegates to support whomever they chose. On the next ballot, I put on a brave face when my vote count actually *fell* to 440, although I was still fourth. I tried hard to hide my disappointment at losing some of my original supporters and I hoped a trickle wouldn't turn into a torrent. My brother Patrick clambered into my leadership "box" — a seating area we had roped off for family and close supporters and where we longed to welcome other leadership candidates who would, we hoped, fall off the ballot before me.

"Things are good on the floor" he reassured me. "Keep smiling."

So I did.

Castrilli was forced off the ballot in the next round, and we all wondered where she was going. Fortunately, she opted to support me, and I welcomed her and her delegates with open arms. Then the excitement for me and my camp really began. Gerretsen, who could have hung in for another ballot, decided to make his move. To me! I was ecstatic when John led his troops my way. Now, undeniably, I was the one with the momentum. The energy we had was palpable on the floor and certainly in my Maple Leaf Gardens box, which was growing happily crowded as I welcomed more and more supporters.

As the night wore on, there was a growing impatience and frustration in the face of the hours it was taking to count every ballot. Of course, I had taken nothing for granted and I worried that the momentum we had worked so hard to create could be stalled. The waiting was torture.

On the third ballot, Duncan found himself in last place. I had leap-frogged ahead of him to land in third spot behind Kennedy and Cordiano. In a move that surprised me and, frankly, surprised many of his own supporters, Duncan decided to back Kennedy. These guys were on different ends of the Liberal political spectrum, with Kennedy on the left and Duncan on the right. Duncan's move helped push Kennedy up to 968 votes on the fourth ballot, but I finished a clear second, with 760. What this meant was that many of Duncan's supporters had chosen to come my way. This was a huge boost for my team. And it spoke volumes about the effectiveness of our strategy to become everyone's favourite second choice. No doubt about it, other delegates were finding a home in the McGuinty camp because we made them feel at home there. They were comfortable with me, my team, how we presented ourselves, and what I stood for.

Luckily, with each ballot we picked up more support — but not enough. Our team had a new objective: win the war of attrition and keep our supporters on the floor. That meant keeping our energy up, constantly circulating on the floor, engaging in endless conversations with delegates, and keeping our entertainment going. We had hired a band to play on the floor, but they could sing only for so long before their voices wore out. Terri and the children hung in by my side though the hour was late, past midnight, charged up on the excitement of the good news and sensing for themselves the momentum Team McGuinty was achieving.

I like to think that on that night my supporters believed I could grow into the job. They were willing to give me a chance. I don't believe they saw lots of royal jelly in me. But they did see earnestness, a commitment to party and public service, and a strong work ethic — somebody who was worth investing in, in hopes of a payoff somewhere down the road.

And while I was still more than two hundred votes behind Kennedy, Cordiano's delegates were now up for grabs. If I could get Joe and his delegates to move my way, I would win. My team worked furiously behind the scenes and on the floor to try to secure the support of the Cordiano delegates. Joe himself kept his own counsel, something for which I admired him. He was going to take his time to carefully consider his options. I couldn't have been happier when he endorsed me. He made his way through the sea of delegates on the floor of Maple Leaf Gardens, climbed up the stairs, and entered my box, where I warmly embraced him and held his arm aloft to tremendous applause. Terri and I looked at each other. We knew this very likely meant I would win. I could tell by the look on her face that there was no separation of purpose between us now. We were both determined to win.

The hour then being 3:30 a.m., I thought it would be a good idea to sneak in a quick shave before the final results were announced. So Doug Lauriault and I made a mad dash to my room at the Toronto Delta Chelsea Hotel. I had been there for only a couple of minutes when I got a call from Judi Longfield telling me, "Get back here right away! They are going to announce the winner!" I dropped my razor, towelled off my face, and ran back to Maple Leaf Gardens.

After the last votes were counted, Kennedy and I were confidentially informed of the results by party officials (we were each handed a slip of paper) so that we could compose ourselves for the public announcement. I paused for a moment before unfolding the paper. My heart was pounding. So was Terri's as she stood next to me. Nobody else in the box knew the result of the final vote. I leaned close to Terri so no one could see what I was doing and unfolded the paper. I had won! I kept a straight face and whispered to Terri, "*I won.*" She hugged me and mischievously whispered back, "You promised you wouldn't win." Terri quietly passed the news on to our children, telling them they had to pretend they didn't know. They could barely contain themselves.

It was 4:25 a.m. on Sunday morning when the results were finally announced. I had won comfortably on the fifth ballot, with 1,205 votes to Kennedy's 1,065. On the outside, I was elated. But inside, I could already feel the weight of this new, heavy responsibility. I wanted to do right by my party and my province, but at that very moment the challenge seemed incredibly daunting. I didn't feel empowered as the winner. I felt humbled.

As I made my way to the stage to be welcomed as the new leader of the Ontario Liberal Party, there was a crush of supporters and media. One of the party officials said, "Step aside and make way for the leader." I immediately stepped aside. It would take some time for me to grow completely comfortable with my new job. Years, in fact.

Right after the final ballot, Terri was asked by a journalist to describe me. She said I was a "good Christian." That prompted some speculation that the Liberals had elected a Christian fundamentalist as their new leader. Terri felt so bad about it. What she had meant was that I was a caring guy. I have never presented myself as a "Christian" politician. For both Terri and me, that exchange was our first acquaintance with the vastly increased significance attached to your words when you are the party leader as opposed to a backbench MPP.

It is fair to say that I was not the choice of the centre-left of the Liberal Party. Gerard Kennedy was their man. I saw myself as more of a centre-right candidate. Since then, however, my politics have evolved. My values have not changed, but I have adopted a more finely balanced, more holistic view of government. I have come to prize a strong economy that creates good jobs and the wealth needed to support great schools and health care. But for me, a strong economy is not the end. It's not the call to arms that stirs my blood. Rather, a strong economy is the means to a higher end, a caring society — the notion that we are all in this together, that what we do affects one another, that we need each other, and that it is right that we work and build something better *together*. For instance, in my first term as premier I emphasized programs to strengthen health care and education. My thinking continued to evolve, however. I learned that a leader needs to reprioritize according to circumstances. So, in my second term, I became more concerned about the economy when Ontario was confronted both by a very challenging recession and by the growing impact of globalization. A new economic reality demanded I emphasize policies to stimulate economic growth. I never lost track, though, of what politics is really all about: making people's lives better. What I learned is that emphasis can change; values cannot.

In the early morning of December 1, 1996, the day after the convention, after saying goodbye to Terri and the kids and after thanking all the candidates and delegates at a morning speech — in other words, after the party was truly over — I walked alone from Maple Leaf Gardens to my Bay Street condo. I was victorious, but I had never felt more alone and more uncertain. I had taken on a huge responsibility and I wondered just what I had gotten myself into. I had been trained to accept responsibility since the day I was born, but that didn't mean I was immune to the weight of it. I had to live up to the expectations of thousands of party members. I had to mount a respectable opposition to the Conservative government, currently under the leadership of the tough and experienced Mike Harris. I had to inspire voters' confidence in the Liberal Party and in me as its leader. At the same time, of course, I didn't want to neglect my family. I felt a heavy burden. And all those things that had freed me up to do what I thought was right and not expedient — I was not mired in party history nor had I made commitments to anyone — meant I was on my own as I faced the prospect of a massive rebuild of our party from the ground up. It was largely through efforts led by McGuintys that I had won the leadership. Now I would need to build a team of my own within the party and at Queen's Park. It was going to take a lot of work. I would have to grow. And so would our party.

The next day, I visited the Opposition leader's office on the second floor at Queen's Park. It was a dark room dominated by a big desk. Not a lot of warmth there. I found a security button, which didn't appear to be functioning. I pressed it and nothing happened. I thought to myself, *Welcome to the powerlessness of Opposition.*

I knew I faced some big hurdles as leader. My first challenge was to reach out to the other leadership candidates and their supporters. I wanted to be inclusive and to heal any rifts before they worsened. A victorious candidate who dismisses his opponents is practising bad politics, and it's not my style anyway. I first reached out to Joe Cordiano, whose endorsement of me at the convention had made me leader. I asked him to serve as my deputy leader. I felt that this was one of the time-honoured rules of politics: if a person helps to put you over the top, you owe him. Joe immediately accepted.

Unfortunately, we were both young and too concerned about maintaining our stature when we should have been more concerned about finding ways to work together for the benefit of the party and the caucus. The caucus began to complain about my deputy leader, about how he carried himself in Question Period in my absence, about how he managed his critic's responsibilities, things like that. In hindsight, none of these were insurmountable challenges. With time and support, Joe would have grown into his responsibilities, as I did. Regrettably, I buckled under caucus pressure. Less than a year after naming Cordiano deputy leader, I fired him. I have always regretted that decision. Others might say I had no choice because I couldn't defy caucus if it was all lined up against Cordiano. But I should have found a way around that obstacle. Six years later, when we formed the government, I named Cordiano as minister of economic development, and he did a fabulous job. He was a shoulder-to-the-wheel, nose-to-the-grindstone kind of guy. Among other accomplishments, he was instrumental in landing a new Toyota assembly plant, Ontario's first new auto plant in some ten years. That alone created more than ten thousand jobs.

I also gave senior portfolios to Gerard Kennedy, Dwight Duncan, and John Gerretsen. They all had political skills and their own support bases and I wanted to turn those to the advantage of my party and Ontarians. But immediately after the convention, there was some lingering bitterness that I had to overcome. Some in the rival leadership camps were reluctant to let the campaign go. They were waiting for me to fail, and they met from time to time to discuss strategy in case I did. Cordiano's people were a particular problem after I fired him.

Annamarie Castrilli was the exception in that she was the only leadership candidate who never really settled into her role as a member of the McGuinty Liberals. Disappointingly, she would later cross the floor and run for the Conservatives in the 1999 election, an election in which she was defeated by one of her former leadership rivals, Gerard Kennedy.

Unfortunately, in Opposition, you don't have much to offer caucus members to keep them onside and engaged. I tried to be as fair as I could in handing out responsibilities and titles but there was always some disgruntlement. Gerry Phillips, a caucus colleague who regularly demonstrated wisdom and leadership at Queen's Park, used to joke that he came away from our caucus meetings feeling worse about our prospects in the next election than

Ontarians made him feel! At first, I devoted too much time toward satisfying the demands of caucus. I eventually learned that at a certain point you just have to get on with the job. Some folks are never going to be as happy as you would like them to be, and a leader has to accept a certain amount of disquiet within the ranks, especially in Opposition. That is only natural; indeed, it's healthy. It's important that caucus members have a place where they can voice their complaints and blow off steam. Better to blow up inside Liberal walls than outside. As party leader, I made it a point to carefully listen to my caucus. (Over the years, as our caucus doubled in size to over seventy, I drew upon the good instincts of Rod MacDonald, responsible for caucus liaison, to help me detect smoke and put out fires before they could spread.) It's amazing what you can learn when you shut your mouth and listen to caucus. I have been blessed with great staff throughout my time in office, but they were no substitute for the advice and opinions of those who practise the art of retail politics. It was only by listening to and learning from my caucus that I felt I avoided getting trapped in the proverbial bubble, oblivious to what was really happening out there. Over time, I would also come to understand that one of the best ways to inspire confidence in me inside the caucus was to inspire it outside the caucus. If I could get Ontarians to start to believe in me, so would my colleagues.

One of the roles immediately thrust upon me as Leader of Her Majesty's Loyal Opposition was to kick off the daily Question Period in the legislature. Think of Question Period as a kind of boxing where opponents use words in an attempt to land solid blows on each other. The Leader of the Opposition's job is to attack, always. The premier's job is to parry attacks and counterpunch. The combatants are egged on by their supporters, and back-and-forth heckling heightens tensions. The exercise (some would call it a spectacle) takes place within the chamber, where the combatants are positioned directly across from each other at a distance of about twenty feet. In theory, Question Period is an important feature of a healthy parliamentary democracy. Governments strive to do good things but they do nothing perfectly. The responsibility of the Opposition is to hold up those imperfections for all to see and for the government to consider. In practice, Question Period has become a metaphor for what ails politics generally. We talk past each other. We seek political advantage instead of policy achievement. We seek to build our side up by taking the other side down. Ridicule and embarrassment are our objectives; instead, we should be promoting thoughtful exchanges leading to policy progress. But I had little considered these things when I first took up my role as lead prosecutor in Question Period. I was just eager to fit in and live up to expectations.

Initially, I felt awkward in Question Period. I was too loud and trying too hard to get the seven-second clip on the evening newscasts. I put far too much time — up to two hours — into my preparation. My legal training was urging me to try to know in advance the likely answers to whatever questions I put forward. However, unlike in a court of law, those being questioned are not required to properly answer the questions put to them. It took me a while to admit that it's just not possible to have in-depth policy debates in Question Period. Maybe that is why it is called Question Period and not Question *and Answer* Period.

Over time, I would grow more relaxed and less severe. I would later discover that being premier and fielding questions is much easier than asking them. I found the role of being accountable for the actions of my govern-ment a comfortable one. I tried to keep the temperature down and, where appropriate, the mood light. Above all, I tried to set a good example by being respectful of the Opposition. I had served there as leader for seven years. I knew how hard the job was. And how important it was.

Another of my chief concerns after winning the convention was put-ting together the office of the Leader of the Opposition. I was free to make whatever decisions I felt would best serve the caucus, our party, and Ontarians. Or so I thought. I chose to name Brendan as my chief of staff. When the news broke, however, it became controversial, the easy assump-tion being that the only reason I was hiring him was because he was my brother. Opposition came both from the media and within my caucus. Foolishly, I bowed to the pressure and rescinded the appointment.

Brendan is the most talented political mind I know. The only other people I would put on the same level are Don Guy, a brilliant political strategist who ran all my election campaigns (and who would serve as my chief of staff when I was elected premier), and Chris Morley, who began as my press secretary in Opposition and grew into a superb chief of staff in the premier's office. Brendan just has a natural instinct for politics. I'm an idealist and I see the best in people. But Brendan understands that some people in politics carry switchblades, and you need to be careful around them. He went on to become chief of staff for Bob Chiarelli when he was mayor of Ottawa. Later and over the years, Paul Martin, Michael Ignatieff, and Justin Trudeau would all try to recruit him to their teams. He has that kind of reputation. Brendan was gracious in the face of my decision: "You can't hire me. They don't want me, so it won't work."

Over time I would learn to insist on what and who I needed to grow stronger. I would understand that getting what you need to be at your best for your party is not being selfish. It's being responsible.

I have always been blessed with great talent to support me in my political roles. And serving as Leader of the Opposition was no exception. I bene-fited greatly from the hard work of capable and dedicated people like Matt Maychak, Monique Smith, Michael Cochrane, Jim Maclean, Kelly Legris, Bob Lopinski, Rod MacDonald, and many others — almost none of whom had ever before worked in a leader's office. We were neophytes. We were all working in the dark for a while. Over the years, I went through a number of staff, rarely firing people. (There is wisdom in the maxim that one should hire slowly and fire quickly.) I tried to develop a strong sense of team and loyalty, but you can't keep people forever. These are thankless, all-consuming jobs. It's easy — and common — to burn out.

Post-convention, I understood that the party faced a long rebuilding process. My first challenge was to get Liberals to believe in themselves. I had to do that before I could convince Ontarians to believe in us. Personally, I also needed to improve my performance. I began to get coaching on how to deliver a speech and conduct media interviews. Over time I would learn that improving my communications skills was something I could never stop doing. There would always be room for improvement. I found acquiring these skills to be very humbling. First, because you have to accept that you are coming up short. And then because you have to be ruthless with yourself in finding out *where* you come up short. I don't want to compare myself to a movie star, but if you watch one on a TV show while a clip of his latest movie is being shown, you'll see he won't watch it, or, if he does, he'll squirm uncomfortably. Not many of us like to watch ourselves perform. And I am no different. I've always hated reviewing a video of a speech or watching myself on TV. Because I'm never satisfied with my performance. In getting coached on delivery techniques, I had to be careful not to let myself be dismantled to the point where I lost my self-confidence. That is, I had to work hard to preserve my own sense of self while I was being told how to stand and sit, what to do with my hands, what to wear, and so on. Over time, I incorporated all the good advice I received and that helped me to be more self-confident and authentic. It actually helped me become comfortable just being me in public. It sounds silly, but in politics, where even the tiniest thing one does is analyzed to death in the media, it is easy to forget who the "me" of "being me" even is.

I also learned a lot about the media and their important responsibility.

My staff wisely counselled that "the media is not your friend," meaning that I should be on guard at all times in the presence of reporters. But I came to enjoy the various characters and personalities that make up the Queen's Park press gallery. By and large, we in Ontario are blessed with a strong and professional media, people dedicated to their craft and journalistic integrity under increasingly trying conditions. There is only about one-third the number of reporters at Queen's Park today as there was in 1990 when I was first elected. Reporters now are expected to file several times a day, to tweet, to blog, and to shoot video. With social media nipping at their heels and a demanding 24/7 news cycle that requires constant feeding — in an environment where there is just not that much newsworthy content — there is little doubt the quality of reported content has suffered. Politicians who organize stunts to attract the attention of reporters under impossible time constraints and grab sensational headlines do not make for a thoughtful presentation of our reality. We are all, media and politicians alike, desperately seeking attention. It feels like a circus, at times. Sadly, the public has become wise to the shenanigans and that is one reason confidence in both institutions has suffered. Reporters, just like the politicians they cover, are less than perfect. In a bid for attention in an incredibly competitive news environment, they can overreach. They sometimes get the story wrong. On occasion they refuse to cover the news we have worked so hard to deliver to them, preferring instead titillating aspects of politics over dry policy. For example, early in my term as Opposition leader there were times when I struggled to get out our story about the shortcomings of the Harris government and, occasionally, I would put out our own policy positions. Not infrequently, these media encounters would be derailed by the interest of reporters in the anonymous criticisms of me emerging from the caucus or elsewhere in the party. I was learning that politics often trumps policy in the news. When my staff thought the media had got it wrong, they would get upset and demand a retraction. I figured that, but for a few exceptions, it all came out in the wash and it was a mistake to attach too much weight to any one story.

I came to enjoy the strange kind of relationship politicians have with reporters. I learned about their personal lives and their struggles to make it in an industry going through painful, disruptive change. But I also understood my friendships with the media were not real in the sense that they were not built on loyalty. Any political misfortune on my part would be professionally welcomed on their part. It's not personal. It's just the way it is. We sometimes forget news is a business. And in the quest for sales and profitability, politics and politicians are a form of content to be presented in a way that promotes the bottom line.

Of all the Queen's Park media gallery characters I came to know, my favourite was Richard Brennan, nicknamed the Badger. The Badger has been around for decades, knows every trick in the book, and loves his craft. As his nickname implies, he is fearless and relentless. But for all his ferocious and unsentimental tenacity, his decency always comes through. He is a true professional. Tough with the questions but balanced in the reporting. And I loved to kid him as much as he enjoyed kidding me. During Question Period, the Badger would sit, godlike, with his colleagues in the media gallery, looking down upon us mere mortals, occasionally expressing his quiet disappointment by shaking his head from side to side. At times, he would ask one of the parliamentary pages to bring me a handwritten note, which bore some terse response to something I had said. His missives included messages like "Nobody's buying that. Resign!" I would fire back my own hand-delivered messages. My favourite: "My dear Badger. I am concerned for your health. I am afraid you are going to fall off your high horse."

In the early years of my leadership, I learned much about the various players on the stage that is politics, media included. But perhaps my most important lessons were about myself. I learned that my continuing growth demanded that I see myself as a work in progress. I needed to keep seeking advice and learning from my mistakes.

As party leader and premier, I was open to advice from just about everyone — a caucus colleague, a deputy minister in a department, a senior advisor in my office, a cab driver, or a security guard at the front desk. Since one can never know everything, it is crucial, I have learned, to utilize the counsel of others.

I have also always tried to set aside time to reflect. We lead lives today where we are drowning in information and thirsting for wisdom. And it seems to me that a prerequisite to wisdom is reflection. Whenever I delivered a speech, conducted a major interview, or led a difficult caucus or cabinet discussion, I would reflect that night and ask myself how I could have been more effective. I was never satisfied with my performance. This would drive Terri crazy. Her stock response to my self-criticism was, "You are being too hard on yourself." When I said I saw room for improvement, she would sigh, "I give up." She may have been right. I was hard on myself — maybe too hard — but I was hopelessly optimistic. I always believed I could keep growing. Without that belief, there would not have been a little part of my mind that responded positively years earlier to Greg Sorbara's suggestion that one day I would be Liberal Party leader.

I had been emboldened to run for the leadership because I believed that I could grow into the job. And because I also believed that it was going to be difficult for my opponents to outwork me when it came to doing whatever it took to grow stronger and smarter.

It was a belief that would soon be put to the test in the form of a provincial election.

CHAPTER FIVE
A Very Public Schooling

Everyone knew there would be an election in 1999. The only question was when. Of course, that was up to the Conservatives. But even before an announcement, the Conservatives launched a series of hard-hitting televised attack ads targeted at the Liberal Party and at me, in particular: "He's not up to the job."

Attack ads were not entirely new to Canada, but they were certainly new to me as a target. I kept telling myself that voters would not be so easily swayed, but deep down I sensed the ads would have an impact. Just how big an effect, I couldn't tell. To make matters worse, our party didn't have enough money to respond with a campaign of our own. This meant that Ontarians, who, by and large, knew very little about me, were being introduced to me courtesy of my opponents. Not surprisingly, my introduction was less than flattering. Well-intentioned supporters reassured me that I needn't worry; the *real* Dalton McGuinty would come through to the public at election time. Their reassurances were less than reassuring.

The Conservatives, for instance, launched an ad that falsely stated I had no health care plan. I remember a couple Terri and I had known for years calling us to say how disappointed they were with the negative ads and how proud they were of me for taking up politics. But then they asked, in passing,

"By the way, what *is* your health care plan?" So, there was no doubt in my mind — the negative ads were having an impact.

Sadly, attack ads have become more and more popular over the last twenty years. The federal Conservatives under Stephen Harper intensified the practice. When asked, people often say negative ads don't have an effect on them, but the truth is they do. That's why political parties use them. There is a risk, of course. The ads can backfire, as they did with the infamous 1993 "face ad" seeking to ridicule Jean Chrétien's physical appearance. Or they can be so over-the-top as to be easily dismissed. Effective attack ads sow doubt and mistrust. I certainly felt that, in my case, the ads had the intended effect. Not having the funds to respond, I felt I was fighting with one hand tied behind my back. After the onslaught of attack ads, I resolved that, in the future, I would make sure people got to know me on my own terms. If they didn't like me, I could live with that — just as long as they rejected the real me as opposed to some fictitious representation concocted by my political opponents. Honestly, though, as harmful as the attack ads in 1999 were, they weren't the cause (or even the principal cause) of my defeat. I had more to do with that than anyone else.

What bothers me still is not so much what those ads did to me personally, but the effect they had on my family. That first barrage of attack ads was a painful learning experience for my family. Children don't like to have a parent publicly demeaned. And they sure don't like being teased about it in the schoolyard. When they were around, I tried to pretend the ads didn't bother me. I would joke about the ads and do whatever I could to make light of them. Looking back, I realize that while I was pretending the ads didn't bother me for the sake of my children, they were pretending the ads didn't bother them for the sake of their father! In the end, we grew stronger as a family through the experience. But that's a side of politics none of us enjoyed. Terri, in particular, was angered by the ads: "How can they get away with that? They're lying!" She was my strongest champion, always ready to pounce on my attackers. Over time, I would develop a thicker skin. I would care less and less about my critics and more and more about simply doing what I believed was right. But not Terri; she was like a mother bear protecting her cubs. The kids would rise to my defence too. I remember I was golfing with the boys and a man yelled,

"Hey! McGuinty!" and was obviously about to launch into a tirade before Liam, then fifteen years old, said, "That's *Mister* McGuinty to you." The man was so embarrassed he turned and walked away.

This would not be the first time that I would experience this phenomenon. People find it easy to caricature politicians as ruthless, ambitious, and self-interested. They seldom see them as regular people. When they do, their perceptions become more complicated, more challenging, and more intelligent.

When it comes to attack ads, Question Period, and politics in general, all of us in politics would do well to respect a basic rule governing private-sector competition: don't attack the category. McDonalds doesn't urge consumers to avoid their competitors' hamburgers. General Motors doesn't badmouth a rival carmaker's products. Samsung doesn't run down Apple's iPhone. Private-sector competitors publicly build up their own products. They don't tear down the other guy's. And that's because they understand that attacks that undermine confidence in their competitor's products — hamburgers, cars, smart phones, whatever — will eventually undermine public confidence in *all* hamburgers, cars, and smart phones. You end up casting doubt over the entire category. Next thing you know, consumers are saying a pox on all your houses. And that's what more and more of our consumers are saying in the political marketplace. In the process of attacking each other, the whole category of politics has been badly damaged. When we seek to demean one politician, we demean all of them, including ourselves. No wonder so few people vote (barely half the electorate turned out in the 2011 and 2014 Ontario elections) and why there's so much cynicism toward politics and politicians. No wonder "you're all the same" has become such a common refrain. Of course there are other contributing factors, but in large part we politicians have brought this plague upon ourselves. I am not saying we shouldn't be critical of each other when it is warranted. Legitimate and thoughtful criticism serves the public interest. But our criticisms should be focused on ideas and not on individuals.

At any rate, the pre-writ Tory attack ads in 1999 put us on notice that it was going to be a very tough election campaign. Premier Mike Harris was a controversial figure, strongly disliked in some quarters but with a solid base of support. He had experience on his side. I was the rookie. I would be quarterbacking my first campaign as party leader. It was going to be an uphill battle no matter what.

We did have Don Guy, who today is one of Canada's premier political strategists. He had been in the Liberal research office in the early 1990s, and I had a nodding acquaintance with him. My staff suggested we recruit him for the election campaign team, so I saw him in my office in the summer of 1998. The meeting was scheduled for thirty minutes but lasted nearly three hours. At the end, I asked him to be my campaign manager. It would be his first time running a province-wide campaign and he would have to do it with a rookie leader up front. As good as he was, that was a tall order. We would all be learning on the job. At times we felt like a small boat being tossed around in a raging sea. There wasn't the precision and predictability typical of a well-developed and well-executed campaign plan fronted by an experienced leader. I was scrambling just to keep up. (Four provincial campaigns later, I can see clearly that I wasn't ready to fight and win a provincial campaign in 1999.)

Our platform was full of generalities but not much detail. We called it our 20/20 Plan, intending to offer a clear vision for the next millennium. We promised enforceable standards for health care, the best education, tough new laws to protect our environment, and a responsible fiscal plan, but we did not give voters a clear road map for achieving these ends. It also contained contradictions, including higher spending in some areas (health care and education), lower taxes for the middle class, and a balanced budget. We were trying to be all things to all people. Many Ontarians had had enough of the Conservatives' hard-right agenda, but our plan failed to inspire them. And in hindsight, it didn't do much to inspire me. I had yet to get on my policy horse and grow excited about what *I* believed were great ideas for my province. That would come later, as would my understanding that what mattered most in my campaigns was not what voters seemed to be looking for, but my belief in what I was offering. For me, it would come down to personal conviction. Best to put on offer what you strongly feel voters need instead of chasing their immediate wants. This won't guarantee success but it does guarantee your authenticity and you just can't win without that.

The 1999 campaign was a great, sometimes painful, and always public, learning opportunity for me. My team was giving me their best advice, but even the best teams can't possibly anticipate every eventuality, which meant that from time to time I had to rely on my own rough and still-very-raw instincts. I was learning on the fly but under the media's gigantic magnifying lens. Failing is one thing, but failing in public is something else altogether. I recall two rookie mistakes in particular. Once, I told reporters I was worried Harris's cuts to education would mean fewer school psychologists and less support for troubled youth who could be a danger to others. The cuts, I said, could lead to more tragedies like the one that had recently befallen a family in Taber, Alberta, who had lost a son in a school shooting. The media gleefully contacted the bereaved father who, understandably, took issue with my comments. I had crossed the line, and I apologized publicly. Another time, I foolishly allowed myself to be goaded by a wily and persistent reporter, Colin Vaughan, into calling Harris a thug. It was another very public, very rookie mistake. I had fallen into an obvious media trap by saying something a reporter wanted me to say instead of saying what I wanted to say. It embarrassed me to have reduced myself to calling an opponent a name. I learned much about the need for greater self-discipline from these mistakes.

Interestingly, we began the campaign against the Conservatives in a statistical dead heat, but polling showed that Harris was way ahead of me on the question of who would make the better premier. Our position was not sustainable. The nadir for us in the campaign was the televised leaders' debate, just two weeks before the June 3 election.

I had worked hard to prepare for it. We had two or three mock debates in a studio, with my friend and colleague Dwight Duncan playing the role of Mike Harris, and Tim Murphy, the always good-humoured and hard-working Ontario Liberal Party president, as NDP leader Howard Hampton. This made me familiar with the format. I practised my message track lines, and I got tips on when to attack. But when it came to the real thing, I was just hanging on. Debates are high-stakes games and participating in them has been one of the more difficult challenges I have faced in my life. Fortunately, the debates got easier for me over time, mostly because I would come to see them as a rare opportunity to speak directly to voters. I learned that, while the media were hoping for conflict and controversy, most viewers were genuinely interested in getting to know my policies and me. This knowledge helped me relax and focus on my message. But the pressure to perform would always be there. I compare it to the pressure put on Olympic figure skaters. They can perform their routines perfectly when practising in empty arenas. But throw in an audience and a live competition, and the pressure to perform well and the odds of making a mistake rise considerably.

I went into the debate desperately wanting to do well for all my supporters and for all those Ontarians who, I felt, would come my way if I could inspire their confidence. Unfortunately for me, things didn't go well. It wasn't just the pressure that got to me; I was thrown off by the tactics Harris employed against me. For example, in debate he would routinely side with NDP leader Howard Hampton, an unexpected and purely circumstantial alliance designed to keep me isolated and on the defensive. Harris went so far as to turn his back on me when I addressed him. (Harris stood centre stage with Hampton and me on either side, these positions having been determined by lot weeks ahead of the debate.)

What really took me back a few steps, however, happened near the end of the debate when Harris misrepresented a statement I had made previously and suggested I had a secret plan to fund private religious schools (this foreshadowed a real and very controversial plan later put forward by John Tory). This was flat-out untrue, but Harris caught me flat-footed and unawares, and to the television audience I must have appeared rattled. In fact, what I was was shocked. I just couldn't believe that a respected colleague — the premier of Ontario, no less! — would make something up and for purely partisan purposes. (Ironically, two years later Harris introduced a substantial tax credit for private schools, which my government later repealed. Only in politics!)

Another low point for me in the debate was when I was thrown by a loaded question from a media panellist. I had expected sharp attacks from my opponents, but not from the media. Live and learn. (This would be the last time media panellists participated in these debates. Panellists were later replaced by a single moderator introducing pre-taped questions received from Ontario voters.) These were all good lessons in the school of politics and debates in particular. I would need to learn to relax at the plate so I could better respond to whatever was thrown my way.

On leaving the debate stage inside the CBC building in downtown Toronto, I was joined by Terri and my son Dalton Jr., who had watched from inside one of the holding rooms made available to the candidates. Terri hugged me and told me I had done a great job. Dalton Jr. was equally proud. I'm sure they both believed it. Terri had been so busy teaching and taking care of the kids back in Ottawa that she had been with me on the campaign trail only intermittently. Whenever she could, she would join me on the bus on weekends and for major events, like the debate. This was a big mistake, and one I would not repeat in my subsequent campaigns.

Truth is, Terri was the most important person on my campaign. Her mere presence helped me relax and be myself. More than that, when necessary she was invaluable at building me up or, when she felt it was appropriate, taking me down. She was a great leveller; she kept me focused and grounded. I could share my hopes and fears with her, thoughts I could never share with others. She was, in a word, indispensable.

In the post-debate scrum, where the candidate's job is to appear relaxed and victorious responding to media questions, I actually did very well. I smiled and looked comfortable, all the while restating my main messages. Meanwhile, as per custom, the three parties had deployed their very best spin doctors to convince the media that their candidate had won. Frankly, I hadn't provided my team with much positive content to "spin." It was no surprise, then, that reviews of my performance were decidedly negative. And because the public tends to follow the media's lead, the instant conventional wisdom was that I had failed miserably. Polls conducted post-debate confirmed it. We went into the debate neck-and-neck with Harris and the Conservatives but emerged 16 percentage points behind. For me, it was a humiliating setback.

My campaign had pre-arranged a post-debate celebration at a local pub. Everyone put on a happy face but the event was uncomfortable for all of us. We all lied and pretended I had done wonderfully in the debate. I was all smiles on the outside but deeply disappointed on the inside. For days afterward I had difficulty sleeping. I didn't tell anyone, not even Terri, but I felt I had blundered away any chance we might have had of winning the election. Oddly, it was liberating. I had nothing to lose, right? So why not go for it? This time, though, I was going to do it *my* way. I stayed up most of the night and rewrote a speech I was to deliver to the Empire Club in Toronto the following day. It was an important speech, and for the first time in the campaign I was able to articulate what I really wanted to say:

At the end of the day, Mike Harris says that we should be against those people who are against him because, in the end, they are all just special interests. I take a different view when it comes to strong leadership. It seems to me that the responsibility of leadership is not to take sides but to bring sides together. Just think for a moment about the opportunities and challenges that await us in the twenty-first century, and all that we must do to find success there. Does anybody here honestly believe that we can continue to enjoy the luxury of infighting and bickering? With all we wish to offer our people in the new millennium, do you honestly think we can afford to continue down the path we have been following?

Mike Harris likes to say that I have made secret deals with union bosses. Well, I want to be on the record. I want to make people understand that from my perspective it is absolutely essential that I have labour at the table. But I also want business at the table. I want nurses at the table. I want teachers at the table. I want doctors at the table. I want farmers at the table. I want miners at the table. I want the forestry people at the table.

Mike Harris likes to stand in front of voters and target the gut area. He will do whatever he can to elicit a visceral response.... It seems to me that fundamentally the job of the leader is not to elicit a visceral response. It is not to reflect our worst; it is to bring out our best. Maybe I am a little bit old-fashioned about this, but it seems to me that the premier of Ontario should be someone that people can look up to, somebody who sets a high moral tone — someone who brings people together.

This evolved into my stump speech for the last two weeks of the 1999 campaign and, because I had written it myself and delivered it with conviction, my confidence rose, and my performance with it. Internally, as I said, I had already come to the conclusion that Harris was going to win the election. So I had nothing to lose. I felt much stronger and more relaxed. I would take every advantage of the rest of the campaign to keep introducing myself to

Ontarians. We closed the gap in the last two weeks and ended up with 40 percent of the popular vote, just five points behind the Conservatives. (It's always interesting to see how the popular vote translates into seats. In the 1999 election my 40 percent of the vote got me thirty-five seats; in 2014 my successor, Kathleen Wynne, would convert her 39 percent of the popular vote into fifty-eight seats — a comfortable majority and a much more efficient use of votes!) Harris had won, but he had a reduced majority, with the Liberals a strong second and the New Democrats a distant third. Some observers said that if the election had lasted another week we might even have won. I don't know about that. But I do know that my first election as leader had taught me a hell of a lot about campaigning and about myself.

On election night, it is customary for the losing candidates to congratulate the victor. I phoned Harris. "Congratulations, Mike, you ran a great campaign." His response surprised me. He said, "Hang in there. I know what it's like." Indeed, Harris had lost his first election too. The thought of resigning never crossed my mind. Regardless of the final vote count, I felt stronger and smarter in the job of leader of my party. I didn't want to throw away all the on-the-job training I had just received. I wanted to build on it. My first task was to convince my party that we needed to continue to invest in each other. I didn't want Liberals to develop a habit of changing leaders after every election defeat. I would convince my party that we needed to keep growing stronger … together.

The Ontario Liberal Party constitution requires a leadership review after every general election. No one openly campaigned against me, but a shadowy "Dump Dalton" movement emerged. I needed someone to take it on. I phoned Greg Sorbara. I needed his great combination of small-p political skills, energy, and idealism. He had been out of politics since the 1995 election, but he had always been a supporter of mine, having backed my bid in the 1996 leadership race. I told Greg I needed him to come out of his self-imposed political retirement and that I wanted him to run for president of our party. I didn't have to push too hard; Greg has always had a strong commitment to the party, and he believed in me. He agreed to come back into active politics, but only for a limited period. That limited period would stretch into more than a decade of public service. He won the party presidency, then ran in a by-election to enter the legislature, and eventually served in my Cabinet as finance minister. Over the years we had the same conversation a number of times. He would say, "I've got to get out now." And I would say, "You can't leave. I need you. Your party needs you. And Ontarians need you." And each time Greg agreed to stay. Eventually, of course, the yes became a firm no. I am forever indebted to Greg for his hard work, good counsel, and friendship over so many years — and his loyalty to the party and to me. From the day that Greg signed on to run for party president and for years thereafter, the Conservatives tried to make mischief by claiming he was after my job. It was an absurd and malicious charge; Greg was never interested in the leadership after he lost his own bid in 1992. His only motivations were loyalty to the Liberal Party, his friendship with me, and a powerful commitment to public service.

Back then, however, my immediate concern was winning the leadership review vote. That required planning and organization. Don Guy had become something of a lightning rod within the party in the wake of the election campaign, so he and I agreed it would be best to keep him out of the fray. I chose Christine Bome, a top organizer who had worked for Dwight Duncan in Windsor, to run my leadership review campaign. Dwight proved to be a huge help and an incredibly valuable asset. A Gerard Kennedy supporter at the 1996 leadership convention, he became a fearless champion of mine, both in Opposition and in government. Such was his loyalty to me that Dwight would later tell me that he would not leave politics until I did. He kept his word.

We ran a good ground campaign aimed at delegates to the convention where the leadership review vote would take place. On the other hand, our opponents in the Dump Dalton group were not well organized in their efforts. It was more a vengeful and spiteful campaign, based on anonymous mailings to Liberals and the media that were filled with internal gossip about me and about members of my team (some of it true, much of it false).

Some of my staff wanted to track down the Dump Dalton people and exterminate them, politically speaking. I said no to that. I did not want to spend a lot of time chasing phantoms. I wanted to marginalize them. So I kept my head down and moved forward with the purposeful objective of having Liberals conclude that I was working hard, that my performance was improving, and that I deserved another chance.

In the end, I won the leadership review by a comfortable 81 percent of the vote. That marked both the end of the Dump Dalton movement and a new beginning for me. My feelings then were markedly different from my feelings after winning the party leadership. With an election under my belt, a larger caucus, and a healthy amount of scar tissue built up from three years in the trenches as Opposition leader, I had grown a lot. I definitely felt stronger. I knew what I wanted and how to go after it.

Looking back at that 1999 campaign, I can say that not only was I not ready to lead a winning campaign, I was also not ready to lead a government. You couldn't have got me to agree to that at the time. I fully believed I could lead a government and lead it well. But hindsight reveals to me that I was too green. I was still learning about myself. Still growing into myself as a leader. What's more, I didn't have a crystal clear vision of where I wanted to lead Ontario. When I did win in 2003 — and again in 2007 and 2011 — I was much more experienced and much more ready. Very few party leaders win their first time out, and with good reason. I was no exception.

I began my march to greater success for my party by focusing on new ideas. I had learned that I loved policy. And the policy that I loved would be the foundation for our electoral success. I would continue to refine my skills as my party's pitchman, but now I understood that it was essential for me to run on a platform I believed in. That's when I was at my best. Our platform in 1999 had been very thin on specifics. It was cobbled together in haste and without a lot of research or critical thought on my part. It was a platform; it wasn't *my* platform. To me, our ideas felt "off the shelf"; I learned that I needed ideas that came from my core. Ideas that would allow me to speak with conviction.

Much of the credit for the 2003 platform has to go to Gerald Butts, a young man I hired as my chief policy advisor after the 1999 election. He had written me a long memo suggesting, among other things, that we hold a thinkers' conference similar in style to the 1960 event Lester Pearson and the federal Liberals staged during their wilderness years. When Butts and I met in the summer of 1999, we hit it off right away. You could say we experienced a *Star Trek* "Vulcan mind meld." We could finish each other's sentences. He had a voracious appetite for policy details, and so did I. We had a friendly competition over who could find the most interesting ideas online from Singapore, Ireland, Germany, South Carolina, or wherever. When it came to new ideas, the world was our oyster. It helped that Gerald's value set and background were similar to my own. He came from a big Catholic family in Cape Breton, and he believed in the nobility of public service. We both felt lucky to be in a position not only to develop ideas, but to actually implement them in government. We were both energized by the opportunity to make real and lasting change. We were like two kids in a candy shop.

With Butts as the chief organizer, we held a successful thinkers' conference at Niagara-on-the-Lake in 2001. Included among the guest speakers were Robert Reich, a professor at Brandeis University and former labour secretary in the Clinton administration; Roger Martin, dean of the Rotman School of Management at the University of Toronto; Dr. J. Fraser Mustard, founding president of the Canadian Institute for Advanced Research; Elizabeth May of the Sierra Club of Canada (and future leader of the Green Party); Toronto chief of police Julian Fantino; Michael Harcourt, former NDP premier of British Columbia; David Johnston, president of the University of Waterloo (and future governor general); and Marc Lalonde and Donald Macdonald, both senior ministers in the Trudeau administration. It was an impressive and diverse lineup, and many good ideas emerged from the conference.

My staff also plugged me into progressive political thinkers in both the United States and Europe. We took trips to Washington, D.C., Boston, Chicago, London, and Dublin, looking for both policy ideas and political advice. In London, Butts and I and my chief of staff, the affable and quick-witted Phil Dewan, met Michael Barber, who was then head of Prime Minister Tony Blair's "Delivery Unit," which made sure the government's priority programs were being implemented. I was very much impressed by Barber's innovative thinking. He would later visit me in Ontario and would become very influential in my own thinking as I looked for new methods to deliver measurable results. We adopted some of those methods when we took office in 2003 and built our own version of Blair's Delivery Unit. Barber told me that for advice on education he relied on Michael Fullan, who was in our own backyard at the Ontario Institute for Studies in Education. Fullan would become one of my closest confidants on education reforms.

We also got advice from David Axelrod, a Chicago-based political consultant who became a key player in Barack Obama's presidential campaign and, later, senior advisor to the president. In 2001 Axelrod had just finished running Hillary Clinton's successful campaign for the United States Senate. Her Republican opponent in that race was Rick Lazio, whose campaign had been run by Mike Murphy, nicknamed the "merchant of mud" for his fondness for negative ads. He had also done work for Mike Harris and the Ontario Conservatives and was a strategist behind the "not up to the job" attack ads aimed at me in the 1999 election. Matt Maychak, a senior aide in my office and a masterful communicator, suggested we reach out to Axelrod for advice on how to combat Harris and Murphy. I took several trips to Chicago to talk to Axelrod and his team. They would put me in front of a camera and critique my performance. They offered a lot of useful advice on everything from how to use my hands and hold my head to what to wear, what words to use, and when to display a sense of humour. It sounds burdensome, but I learned that if you incorporate that advice properly, you do not actually think of the techniques as you are speaking; they become second nature. This helped increase my confidence level and made me more relaxed. That helped relax my audiences, making them more receptive. The overall effect was that I began to come across as someone who was comfortable with himself. And I could feel it. It had often been said of me that I was wooden on camera. That was a fair criticism. But I was changing and I enjoyed audiences' reactions to the real me, which clearly clashed with the perception the media had fostered. Later, I would come to rely on Toronto television executive Jack Fleischmann for his sound advice on communications. I will never forget his wise refrain: "Slow down and let the words breathe."

I can recall an early occasion where, in an effort to get me to loosen up before an on-camera exercise, Axelrod said to me, "Tell me about Terri." I said, "She's a great teacher." The room erupted in laughter. Here I was asked to speak about my darling wife of (then) over twenty years — to say nothing of the fact that we had earlier dated for seven years — and the mother of my four beloved children, and all I could come up with was "She's a great teacher!" It would take time but I would learn to grow more open and to share a little more of myself and my family. I would come to better understand and respect people's natural curiosity about their political leaders. People want to know who you are as a person. You don't have to tell them everything, but you do have to open up a bit. It's only after people see you as a human being that you can begin to form an emotional bond with them and hope to inspire them with your leadership. Throughout my seventeen years in leadership politics, I would tell countless stories about my family and my own personal experiences. The majority of these were humorous and self-deprecating. And they always had the desired effect. People got to see me a bit more clearly and they always appreciated someone who could laugh at himself. Axelrod and his team were much more than just experts in communication. They also offered advice on strategy and policy. While they had a successful track record south of the border, including Hillary Clinton's successful Senate run, I wondered if what they offered was relevant to Ontario voters. Greg Sorbara, whom I had named chair of our election campaign team, was even more negative. He thought Axelrod was too expensive and, more important, knew nothing about Canadian politics. So we parted company before the 2003 campaign began in earnest.

Heading into that campaign, we had a thorough policy development process designed to produce a platform that was much more extensive than we had had in 1999. I insisted the caucus be given real opportunities to help shape the platform, although in the end it was my call. I stayed strong on this because I knew that a platform I believed in was the best chance we had of winning. Toe Blake, legendary coach of the Montreal Canadiens, used to say you should never break up a winning combination. My communication skills were improving and I really believed in my message. I was connecting with voters. Why mess with that?

———————————

There were some internal disputes over platform plans. But I learned that sometimes the best way to address internal doubts was to secure external support. On more than one occasion, I would deliver a speech in the riding of a wavering caucus member to give them an opportunity to witness how well my message was being received by their constituents. It's not supposed to be that way, but sometimes in politics the best way to build support is from the outside in. In the wake of the 1999 campaign, I knew I had to run on the things I really cared about: education, health care, the environment, and, later on, innovation and the economy.

Our 1999 platform was just twenty-seven pages long. In 2003 the platform consisted of seven booklets totalling 146 pages. Included were promises to:

- balance the budget while holding down taxes;
- attract more investment in the auto sector;
- invest more in colleges and universities;
- make attendance at school mandatory until age eighteen (up from sixteen);
- put a hard cap of twenty students on class sizes from kindergarten to grade three;
- create "turnaround teams" to tackle problems at under-performing schools;
- guarantee that 75 percent of students meet or exceed the standard in province-wide tests (up from about 50 percent);
- reduce wait times for cardiac care, cancer treatment, joint replacements, and MRIs;
- increase the number of family doctors and nurses;
- legislate family medical leaves;
- accelerate the accreditation of foreign-trained doctors;
- shut down all the coal-fired power plants by 2007;
- boost public transit with a dedicated gasoline tax and a GTA-wide planning authority;
- curb urban sprawl with a greenbelt encircling the Golden Horseshoe;
- ban self-promotional government advertising;
- establish fixed election dates;
- hold a referendum on electoral reform.

I am proud to say that we were able to deliver on almost all of the above. Shutting down the coal plants took longer than expected but we eventually got the job done. And I did raise taxes. Most important for me and for our party, I ran on a program I was personally committed to and absolutely determined to deliver. It was an ambitious platform, one the party and caucus had embraced and one I hoped Ontarians would embrace as well. No one could mistake the "activist" profile of my government. We were not going to be the dog that caught the car. We knew exactly what we intended to do in government.

I don't pretend voters were galvanized into voting Liberal because of our detailed platform in 2003. Voters could hardly be expected to carefully scrutinize our 146-page program. But they did want to be reassured that what we were offering by way of change was grounded in substance and represented the culmination of deliberate and thoughtful consideration of the times and what they called for. For me, ideally, I hoped our platform would give voters a sense that our party was playing the long game for Ontario's benefit rather than a short game for today's voters only. Hence, for example, my refusal to promise tax cuts at a time when many pollsters and pundits believed tax cuts were the price of admission into government.

———————

Besides an energizing platform for me, the other key difference between the 1999 and 2003 campaigns was our opponent. Mike Harris had quit politics abruptly in 2002. Ernie Eves, finance minister under Harris before leaving to take a job on Bay Street, had returned to win the Conservative leadership and assumed office as premier. Immediately, the pundits decided I was in trouble. The way they saw it, Eves was a Red Tory and my chances of becoming premier would have been better had his opponent, Jim Flaherty, won.

I never got the sense that Eves was driven by a powerful desire to bring about change. I'm certain he enjoyed the job of premier but, as I have learned, that isn't enough. The trappings of the office just won't sustain you. You need a burning desire to do something. You need to be leaning into the job. Eves was also trapped in a paradigm that was not of his own making. He was more moderate than Harris, but his campaign was being run by Harris's team, and that meant he was running on a right-wing platform that included more tax cuts and more attacks on teachers and immigrants. This platform was just not a natural reflection of Eves or what he really believed, and I believe voters sensed that. Additionally, voters were just plain tired of all the fighting. They wanted progress, as they always do, but now they wanted peaceful progress.

In any case, Eves made a critical mistake. He delayed calling the election for more than a year after he became premier. That gave us a chance to mark him up in the legislature and expose his personal discomfort — if not with the direction of the Harris government, than certainly with the divisive methods it had adopted. Worse, Eves was hit by a pair of crises that no one could have predicted: the SARS outbreak in Toronto in the spring of 2003, and the North American blackout that summer.

My NDP opponent was Howard Hampton. Hampton was nothing if not dogged. He had been made NDP leader following Rae's resounding defeat at the polls. Although in politics we never say never, it was a given that it would be some time before the NDP were again returned to government in Ontario. This meant that, in some ways, Hampton had a harder job than I. Realistically, he could not win. I had a chance. Having a real shot at government instills some discipline in your caucus. If it looks like you can win, they want to be onside. I sometimes saw Hampton arguing openly with his caucus colleagues in the legislature. Although circumstance brought us together in opposition to the government, I found him hard to get to know on a personal level. Hampton and his spouse, Shelley Martel, also an NDP MPP, were raising two young children and I understood how daunting a challenge it must have been to balance their political and family responsibilities. On one occasion, Hampton came under attack for his MPP travel expenses (incurred largely as a result of wanting to be with his children). I publicly defended him in his desire to spend time with his young family. He never acknowledged my support. On public occasions we were sometimes seated next to each other. But try as I might, I could never get him to open up and just chat about life in general. He never let his partisan guard down.

Still, despite all of this, I entered the 2003 campaign as the underdog. Even though my party was running slightly ahead of the Conservatives in the polls, at the outset of the campaign the voters had a more positive impression of Eves than of me, and the media were expecting me to fail. Being the underdog is a position that I came to relish in all my campaigns. I just felt better running from behind than trying to protect a lead as the front-runner. I enjoy the happiness of pursuit.

In 2003, apart from a platform I could go to the wall for, I had a number of other advantages I had lacked in 1999. For one thing, I was now an experienced campaigner. Before, I was just hanging on by my fingernails. In 2003 I felt confident, like I was in the driver's seat. The whole campaign team felt stronger. We had a lot more talent this time, including Warren Kinsella, a superb political strategist who ran our "war room." And this time, Terri was on the campaign bus with me. That made a huge difference. She kept me on an even keel when we were on the bus and it was wonderful having her by my side at all the stops along the way. She helped me relax and smile — powerful weapons in the battle for votes. The kids also rotated in and out of bus duty and injected a lot of fun into what was a highly pressurized environment.

This time around, I had a game plan and I knew it would take discipline to execute it. That meant avoiding distractions. One of the best pieces of campaign advice I received, and religiously followed in every campaign thereafter, was from former prime minister Jean Chrétien. "Dalton," he said, "you must completely ignore the media. That means no TV, no radio, and no newspapers. Just get in your zone and stay there." So I worked hard to get in my zone and stay there. If something happened during the campaign that was really important for me to know, somebody would tell me and I would adjust.

———————

Media interactions required lots of discipline from me. Reporters had their own stories they were pursuing and I had my own message I was trying to get out. TV pictures are very important in a campaign and my job was to look confident and relaxed. In a subsequent campaign, former premier Bill Davis impressed upon me how vitally important it was to keep smiling. "How can anyone believe all those bad things your opposition is saying if your reaction is a smile?" I compare the whole thing to walking on a tightrope without people knowing, because all the camera shows is your face. And that face had better be relaxed, confident, and smiling.

The whole 2003 campaign had a different feel from the get-go. We were all leaning into it with confidence. Starting from behind in the polls made all of us comfortable, especially me. The Conservatives again ran negative ads against me, this time with the tag line: "Dalton McGuinty, he's still not up to the job." My team and I resisted responding in kind. We felt the Tory ads smacked of desperation and would be seen as such. We ran positive ads speaking to Ontarians about our positive agenda. After the first week, we could feel the momentum building at every bus stop on our tour.

My first campaign had taught me just how important the campaign bus is. It's a rolling office, fully stocked with technology, food, and clothing changes — everything you need for long days on the road — and "wrapped" on the outside with pictures and slogans. But the most important ingredient on the bus is the people. These include the driver, a police officer (supplied by the OPP to all leaders during a campaign), and four others who were part of my political team. Apart from my brother Brendan, who was a constant, these four would vary a little bit from campaign to campaign. All the members of our little corps had to be cool under fire and possessed of a good sense of humour. The last thing I wanted inside the campaign-bus pressure cooker was an explosive personality. In 2003 I had been given the opportunity to design my own space in the rear of the bus. I included a couch, a La-Z-Boy chair, a desk with chairs, and a TV for movies, which I never watched. There was also a big clock, a vanity mirror, and a calendar so I could cross off the days as they went by, something I enjoyed very much. The bus was stocked with plenty of goodies of the fattening and non-fattening variety. I had lost too much weight during the first campaign and had resorted to food-supplement drinks. This time around there was lots of food to keep my team and me going.

As a matter of daily routine, we would pile into the bus early in the morning and hit the road, with three or four stops along the way. I was sometimes afraid of being asked where I was and not knowing. We would play loud music just before each stop to ramp up our emotional level, and Terri and I would position ourselves by the door, ready to exit as soon as we stopped. My objective when I stepped outside was to enjoy the experience of meeting supporters and deliver a clean message through the media, all the while avoiding the dreaded gaffe and the ensuing "orchestra pit phenomenon." This is where a politician delivers an inspiring speech on, say, how to bring lasting peace to the Middle East but accidentally falls into the orchestra pit. Guess which event will generate more news coverage? Not the speech.

Relaxing at the plate in the 2003 campaign meant we could take advantage of opportunities when they arose. For instance, at one point during the campaign an overzealous Conservative campaign worker labelled me an "evil reptilian kitten-eater from another planet." As luck would have it, when the news broke I was visiting a farm and a barnyard kitten presented itself. I approached it hoping it wouldn't run away or start scratching me. The kitten behaved beautifully and allowed me to pick it up and cuddle it. This made for great TV and newspaper pictures. In 2003 even the cats were with us.

The 2003 televised leaders' debate was uneventful. Which was exactly what I was hoping for. In contrast to my previous outing, I was relaxed, confident, and much better prepared. I also better understood my objective: seize the opportunity to speak directly to Ontarians — and that is what I did.

We won the election handily — a majority of seventy-two seats out of 103. The Liberals garnered 46.5 percent of the popular vote, more than the Harris Conservatives in either 1995 or 1999. It was an emphatic victory. Our last victory at the polls had been sixteen years earlier in 1987. So this triumph was a great cause for jubilation. But on election night, in keeping with the McGuinty nature, I was privately more daunted than jubilant, already beginning to feel the weight of expectations and thinking about the work ahead and how I was going to get it done.

CHAPTER SIX
Leading Change

Becoming premier meant big changes in my personal life. Of course, the biggest change was that Terri and I had to move our family to Toronto. In my thirteen years in Opposition we maintained our home in Ottawa. That minimized the disruption for my family, and I could always come home on weekends. But once I became premier, Toronto had to be my home base. Greg Wong, at the time the tireless president of the Ontario Liberal Fund came up with a creative solution: the Liberal party bought a house for us to live in, in midtown Toronto. Terri and I were very grateful as this meant we would not be forced to sell our home in Ottawa, one we wanted to return to after politics.

I had one more surprise. As premier, I would be under the watchful eye of an Ontario Provincial Police detail. The remarkable men and women of this detail proved to be one of the highlights of my job. They were warm, considerate, thoroughly professional, and, when circumstances permitted, almost invisible. Many days I spent more time with these police officers than I did with my family. From time to time there would be some kind of threat made against me, but this never stopped me from doing my job or pretty well anything else I wanted to do. Each family member was briefed on safety issues and we all quickly settled into our own routines. Although it raised a few OPP eyebrows, Terri and I regularly took our dog, Mikki, for walks in the local park without OPP supervision. And although I was never supposed to drive, I did sneak out in our car on a few occasions.

A typical day on the job as premier began with the OPP picking me up first thing in the morning after my exercise routine. On the way to Queen's Park, my staff briefed me by phone on the latest news developments. I would also get in a few calls that had been previously arranged. At Queen's Park, I always said hello to Don, the affable security guard outside my door. Generally, I took breakfast at my desk: a plain whole-wheat bagel and orange juice until later on, when I graduated to fresh ginger tea made by our office den mother, Wendy Wai.

Office time was generally spent in an endless series of meetings and telephone calls with staff, bureaucrats, ministers, and others — meetings and calls that were interrupted by my attendance in daily Question Period, a weekly caucus, Cabinet meetings, and scheduled events throughout the city. Frequently, I would meet with the media. And, of course, there were meetings with Ontarians who had obtained an appointment to meet with the premier. As time wore on, I began to master my schedule and to insist it better serve my purposes and help me move my agenda forward. I learned how to balance the list between those who wanted to see me with those I wanted to see. I also had to insist on time to review briefing materials and to reflect. There was no shortage of information for me to consume, but I was frequently time-challenged when I needed to process all of it in my head.

As part of my routine, when I paid a visit to some place outside of the legislature, for example a school (my favourite "field trip" destination), hospital, or manufacturing plant, everything was "advanced" carefully by staff so we knew exactly what we were getting into and how everything was going to unfold. Always, time was of the essence and I often wished I had more time to chat with my hosts and learn more about them. My team had to keep me moving. There was always the next appointment to be kept. But not everything could be controlled. On a couple of occasions as I was delivering a speech to audiences in Ottawa and Toronto, the room was stormed by demonstrators. I simply remained at the podium and waited for the whole thing to blow over. Once the demonstrators had made their point, they left. I would turn to my audience and say, "If that interruption is the price we have to pay to live in a healthy democracy, I consider it a very small price."

Most evenings I travelled directly from Queen's Park to various events, sometimes several, most often speaking to the assembled. This, like so many other parts of the job, required that I develop the ability to quickly change gears and be "in the moment." My responsibilities could take me in short order from a celebratory cultural event to a solemn memorial.

At day's end I would arrive home, usually around nine o'clock, sometimes later. It was only then that I had dinner. I almost never ate at events. I cherished my quiet dinners at home. These were an injection of sanity into what could be an otherwise crazy day. Later in the evening I would open the file my staff had sent home with me and review my briefing materials in preparation for the next day. The days were long but they were also incredibly stimulating. I rarely felt tired and I looked forward to the work.

Along with the changes in my own life were the changes that accompany a new government. When governments change hands in our parliamentary system, there is a very short transition period — a couple of weeks, no more. The incoming premier has to scramble to get ready to govern.

One of my first tasks was to sit down with Ernie Eves, the outgoing premier. I hadn't seen him for several days and I thought he looked years older. The campaign and the loss had obviously been wearing. Our conversation was brief and, I thought, forced on his part. This was understandable. He was extending me a traditional courtesy, one he had hoped never to extend. I felt for Eves. It is one thing to run and lose your first election at the beginning of your career as a leader, as I had. But it is quite another to face a first defeat at the end of a successful career. I sensed strongly that Eves had not been prepared to lose, whereas I understood that losing was a real possibility at the time of my first election. For years afterward, it seemed to me that Eves continued to define himself by his election loss.

When he returned to Queen's Park nine years later for the hanging of his official portrait (a privilege granted all former premiers), I spoke at the event. I was very complimentary to him and was surprised when he took some thinly veiled shots at me (and others) in his own speech. I remember a TVO dinner event celebrating host Steve Paikin's twenty years at the helm of its program *The Agenda*. Eves had been invited to speak and again, he stood out as a guy with a chip on his shoulder. Strangely, I saw Eves as a guy who had enjoyed a remarkably productive and successful political career.

While I was grateful for his contribution, he seemed to see himself only as a guy who had lost his last election.

Eves' staff and mine worked well together to ensure a smooth transition. And the bureaucracy had already prepared for the change in government with binders of documents. This proved to be a troublesome practice later on when the bureaucrats, as required, prepared costings for our campaign promises, estimates that became public and with which we did not agree. Independent of this minor kerfuffle, Tony Dean, secretary of the Cabinet (the top public servant in the province) under Eves, came to see me and tendered his resignation. Dean believed the choice of Cabinet secretary was the premier's alone, and as there was a new premier at the helm it was only right that he vacate his position. I didn't know Dean that well, but I had heard good things about him. I thanked him for his offer but asked him to remain. He accepted, and in retrospect it was one of the best moves I made. Dean was a consummate professional who knew his way around Queen's Park like no one else. He said, "Count on me for fearless advice and loyal execution." For the next five years until he retired, I did just that. Dean helped me understand which of my ideas were sensible and which ones were problematic. He and his colleagues in the civil service would prove to be valuable partners as I sought to convert ideals and ideas into sound public policy.

In my election night speech, I had told the public service that I was looking forward to working with them. Under the Conservatives, public servants had often been portrayed as the enemy. I thought it was important to send an early signal to Ontario's public servants. I was genuinely eager to work with them, and I knew I would have to count on them. The fact is, premiers and their governments come and go. But the civil service is always there. They provide the continuity, the stability, and the institutional memory that informs good political judgment. Any government that fails to draw on that resource does so at its peril and to the detriment of the public it serves. Until I was elected premier, I had never set foot in the Cabinet room! I absolutely had to count on Ontario's public service to guide me.

Just before being sworn in as premier I agreed to an interview with two reporters from the *Globe and Mail*, Richard Mackie and Murray Campbell. Mackie asked how I was feeling about it all. I took a long pause. Mackie said, "I can see movement behind your eyes. How are you feeling?"

"I just don't want to screw up."

It was the old McGuinty response to a grand occasion I had worked so hard to make possible. I was about to be sworn in and I could not sense celebration. I felt only humbled. I could feel the weight.

I would not be sworn in alone. I had chosen a Cabinet. I had consulted a few people — not on whom to choose but on the principles to rely on in making such choices. Again, some of the best advice came from Jean Chrétien, who was still prime minister at the time. He told me to put my strongest people — the ones with the best political skills — in the toughest jobs. Seems obvious, only it isn't — especially when you are up close to the decisions. I had another rule I followed: create balance by ensuring regional, ethnic, generational, and gender diversity. In order to achieve that diversity, I realized it was necessary to appoint some people who were politically untested; it was risky, but I thought the risk justified. I wanted Ontarians, young and old, to see themselves in the makeup of my Cabinet.

John A. Macdonald once said, "Give me better wood and I will make you a better Cabinet." Better wood was not a problem for me in 2003 or later on; I was fortunate to have a big and talented caucus to choose from. Indeed, my biggest dilemma was deciding which of many worthy candidates I would have to pass over. Choosing a Cabinet is a wrenching experience for members of the caucus too. Each sees him- or herself as worthy of Cabinet promotion, but only a few are tapped. The process leads inevitably to disappointment. For most, the sense of loss dissipates with time. For a few, it never does, and resentments metastasize. I did what I could to validate those who felt left out or unappreciated. I gave them other responsibilities and always demonstrated respect for them. But at some point, you have got to accept disappointment and disgruntlement and get on with the job of governing.

I wasn't elected premier to be everyone's best friend.

It came as a mild surprise to some that I tapped Greg Sorbara for finance instead of Gerry Phillips, who had been a superb finance critic in Opposition. Actually, it was an easy call: Phillips had made it clear to me that he would prefer a lower-profile ministerial position. I also respected Sorbara's judgment. I thought he would make a great finance minister, and he did not disappoint me. He was an excellent steward of the province's finances throughout our first term in office. He was forced to take a six-month hiatus from finance, however, after he was wrongly named in a search warrant during an RCMP fraud investigation into Royal Group Technologies (where he had been on the board of directors). Greg's connection to the case was always spurious, but he and I agreed that it was best for him to step aside while the investigation continued. The period of the investigation was very hard on Greg and his family, but they managed through it with inspiring grace and dignity, and a judge subsequently determined there was no cause for including Sorbara's name in the warrant. I immediately reappointed him as minister of finance.

Another surprise for some was my decision to make Joe Cordiano minister of economic development. He himself was surprised, given our falling out when we were both in Opposition. But I had never felt right about yanking him out of the deputy leader's job, so I was keen to make amends by offering him a senior portfolio for economic development. I told him I had every confidence in him, and he responded in an exemplary way. Among other things, he was the architect behind the Ontario Automotive Investment Strategy, which helped Ontario leapfrog ahead of Michigan as the largest auto-producing jurisdiction in North America, a leadership position we held for the balance of my three mandates. I was sorry to lose Cordiano three years later when he retired from politics, but there was a silver lining: this was an opportunity for me to bring a very promising colleague, Kathleen Wynne, into Cabinet.

In addition to Cordiano, all my other opponents in the 1996 leadership race got senior positions — Dwight Duncan in energy, John Gerretsen in municipal affairs, and Gerard Kennedy in education. (I couldn't put Annamarie Castrilli in Cabinet because she had crossed the floor to the Conservatives and then lost her seat.) It was a "team of rivals," to borrow the title of Doris Kearns Goodwin's book on the presidency of Abraham Lincoln, and by and large it worked, because I put the right people in the right positions. The advantage I enjoyed is that I had been in caucus a long time and I knew these people. I knew their qualities and their talents, and they did not disappoint me in their roles. Some leaders constantly tinker with their Cabinets, but I was not eager to make changes. It takes a long time for cabinet ministers to get up to speed. They need time to grow into their jobs and develop confidence based on knowledge acquired and experience gained.

I regularly impressed upon my cabinet ministers that they ought to feel privileged to be at that table and I insisted they remain sensitive to the needs of caucus. In our caucus meetings I made it clear that I wanted to hear from cabinet ministers only if time permitted. Ministers had lots of opportunity to speak up at Cabinet meetings. I wanted us to hear from the rest of caucus.

Over the years, my experience with cabinet ministers led me to be on the lookout for two problems that can arise from time to time. *Mission creep* is what can happen when a cabinet minister becomes so increasingly infatuated with a particular area of policy that they veer off in unanticipated and often unapproved directions; it becomes a race with no finish line. There is no shortage of things to be done, but there is a limited amount of time, money, and political capital. We had to respect those limitations. We needed the discipline to say no to distracters.

Cabinet ministers can also be afflicted by *ministeritis*. They can get too full of themselves. A car and driver are at their disposal, everyone addresses them as "minister," doors are held open for them, invitations pour in for them to speak at events, and so on. I wanted all of us to keep our feet on the ground. I didn't want us to confuse the trappings of power with our real privilege: to serve the public. On a few occasions I found it necessary to bring a wayward minister in for "the talk." They were sheepish but, without exception, they picked up their game. As for who would give me the talk if required, my most senior staff had the job of correcting me when required. I like to think I was a good student.

Ministers are regularly sought out and lobbied by "stakeholders," people and organizations who can be directly impacted by the minister's actions. For example, teachers lobby the minister of education and nurses lobby the minister of health. Where stakeholders are concerned, I believe there is an important distinction between the role of individual ministers and the role of Cabinet. I explained to my Cabinet that "as ministers, you will all come to know your stakeholders well. Your job is to work closely with them and to make all of us at this table aware of their issues and concerns. But as a Cabinet, we are a little apart from stakeholders. Instead, we stand close to that vast majority of Ontarians who never come into contact with us. These people are counting on us to never forget them and to always be fair."

To boost the role of my backbenchers, I took the unprecedented step of having all of them take the oath of secrecy so that they could participate in Cabinet decision-making. "For the first time in Ontario history, every MPP in the government caucus will sit on Cabinet committees," I said in my speech at the swearing-in ceremony for the new government. "And those committees will be chaired by non-ministers. In keeping with our parliamentary traditions, decisions will remain with Cabinet. But with this innovation, MPPs will have real, meaningful input into those decisions. When it comes to policy-making in our government, there will be no backbench." I had been warned that giving the backbench access to Cabinet secrets would lead to damaging leaks. It never happened.

With the ministers themselves, I adopted an approach that was articulated by Michael Barber, an advisor in Prime Minister Tony Blair's office: *intervention in inverse proportion to success*. A minister who was performing well would not hear from me. But if there were problems, I would get involved.

I borrowed another Tony Blair innovation: a "results table" for the major portfolios (such as health and education and, later, justice). I would meet periodically with the ministers and their teams, including the deputy ministers, but I also insisted that we be joined at the table by outsiders who were experts in the field — the CEO of a hospital, for example, if it was the health portfolio. I chaired the meetings, and the minister and the deputy would start with an overview. I then would call on the expert for a "real world" perspective. That is how I was able to hold our government's feet to the fire as we pursued specific targets, such as wait times in health care and test scores in schools. We would compare the results we were measuring to the targets we had set for Ontario. Then I would ask what I could do as premier to help us reach our targets. It was a focused intervention on my part. And it worked.

In the past, governments had rarely so explicitly set the bar for their own performance. Instead of measurable outputs, governments had traditionally measured their own success in terms of inputs — more money, more people, more buildings, and more roads. Inputs are easier to manage than outputs, and that makes "success" easier to achieve. But all those inputs sometimes do little to improve outcomes. I thought it was time for us to start focusing on outputs that were measurable, like our high-school graduation rate, or wait times for a hip operation, or our court backlog. We needed to move the needle in these and other areas, and I knew that just putting more money into the system was no guarantee of progress. We needed to objectively measure these kinds of things, make those measurements public, and drive strategies to achieve our targets. By making our targets public, we were throwing our hat over the wall, and we had no choice but to find a way over to retrieve it.

In the early days in government, I was also influenced by the book *Reinventing Government: How the Entrepreneurial Spirit Is Transforming the Public Sector,* by two Americans, David Osborne (who later became a senior advisor to Vice-President Al Gore), and Ted Gaebler. Most people assume from the book's title that it is a right-wing tract advocating the downsizing of government. But the book's real message is how to make government more effective, not necessarily smaller. The authors' thesis is that government should steer, not row. And I was eager to find opportunities to engender public-sector entrepreneurialism. For example, we introduced "pay for performance" for hospitals. Hospitals that delivered a procedure at lower cost got funded to do more of these procedures than their higher-cost counterparts. We were incenting outputs, and it didn't take long for hospital administrators to catch on and make productive changes.

And then there was the challenge of birth certificates. I was embarrassed because my government was taking up to a year to deliver these. I used to joke that I was afraid a child born in Ontario would get their driver's licence before their birth certificate. It was a relatively small issue, but I thought it readily lent itself to public-sector innovation. I spoke to Gerry Phillips, the minister responsible, to let him know there was private-sector interest in taking on the job of reducing birth certificate turnaround times. Phillips wisely pleaded with me for time to resolve the issue in-house. I told him we needed a money-back guarantee: the birth certificate would have to be delivered within a certain period of time or it would be free. Phillips talked to his senior bureaucrats, who got creative and came back to us with an innovative proposal, a first for North America, to shift to an online application service with a guaranteed delivery within ten days. They pulled it off — the cost was lower and there was a 99.9 percent success rate! That was a wake-up call to the rest of the bureaucracy that they could compete with the private sector on these sorts of services. We later expanded the money-back guarantee to other services, like marriage certificates and personalized license plates. Then we adapted the model for GO train riders, refunding their fare if the train was late.

Shortly after we formed the government, we were informed by the Ministry of Finance that, contrary to what the Eves government had claimed, the budget was not balanced. In fact, we had inherited a *hidden deficit* of $5.6 billion! I was stunned. I thought to myself, *Welcome to government and realpolitik.* I was trapped between a rock and a hard place; I was definitely about to experience some political pain. On the one hand, I had promised to invest in the restoration of public services, like health care and education. On the other, I had made a specific and very public commitment to not raise taxes.

On September 11, 2003, during the election campaign, I signed the so-called Taxpayer Protection Pledge to hold down taxes. The Conservatives were telling Ontarians I had a secret plan to raise taxes, and my team insisted we had to inoculate ourselves against those attacks by signing the pledge. Given the Eves government's assertion that the budget was balanced, I felt confident in making my commitment. But now none of this mattered. I was about to break a promise and I hated it.

I struggled for weeks with my unappetizing choice. I slept poorly and lost my appetite. I kept hoping officials in the Ministry of Finance would come up with some magic. But there was none to be found. It fell to me to decide. In the years following, I would come to understand that if you have to swallow a toad, you shouldn't stare at it for too long. Waiting just doesn't help. Better to get on with it. Don't waste your energy in useless fretting. Save it for the hard part: communicating the reasons for your decision and why you believe what you did was the right thing.

After much reflection, I decided my highest obligation was to improve public services — in particular health care and education. Everything else was secondary. That meant I had to break my commitment on taxes to make sure we had the revenue to improve public services. I knew there would be a backlash.

My broken pledge was later made the subject of a legal challenge. I was pleased when the court ruled in my favour: "From the record," the court stated in its ruling, "it is apparent that upon taking office and assessing the situation, the government believed that it would be contrary to the public interest to keep the promise made during the election.... This decision not to keep the promise does not mean that the promise, when made, was untrue, inaccurate, or negligent." I was happy to have the court onside, but the court that really mattered was the court of public opinion.

Of course, the budget was the direct responsibility of finance minister Greg Sorbara. He and I met on numerous occasions prior to the tabling of our government's first budget in the spring of 2004. We were bubbling up options and considering alternatives. We came to the conclusion that we had to raise taxes, but Greg got there more quickly than I did. In that first budget, we imposed a tax in the form of a health premium, ranging up to $900 for Ontarians with a taxable income of over $200,000. (Families with incomes below $20,000 were exempt.)

There was an immediate uproar. "Fiberal," shouted the *Toronto Sun* on its front page, with a caricature of me growing a Pinocchio-like nose. This was a gift for the right-wing media, like the *Sun*. I should have charged them a fee for the two-by-four I gave them to whack me over the head.

I toured the province to pitch the budget's merits, including higher spending on health care and education. I knew it was going to be challenging politically, but I did not fully anticipate the extent of the anger and feeling of betrayal. I remember getting death stares on the street and in airports. However, I firmly believed I was doing the right thing *and* that we had time to recover. We needed to convey to Ontarians that this was not a capricious decision or part of a nefarious plot that we concealed during the campaign. Rather, the tax increase was a reasoned and responsible response to extraordinary circumstances — a massive deficit that had been hidden from us by the Eves government.

Even so, by the time the next election rolled around in 2007, lingering resentment and anger over the tax hike was still part of the political picture; we challenged voters to consider our overall record, not just the tax hike. We succeeded, although not without some help from the Opposition.

To ensure that no new government would ever again be surprised by a hidden deficit, we passed a law requiring the government's financial books to be audited *before* an election. This is another responsible-government innovation I am very proud of.

My first and highest personal priority in office was always education. My grandparents had never made it to high school. Two generations later I was premier. To me, this was nothing short of miraculous. It spoke to Canada truly being a land of opportunity, a nation where our past in no way limits or determines our future. It spoke to the love, support, and encouragement given to me by my parents. And of greatest importance to me as premier, it spoke to education as the true ladder of opportunity. And now I was in a position to make education even better and more accessible to more families working hard to get ahead. I wanted every child in every family, regardless of their socio-economic circumstances, to achieve their potential through a great system of public education. I firmly believed that, unlike in the days of our parents and grandparents, the strength of our economy was now directly related to the skills and education levels of our people. Quality education for all of us was now more than a moral imperative. It was an economic necessity.

I felt for my various ministers of education because I often had my nose in their files. My first minister, the one who really set the tone and pace for the dramatic progress we made, was Gerard Kennedy. He and I were old leadership rivals, and he had a loyal cadre of supporters that refused to disband. I didn't mind. In fact, I admired that kind of loyalty. I was happy to have Kennedy as part of my team of rivals. I gave him what, for me, was my most important file: education. And he did not disappoint. He was creative and worked well with teachers. Among other things, Kennedy demonstrated real skill in getting four-year labour agreements with our teachers, something that had never before been done. This set the table for all the progress we were to make in our schools. Most important, he helped me get real, measurable progress in our test scores and high-school graduation rates.

Over the years I was blessed with an exceptional team of education ministers, including Gerard Kennedy, Sandra Pupatello, Kathleen Wynne, Leona

Dombrowsky, and Laurel Broten. To Broten fell the difficult challenge of constraining costs in the aftermath of the 2008–2009 recession, and in this she acquitted herself very well.

When we formed the government, our schools were suffering from neglect, poor performance, and low morale. Labour unrest was the order of the day. Parents had lost confidence in public education. Record numbers of students had left public schools for private alternatives. Only 54 percent of students were meeting the provincial standard for literacy and numeracy, and only 68 percent were graduating from high school.

We had campaigned on a plan to improve our schools. We had promised peace, stability, respect, smaller classes, higher test scores, and higher graduation rates. And we kept all those promises. We capped class sizes in the early years at twenty-three, with 90 percent of classrooms having twenty or fewer students. Some eleven thousand additional teaching positions were funded, with an emphasis on more specialists in physical education, music, and art. And we made a massive investment in school building projects. Most important, we got results. Our test scores went from 54 percent to 70 percent, while our graduation rates increased from 68 percent to 82 percent. The gap in student achievement between our non-English-speaking students and others dropped from 24 percent to 11 percent. And our international rankings put us in the top five in science and reading.

I was pleased with all the progress we made in education but, as in every other area where our government achieved progress, I felt there was always room for improvement. I kept remembering the Belgian car that broke the world land speed record in 1899 by going one hundred kilometres per hour. The name of the car was La Jamais Contente (The Never Satisfied). We could all be proud of the progress we had made in our schools, but I did not think we should ever be fully satisfied. There was always more to do, more to be learned. And what I learned along the way about education reform can be briefly summed up in seven lessons:

Lesson One

The drive to make progress in our schools can't be a fad. It has to be an enduring government priority backed by resources and an intelligent plan.

Lesson Two

Education reform is not important to the government unless it's important to the head of the government, personally. As premier, I took personal responsibility for driving academic achievement.

Lesson Three

It doesn't matter how much new money you invest in schools; you won't get results unless you enlist your teachers in the cause of better education.

Lesson Four

To succeed, you can't just issue orders from on high; you have to build capacity in the ranks. Among other things, you need to invest in teacher training and encourage the sharing of best practices among schools.

Lesson Five

Settle on a few priorities and pursue them relentlessly. We chose class sizes, test scores, and graduation rates. Exercise discipline by saying no to distracters.

Lesson Six

Once you start making progress, you've got permission to invest more. Nobody wants to invest in failure, but investing in success is another story.

Lesson Seven

You're never done. You're never done learning about how to do things better and you're never done applying those lessons.

Health care was another major challenge for us when we took office. During their tenure in office, the Conservatives had closed hospitals and laid off nurses to save money, but they did not tackle the sort of systemic change that would make our universal health care system sustainable in the long run.

To tackle the challenge, I appointed George Smitherman as minister of health. He was a quick study who was well-suited to the challenge of a complex file, and a take-no-prisoners kind of guy who could drive the sorts of changes we needed to make. There were a lot of defenders of the status quo within the system. We needed to quickly overcome this inertia to achieve our ambitious goals, which included improved access to family care and shorter wait times for cardiac care, cancer treatment, joint replacements, and MRI/CT scans. Later, we would add emergency-room wait times to our list of targets. The wait-time situation was acute when we took office. For example, only 31 percent of cancer patients were receiving radiation treatment within the recommended four-week window.

Like the approach we brought to education, our health care reform demanded that we publicly report on our chosen indicators (wait times), set public targets we wanted to achieve, and implement a comprehensive strategy to drive successful change.

I put Dr. Alan Hudson in charge of the wait-time file. A brilliant neurosurgeon, Hudson had been president of Toronto's biggest hospital complex, the University Health Network. One of his best attributes was that he could smell "bull" a thousand miles away. Defenders of the health care status quo would say we can't do this or we can't do that, and Hudson would call them on it. He broke a few eggs along the way, but he succeeded in bringing wait times down dramatically. Without his smarts and Smitherman's determination, we would not have achieved what we did. Later, I put Hudson in charge of eHealth, the agency charged with digitizing Ontario's health records. That did not turn out as well, as we shall see in a subsequent chapter, though Hudson was not to blame.

As in education, we got measurable results in health care, including some of Canada's shortest wait times, access to a family doctor for 2.1 million more Ontarians, electronic medical records for nine million Ontarians (up from seven hundred thousand), and Canada's most comprehensive newborn screening program. Of course, just as with education, the job of improving health care — and that includes ensuring that any improved service is sustainable — will never be done. But that should not deter us. It's a magnificent Canadian challenge, and one I feel we are more than up to.

It so happened that the health file was my introduction to government labour negotiations. We had been negotiating with Ontario doctors to land a new agreement that would determine how much they would be paid for their services. After nine months of negotiations, things were getting sticky, and Smitherman recommended that we pay a visit to the team leading the talks on behalf of doctors. I was to let them know politely but firmly that we had reached the end of our rope. I did not feel entirely comfortable inserting myself into the process, but it needed doing and I got it done. I was eager to get beyond pay negotiations and move on to our wait-time reduction agenda. Happily, we settled on the money that was on the table with some adjustments within that envelope.

Energy was probably the most difficult file we faced in our first term, one even more difficult than health. For one thing, the challenge energy presented was definitely more urgent. One of the shockers for me upon assuming office was the magnitude of the infrastructure deficit that existed in the electricity sector, the product of years of neglect by a succession of governments of all stripes.

Under the previous government alone, generation had fallen by 6 percent while demand had grown by 8 percent. What's more, the Conservatives had more than doubled the amount of power supplied by burning coal. My party had committed to eliminating all coal-fired generation — a very ambitious goal, but one I felt was entirely achievable. It would take us significantly longer to get this done than we had wanted, but I was very proud when Ontario achieved a North American first: shutting down all of the province's coal plants. This action was the equivalent of taking seven million cars off the road.

I am proud of this action, but I would be remiss if I did not acknowledge the leadership of Jack Gibbons and the Ontario Clean Air Alliance in this fight.

From the outset, it became apparent we needed to invest many billions of dollars installing new wires, retrofitting old nuclear plants, and building new generation capacity. The whole energy system was stretched so thin that there was a genuine concern in our first year that the province would suffer brownouts. This was the reason we could not shut down all the coal-fired power plants as quickly as we wanted.

There are established entities in the electricity sector with their own power structures, such as Hydro One and Ontario Power Generation, the two successor companies to the old Ontario Hydro. I learned that despite being progeny of government, these bodies had greatly outgrown the parent in terms of knowledge and sophistication. It is not easy for the politicians (or even the bureaucrats in the energy ministry) to understand what is going on inside those companies. I tackled this monopoly in part by opening up new generation opportunities to the private sector.

I made Dwight Duncan my minister of energy. Duncan, like his fellow Windsorite, the irrepressible and very effective Sandra Pupatello, had impressed me in Opposition with his superb political skills and sharp mind. (There must be something in the Windsor water. On a per capita basis, no Ontario community seems to produce more political smarts.) I was confident that if anyone could get his arms around these Ontario energy behemoths, Duncan could.

Like all premiers, I also kept an eye on the energy file. At first, I tried a Boy Scout–like, hands-off approach. I said we would follow the advice of the experts on issues like hiking hydro rates and locating new plants. That sounded wonderful in the abstract. But the first issue we had to deal with was skyrocketing electricity prices in northern Ontario. When combined with a declining market for paper and a rising dollar, the higher prices were doing serious damage to our pulp-and-paper mills in the north. We decided we had to intervene with subsidies that brought down the electricity rates for the mills by 15 percent. It would not be the last time we had to intervene in electricity pricing.

In hindsight, this was another lesson in the school of hard-knock politics. I would learn that while it made sense to delegate certain issues to the experts, I could never delegate political accountability. If something went off the rails, I would be accountable. This is how it should work in a healthy democracy. I would learn the hard way that my government and I should have been more diligent in our oversight of agencies like eHealth, Ornge (the Ontario air ambulance service) and our public energy companies. For example, I failed to recognize that delegating the decisions on locating gas plants to an arm's-length agency was asking for trouble. In the end, it wouldn't matter that eighteen of twenty plants were sited correctly, including plants in Brampton, Windsor, and Toronto. All the attention would be focused on the two they got wrong. And I would be accountable both for righting the wrong and for the ensuing costs.

One reform we implemented was the publication of a long-term energy plan that clearly laid out projected demand for electricity in the province as well as our proposals to meet that demand with new supply. Such a public plan seemed so sensible it's hard to imagine why it had not been an Ontario practice. It gave businesses and the public — and us politicians — both a clear and transparent picture of our energy reality *and* a working basis upon which to make decisions. And because we required the plan to be revised regularly, we were able to adjust it in keeping with a fluctuating economy and demand.

The nuclear file was an endless trip to the dentist for us. Our energy plan increased our capacity at Niagara Falls, increased our investment in gas plants, exploited promising new hydroelectric opportunities, retrofitted our existing nuclear plants, and equipped homes and businesses with smart meters to help drive conservation. Even so, the experts were telling us we still needed to build a brand new nuclear facility. This was a daunting prospect.

We looked at other nuclear projects around the world, only to learn they were running over budget and behind deadline. We had a number of meetings and agreed that in order to protect the Ontario taxpayer, the risk of cost overruns needed to be shifted to the private sector. But when we undertook an RFP (request for proposals) process, the answer we got back from the private sector was, predictably, the more risk we shifted over to them, the pricier the new nuclear facility would be. News reports estimated building the new plant would cost in the $26 billion range, or about double the cost of the Darlington plant completed twenty years earlier. So we danced back and forth. The experts insisted we had to build, but I was doubtful. On most public policy matters, after wrestling with the various options, I would sooner or later (I preferred sooner) come to a landing. Given what was at stake here, meeting the long-term energy needs of Ontario, I resisted the temptation to rush in. Eventually, the recession caused electricity demand to plummet, and we put the whole decision on hold. In the end, it worked out for the best. We didn't build a plant we didn't need.

Whatever ups and downs lay ahead of me or behind me in government, I would remain determined to keep driving change. I wanted to lead an activist government and I was proud of the change we had begun. But there was still much to be done.

CHAPTER SEVEN
Growing into the Job

While health care, education, and energy were the meat and potatoes of my government's responsibilities, and we were driving hard on those files, I was equally excited by the possibilities in the area of the environment. This led to our creation of the Greenbelt around the Golden Horseshoe, the heavily urbanized area around the western end of Lake Ontario that includes Toronto and Hamilton. The Greenbelt today permanently protects nearly two million acres of environmentally sensitive areas and farmlands from urban development and sprawl. It is the world's largest such area. When my environmental advisor, Dave Harvey, first showed me the proposed map of our Greenbelt, he expected me to be astounded at the expanse it covered. Instead, I asked, "How do we make it bigger?" I understood just how momentous an opportunity this was. If we didn't claim this land for future generations now, chances were it would be lost forever. It's hard for me to exaggerate the pride I take in the Greenbelt, knowing families in one of the fastest growing regions in North America will always have green space to enjoy. I had the good fortune of spending much time outdoors, close to nature, working at the McGuinty summer camp, and I had taken my own sons on several canoe trips up north so they, too, could connect with the planet that sustains us. For me, the Greenbelt was our government's way to make sure the opportunity to make that connection was there for millions of Ontarians long into the future.

Our Greenbelt initiative was accompanied by our "smart growth" policy encouraging new development in built-up areas in an effort to check urban sprawl. These two initiatives were not easy goals to achieve. We faced stiff resistance from some developers and municipalities — and even from the general public when smart growth meant intensified development in their neighbourhoods. (Rob MacIsaac, the one-time mayor of Burlington, once said, "The only thing that people oppose more than sprawl is intensification.") But we were committed to the goals and pushed them through, and I believe they have contributed significantly to enhancing quality of life in the GTA.

John Gerretsen, as minister of municipal affairs and housing, was in charge of our land reforms. John had a dogged determination that served us well. I recall first meeting John in his Kingston riding, where I had been sent by the party to help him launch his 1995 campaign. As it turned out, the wily Gerretsen, mayor of Kingston at the time, needed no help from me. He won handily and became an important member of the government.

Our government also managed to pass a new City of Toronto Act, which gave Canada's largest metropolis more freedom to look after its own affairs without always having to come to the provincial government for approval. I think it helped that I was not from Toronto. I could look at the matter objectively and not worry about being accused of a pro-Toronto bias. It was obvious to me that Toronto, an extraordinary municipality in terms of its size and economic clout, needed extraordinary powers. As I said at the time, "Toronto is the engine of economic growth in Ontario and much of Canada.... It's a miracle it has delivered prosperity for so long and to so many, despite living in a legislative and fiscal straitjacket that would baffle Houdini."

I wanted the new legislation to be permissive instead of the old "father knows best" prescriptive approach that had always defined our relationship with Toronto. The act made that very clear: "The assembly recognizes that the city is a government that is capable of exercising its powers in a responsible and accountable fashion.... The city may provide any service or thing that the city considers necessary or desirable for the public."

A number of members of caucus and Cabinet were opposed to my initiative, feeling we would take the blame for anything that Toronto did with its new powers, such as raise taxes. (Toronto's council did subsequently raise land transfer and vehicle registration taxes, initiatives for which my government was never seriously criticized.) They said we could not trust the Toronto politicians. But I argued that it was time to show some respect for Toronto and to empower the city to grow stronger. To me, it was both good politics and good policy.

Toronto mayor David Miller and I worked well together on the rewriting of the City of Toronto Act. I hoped that over the ensuing years the new legislation would fire up the imagination of city leaders. Having had the opportunity to travel to many big foreign cities, I can say that Toronto is incredibly attractive by virtue of its rich quality of life and cultural diversity. I sometimes quietly lamented that all Toronto needed in order to create an inspiring vision of its future was to see itself as the world sees it: strong, confident, innovative, diverse, and friendly — in short, built for the future.

I wanted all Ontarians to take pride in their capital city, so we invested heavily in its cultural character, revitalizing iconic attractions like the Royal Ontario Museum, the Art Gallery of Ontario, and the National Ballet School. We also invested in brand new institutions like the Four Seasons Centre for the Performing Arts and the TIFF Bell Lightbox, the centre for the world-leading Toronto International Film Festival. And then there were the Pan Am Games.

Landing the 2015 Pan Am Games in Toronto was an uphill battle too. When I first broached the idea of making a bid on the Games with the Cabinet, my proposal was met with deafening silence. I understood the reasons for my colleagues' lack of enthusiasm: these kinds of events often had serious cost overruns. No one needed reminding, for instance, of the disaster that was the Montreal Olympics. Nobody (except a very small group of Pan Am supporters) was breaking down our door to get us onside. No doubt about it, the safe play would have been for us to keep our heads down. But by this time I had grown comfortable in my leadership; I knew I didn't like playing it safe when doing so betrayed the public interest. I believed we had good reasons to get behind a bid for the Games: our investment in sporting infrastructure and housing would deliver short-term economic stimulus and long-term value to Ontario, new training facilities would be a boon to local athletes — many of Ontario's elite amateur athletes were forced to train in cities like Vancouver, Calgary, and Montreal (each of which had hosted an Olympic Games) — and I felt it was high time Toronto got back on its horse after losing a bid in 2001 for the 2008 Olympics. What's more, I believed we could win. So I worked hard to garner the necessary international support. I flew to China, Denmark, and Mexico to meet with voting officials, and hosted them in Toronto. I am indebted to long-time Liberal and international games entrepreneur Bob Richardson, as well as former premier David Peterson, for the invaluable roles they played in helping us land the Games.

One first-term highlight was something we did *not* do: allow the introduction of Sharia law in Ontario.

Like most Ontarians, I was unaware that there were religious courts in the province — Catholic, Jewish, and others. To settle family law disputes, the Rae government had quietly changed the rules to allow couples to turn to their places of worship if they preferred. This practice had gone largely unnoticed until 2004, when the Ontario Islamic Institute of Civil Justice proposed to establish a Sharia court to conduct binding arbitrations according to Islamic law. This gave rise to strong opposition by many, but especially by women's groups, including Muslim women, who argued that Sharia courts discriminated against women. This created a controversy almost instantly. Attorney general Michael Bryant suggested we get former NDP cabinet minister Marion Boyd to study the proposal.

Bryant had impressed me early on. When I first met him, he was leading a successful life as a Bay Street lawyer. He had come to see me in my office while I was in Opposition to seek my advice on running as a Liberal. He had impressive credentials and a quick mind, but there are any number of dilettantes who flirt around the edges of politics, never getting into the game, never taking any real risks. So I told Bryant that if he was serious about getting elected he should quit his job and start knocking on doors. To my amazement, he did just that.

Anyway, I approved of Bryant's decision to appoint Boyd. She came back with a report in support of Sharia law, but with a lot of conditions. Something didn't sit well with me about Boyd's advice, however. It didn't feel right. I knew where she was coming from but I didn't feel it would take us where we wanted to go.

I believe that as Ontarians and Canadians, embarked together on our wonderful adventure in pluralism, we have found strength in our diversity in a way that is largely without precedent anywhere. But there are, nonetheless, limits to what we will accept. There is, in fact, an end to our accommodation. While we warmly welcome faiths, cultures, and traditions from around the world, there has to be solid bedrock upon which we are building together. And for me, that bedrock must be our law. There can be only one law for all of us. We should not have people going off to different authorities interpreting different laws to settle disputes, whether family disputes or any other kind. This thinking led me to turn down the request for a Sharia court in Ontario. Contrary to what many believe, we didn't decide to ban religious arbitrations in Ontario. But we did prohibit any and all religious arbitrators from using religious law in their arbitrations. Now, all family law arbitration in Ontario can be conducted only in accordance with Canadian laws. And, for good measure, we now regulate Ontario family law arbitrators and require that they undergo training.

I believe our government struck the right balance. Most Ontarians thought it was a sensible limitation, although I believe Marion Boyd and Michael Bryant may have felt I had undercut them. But that's the job of a premier. You have to intervene when you think it's warranted. This was something else I had learned: you should never substitute an advisor's judgment for your own. You need to be comfortable with the call because you're the one making it and you will be accountable for it.

The issue of religious courts had struck a chord with the general public. It had become water-cooler and dinner-table talk. For me this was more than just an ordinary, everyday political issue. It was a rare opportunity to further define ourselves as a society. I always enjoyed such opportunities. Later on, another such opportunity arose in the form of gay-straight alliance clubs (GSAs) in our high schools. Catholic school boards were adamantly opposed to GSAs and insisted that we could not impose them on their schools. I listened carefully to the objections raised by Cardinal Thomas Collins, the archbishop of Toronto. It was obvious he was under huge pressure from some members of the Catholic faith to oppose GSAs. I had to respectfully disagree. Interestingly, while some parents and school trustees remain opposed, Catholic students themselves have embraced GSAs and the idea behind them. So, too, have a number of Catholic school boards. Again, I saw this as an opportunity to further define the kind of caring, accepting, and progressive society we were building together. I was proud of the way Ontarians debated these and other contentious issues during my term as premier. While there was often strong disagreement, overwhelmingly, opposing voices were heard and respected.

Although citizens of Ontario might think that such issues as the treatment of Sharia courts or gay-straight alliances in Ontario are of interest to Ontarians only, my travels abroad as premier taught me that what we do here in Ontario (and Canada), how we get along, and how we treat each other is of more than passing interest to others. I recall one occasion when I was on a trade mission to Pakistan, the first one ever led by a Canadian premier. I was giving a speech at the prestigious Lahore University of Management Sciences. My audience was warm and attentive. After I had finished speaking a young man said to me, "Premier McGuinty, I understand that you rejected the advice of your own adviser, Marion Boyd, and that you are refusing to allow decisions based on Sharia law in Ontario. Why are you rejecting this advice?"

I was surprised to learn that anyone in Pakistan was following or even cared about what we were doing in Ontario. But I was astonished when, as I was giving my answer about the need to build our society on the bedrock of Canadian law, it seemed to me that every woman in my audience was nodding her head in agreement. This told me that what we were doing back home could be very meaningful to other people elsewhere. We could be a source of inspiration, a beacon of hope.

Just as I was called on to represent Ontario in travels outside of the country, one of the key roles for any premier is interaction with other premiers, notably at their annual conference. By chance, it was Ontario's turn to host the conference in my first year as premier in the summer of 2004. The conference was in Niagara-on-the-Lake, an idyllic setting. I soon learned that we often made more progress *after* the meetings over a drink than we did during them, when it was easier to dig in and hold your line. Not that I always succeeded in changing a colleague's mind in a social setting, but we always developed a better understanding of each other's position.

Coming together as premiers, I felt our greatest priority should be to find ways to work together to advance the interests of Canadians. I soon discovered this put me in a very small minority. It quickly became apparent that, as a collective, our greatest priority was invariably to get money and/or power from the federal government. I didn't like banging my head against that wall. To me, it made us look weak. Better to do what we could on our own to make progress for Canadians. We were hardly powerless, so why not embrace our opportunities to collaborate? To be fair, we did take on important tasks, such as reducing interprovincial trade barriers and working together to reduce drug costs, but these never mustered up the same enthusiasm among my colleagues as a full-on attack of the feds. My lone ally in my efforts to direct our constant attention away from Ottawa was British Columbia premier Gordon Campbell. We did not have much success.

Quebec premier Jean Charest was always a force at these conferences. I would come to know Charest well as a colleague and friend. He was one of the savviest politicians I have ever met, with a superior ability to read his electorate and champion their causes. Throughout my time as premier, I took some comfort in having Charest as my provincial neighbour and someone of my generation and political stripe, a fellow premier who was living many of the same kinds of political challenges as me. We had much in common.

In 2003 Charest persuaded the other premiers to restyle themselves as the "Council of the Federation," rather than just a group of guys (we were all men back then) who met once a year. He also wanted to buy a building in Ottawa — ideally, right across the street from Parliament Hill — to let the federal government know we were not going away. I worried that buying a building in Ottawa would be difficult to justify to our voters back home, and I was always able to persuade the other premiers not to go there. Besides, I didn't like the in-your-face symbolism of the building. Maybe I was being naive. Or maybe I was just too Ontarian. Maybe I was both.

It was fascinating to observe the impact of a growing cohort of female premiers at our meetings. When I began as premier, we were all men.

When I left, the premiers of British Columbia (Christy Clark), Alberta (Alison Redford), Quebec (Pauline Marois), Newfoundland and Labrador (Kathy Dunderdale), and Nunavut (Eva Aariak) were women. I found the presence of women made for more collaboration and less posturing at our meetings. It made us more likely to achieve some consensus. And women had this influence without in any way giving up sharp elbows when circumstances required.

During my decade in office, the premiers were an assembly of vastly different personalities. They were all in politics to make a difference, each a product of their own life experience, which included, of course, the way in which their views had been shaped by life in their province or territory. We all shared a concern about protecting our flanks and we all wanted to make the folks back home proud. I enjoyed their company and the spirited exchanges I had with them about mutual challenges, but I sometimes despaired about our inability to do anything substantive together. At the end of our meetings we would spend three or four hours behind closed doors, arguing over the wording of a resolution that didn't bind us in any legal way. What, really, had we accomplished?

When we prepared to meet the media afterward, we would talk about staying in sync. By tradition, the host premier was the chair of the meeting and the one designated to speak for all of us. But when we emerged, someone would always go off script. Alberta's Ralph Klein and Newfoundland's Danny Williams excelled at this; both were adept at offering colourful off-the-cuff quotes the media found irresistible (a talent I envied). The prime minister of the day would answer back that he would like to work with us but he was getting mixed messages. As a result, nothing would get done.

Klein was an interesting study. He would often show up late for our meetings, say very little, and leave early. When he did speak, it was invariably to make a strong case for Alberta. I saw Klein later, during my cross-Canada tour to promote understanding of the fiscal gap between Ottawa and Ontario. Ontario taxpayers were sending $23 billion more to Ottawa than we were getting back by way of federal transfer payments. (By 2015, the time of this printing, the gap is closer to $11 billion.) Klein was cordial during our talk, but I got the sense that he just wasn't interested. He saw me first and foremost as a Liberal. What's more, to

Klein I was too young, too left, too modern, and too Ontario. I was not, as the saying goes, Ralph's cup of tea.

As premier I confirmed for myself what Ontarians already knew: there is some resentment of us in the rest of the country. That meant I had to be very measured in my remarks to my provincial counterparts; when I spoke it, was easy for me to get the other premiers' backs up. I did not fully understand that at the beginning, so I would speak enthusiastically about our achievements (such as our progress on wait times) and invite the other premiers to communicate with my government for some ideas. The unspoken reaction of the other premiers seemed to be: *There goes Ontario again. It gets all the attention and it thinks it's got all the answers.*

I had the sense that the premiers expected Ontario to play the honest broker among the provinces, even at the expense of its own interests. That made it especially challenging for me to say Ontario was getting the short end of the stick and was tired of it. Among the provinces, there is no sympathy for Ontario. Time and again the federal government exploited this political reality and used it against me. Peter Van Loan, one of Harper's ministers and an Ontarian himself, called me "the small man of Confederation."

I admit I resented having to champion fiscal fairness for Ontario. I longed for the days of old when Ontario could afford to avoid the difficult topic of how Canadians' money was being divided, and concentrate on nation building (although I quickly learned there would be no nation building on Prime Minister Stephen Harper's watch). But such was not my lot. We were being shortchanged and my job, like it or not, was to try to do something about it. This would make me as unpopular at the premiers' table as it would in Ottawa (especially among my Liberal cousins), and even among some Ontarians who preferred that we keep up appearances and not talk about something that could diminish us in the eyes of the neighbours.

I understand the psychology here; if you live in the biggest house on the street, people do not want to hear about your financial challenges. Combined with the perception that Ontario is overly privileged is the reality that no other Canadians feel less attachment to their province than do Ontarians to Ontario. So it was not easy to get Ontarians riled up about the fiscal gap. Ontarians aren't used to standing up for Ontario. That made it possible for Ontario's MPs to ignore my efforts to address the fiscal imbalance. In this, as I discovered, Ontario is very different from the others. I used to joke that on Parliament Hill there are conspiratorial meetings in each party's Maritime caucus, western Canada caucus, and Quebec caucus, each with the purpose of plotting to their region's advantage. But when Ontario caucuses met, they fretted over needs in the rest of the country. There is much truth to this. It's just who we are as Ontarians and how we think.

There is one Ontarian in particular whose life was made complicated by my position on the fiscal gap and my actions generally as premier and leader of the Ontario Liberal Party — the Member of Parliament for Ottawa South, David McGuinty. When David went about his work on Parliament Hill, or when he was knocking on doors looking for support, he was often a lightning rod for those unhappy with his older brother. I could never be accused of making his political life easy. First elected a Liberal MP in 2004 (one year after I had become premier) and re-elected several times since, David has had the burden of running on my record as well as his own. One time, when I was knocking on doors in our riding in support of David during a federal election, a woman mistaking me for him said, "All right, you have my support this time but if that premier brother of yours keeps screwing up you won't get it next time!" I assured the woman I would deliver the message to the premier and quickly moved on to the next door. Anything unpopular or controversial emanating from me stuck to David. It was guilt by association. But he kept his head up and kept winning his elections. I will be forever grateful for sharing a riding with my brother, who provided his unremitting support and good counsel to me as premier while taking it on the chin for me in the alleyways of politics.

Given the alliances formed by some of the other provinces, I suggested to Charest that our two provinces should start collaborating. We began holding joint Cabinet meetings to discuss matters of mutual interest, including the best strategies for dealing with Ottawa. I liked how these meetings made all of us feel, a feeling that hearkened back to the historical ties that bound Ontario and Quebec, originally Upper and Lower Canada, together in a special relationship. I was quite proud of how we had brought our two provinces together and of where I thought we were headed. Unfortunately, Pauline Marois and the Parti Québécois were elected and that brought an end to our nascent efforts. However, I am glad to see that the relationship has warmed up again now that the separatists are out of power in Quebec.

Back in 2004, there was an issue on which all the provinces could agree: Ottawa should be contributing more to the financing of health care. Spending on health care was increasing at a rate much faster than inflation, but federal contributions had been slashed as part of Paul Martin's deficit-fighting budgets. In truth, Martin balanced the federal budget on the backs of the provinces. By 2004, Ottawa had a healthy surplus, and the provinces were still trying to make ends meet. We wanted some of the federal surplus to be spent on health care. The matter came to a head at a first ministers' conference in September 2004.

The conference started badly. We met with Prime Minster Martin over dinner at 24 Sussex. Federal officials had already leaked their offer to the media, and Martin told the premiers at dinner that it was a take-it-or-leave-it proposition. Every premier left unhappy but hopeful of changing Martin's mind at the formal meeting in Ottawa's government conference centre the next day. Martin remained intransigent at the meeting and later that day we again retired to 24 Sussex, where the meeting, now essentially a round of negotiations, continued informally with the premiers in the living room on the ground floor and Martin upstairs. I was the go-between as we began the messy process of making a deal.

Martin had the money and the premiers had the needs. I understood that Ottawa could not, without conditions, just hand over a bucket of money for health care. Earlier, I had suggested to Martin that he insist on a quid pro quo: the provinces would have to commit to measurable improvements in wait times. We all eventually agreed on five areas: diagnostic imaging, cancer treatment, cardiac care, joint replacement, and sight restoration. (Four of the five were already Ontario priorities.) We also agreed on the creation of a new body, the Health Council of Canada, to measure outcomes. I went up and down the stairs between Martin and the premiers three or four times. As chair of the Council of the Federation at the time, I considered it my job to try to broker a deal, and I was determined to get the job done. I presented offers and counter-offers over the course of several hours. I took turns listening to both sides as each insisted the other was being completely unreasonable. A few of the premiers were especially incensed and Newfoundland and Labrador's Danny Williams threatened to walk. In the end, and happily for Canadians, we struck a deal. Collectively, we came around to the view that it was better to have a long-term deal than a short one. Martin called the agreement "a fix for a generation," which was a bit of an exaggeration but understandable; he clearly wanted the issue off the table before another federal election. Our agreement meant $41 billion in new federal funding over the next ten years. It was a lot of money, and it was good news for Canadians. We landed the deal at one o'clock in the morning and made a joint announcement later that day. Everyone was positive and upbeat. That was a rare occasion in my ten years as premier — the premiers arriving at a manifestly positive outcome for Canadians as a result of their collaborative efforts.

We came pretty close on one other occasion.

In 2005 we all signed on to the Kelowna Accord to improve housing, health, and education for our Aboriginal peoples, while also making everyone more accountable for how the money was spent. All the first ministers were there, as well as the key Aboriginal representatives, and everyone signed off on the $5 billion deal. It was probably the closest we got as first ministers to a nation-building moment. I was very impressed by Prime Minster Martin's determination to improve opportunities for Aboriginal Canadians. This was a complex issue and, while it did cry out for reform, it would have been easy to bury it under other issues more prominent in the daily lives of Canadians. But Martin lost the federal election that came quickly on the heels of the Kelowna gathering, and the new prime minister, Stephen Harper, decided to scrap the accord. I was deeply disappointed by this turn of events.

Martin and Chrétien both displayed a much greater desire to work in a collaborative way with the premiers than did Harper. During his short tenure as prime minister, Martin met with us twice. Chrétien met with the premiers seven times. (Before that, Brian Mulroney and Pierre Trudeau had hosted fourteen and twenty-three meetings, respectively.) Harper met with us only twice in nearly a decade. He did so because his hand had been forced by the 2008–2009 recession that was ravaging Canada and the world. I believe it was a mistake for Harper to refuse to collectively engage Canada's premiers. We could have and should have done more, together. Our federation works best when we make sincere efforts to understand each other, find common ground, and build progress. All of this begins with coming together in the same room.

Harper had plenty of one-on-one meetings with premiers — usually on his terms. My first meeting did not come until 2007, more than a year after he took office. The feel was all wrong. While the meeting was to take place in Toronto, the prime minister insisted it take place in his hotel suite, not in my office, and that there be no photographers to record the event. This restriction came after he had already held numerous meetings with Charest with built-in photo ops.

These thoughts were in my head as I entered the outer room of Harper's hotel suite, where the Mounties and Prime Minister's Office staff were buzzing. Then I was ushered into the inner sanctum to meet the prime minister. It was a very stilted encounter, civil but not convivial. I got the impression that it was pro forma on his part — something he knew he had to do but did not want to do.

In Harper's eyes, I was from the wrong party. To make matters worse, I kept hammering the federal government on the need for fiscal fairness, which meant taking less money out of Ontario for distribution to the rest of the country. In spite of this backdrop I felt that, no matter what our differences, it was my responsibility to Ontarians to go the extra mile with Harper to find common ground. I took the opportunity to assure him that if we ever did a public event together, I would not embarrass him. No matter how much the media might try to goad me into saying something unflattering or critical about him, I would not accommodate them. I wanted to give him that comfort level and to establish a personal relationship that would enable me to pick up the phone and talk to him about an issue.

We never got there.

Interestingly, shortly after Harper lost the 2004 election, I phoned him (as I did all federal party leaders) to thank him for his contribution to the democratic process. Harper sounded very dejected. I said to him, "You just got a lot of good experience on the campaign trail. That's a good thing for you and your party. It's not all bad news." He thanked me for the call. He wasn't in the mood to talk.

Two years later I phoned Harper again just after voters had made him prime minister. I congratulated him on his victory and asked him to reconsider his plans to cut funding for child care. He was resolute. I hung up the phone, turned to my staff and said, "This guy will be prime minister for a long time. He knows what he wants to do and he won't budge."

The relationship did get a little warmer over time. We eventually arranged a couple of public events together. Whenever we met, I would begin by finding some way to thank him for something the federal government had done. I did not want to be seen as a griper, but rather as someone who was fair and balanced and advanced only legitimate concerns. I tried to make small talk, but Harper would never allow me to forget that he was the prime minister and I was just a premier. That hierarchical distinction was always front and centre. As was his partisanship. It had a stranglehold on him. Clearly, those who were not of his political stripe were not to be trusted. I have met many politicians over the years but none as partisan as Stephen Harper. And that's a shame. If Canadians should be able to look to one among us who can see beyond our differences, someone who can rally us together, it ought to be our prime minister.

I suspect Harper was too much influenced by the weighty presence of Mike Harris's old team in his government. Three senior members of Harper's Cabinet — Jim Flaherty, Tony Clement, and John Baird — had been ministers under Harris. Another Harper Cabinet minister, Peter Van Loan, was provincial party president under Harris. None of these men were McGuinty enthusiasts.

Anyway, after our first meeting in 2007, Harper walked from his hotel room to the adjoining convention centre to attend a major fundraising dinner for the provincial Conservative party. With a provincial election looming, Harper's role at the dinner was to introduce the featured speaker, Ontario Conservative leader John Tory. He introduced Tory as "the next premier of Ontario," a prediction I was determined to prove wrong.

CHAPTER EIGHT
A Head of Steam

I was up against yet another Conservative leader in the 2007 election. John Tory, who had replaced Ernie Eves in a tightly fought leadership contest, was as different from Eves as Eves was from Mike Harris. He was very much of the Bill Davis mould of Conservative, a moderate, whereas Harris was a right-winger and Eves was somewhere in between the two. That is not surprising, because Tory worked from 1981 to 1985 in Premier Davis's office as principal secretary.

Tory is a genuinely decent man, and I could not help liking him, even though he was my political opponent. He made a sincere effort to bring decorum, dignity, and responsibility to the role of Leader of the Opposition, something I would dearly miss when I had to confront his decidedly different successor.

A good indication of the tone of our relationship involves, oddly enough, his daughter and one of my nieces. A few years after John had left provincial politics, our two relatives were residents together in internal medicine in Toronto. For a Christmas party, they did a video skit that spoofed the rivalry between John and me, and they invited both of us to play a role. In the video, the two young doctors spend their time trying to sabotage each other. Then the camera pulls back and shows John and me watching the video together over a beer and wondering what is wrong with these kids. John and I genuinely enjoyed this opportunity. It made our partisan differences seem small.

I was delighted when Tory was elected mayor of Toronto in 2014. He brought civility, stability, and intelligence to the office at a time when Torontonians and, indeed, all Canadians were thirsting for these qualities in the mayor of our biggest city.

Those qualities were not evident in Tory's mayoral predecessor, Rob Ford. Let me provide some insight into him. Shortly after Ford's election in 2010, I invited him to Queen's Park so I could formally welcome him there. I felt it was important to try to get off on the right foot. Ford had already been making demands in the media for provincial government dollars. That didn't bother me. It was the usual course of action taken by newly elected Toronto mayors. Of course, Ford's reputation as a rough and ready guy had preceded him, and I was looking forward to meeting this unusual character. (There were no public stories then about his addiction problems). I considered it a test on my part. Although Ford and I were as different as night and day (from a media perspective, he was incredibly exciting and I was boring), I was intent on striking up a relationship that would serve both of us well.

My office had asked Ford to show up at nine o'clock in the morning and had invited the media to be there to get some pictures of me formally receiving him and shaking his hand. But Ford chose to avoid this public welcome by showing up at my office a half hour early. Ford's relationship with the media was, at best, strained, and he wanted to avoid them. I thought it was important that Torontonians see their mayor and premier working together, so I invited the media in for some pictures of us sitting down at my boardroom table. After the media left, I tried to engage the mayor in some small talk, but he seemed decidedly uncomfortable, fidgeting and perspiring heavily. It seemed to me that the last place he wanted to be was in my office, having to make nice. He wanted the whole thing to be over as soon as possible.

Ford quickly laid out his "asks" in a rough and rudimentary way — about $50 million to offset welfare program costs and my consent to stop collecting the city's car registration tax. He also wanted my commitment to work with the city on its ever-evolving transit plan. My staff had anticipated these requests, and I agreed to them in short order. I had hoped we might then consider some other big issues facing Toronto, but it quickly became apparent that the mayor's staff had him on a very short leash. Ford had been given some very specific and limited speaking points, and he was not to freelance beyond those. This meant we had twenty minutes to kill and nothing more we could talk about.

Ford's assistant was visibly nervous about his boss and what he might say or do. This became most apparent when I observed him prep the mayor for his unavoidable encounter with the media, who were lying in wait for him outside my office doors. The mayor's assistant treated him as you might an unruly, fidgety child who wanted nothing more than to go outside and play. He urged the mayor to focus on the job at hand, to stick to his basic speaking points, and not to answer any other kinds of questions. It was painfully obvious to me that the man was in over his head. I could not help but feel that those nearest and dearest to Ford — his family, closest friends, and political confidants — had not been honest with him. Had they been, they would have told him that, for a host of reasons, he lacked the capacity to serve Torontonians as their mayor. Instead, he acted in a fog of delusion.

Looking back, I find the whole Ford debacle to be more tragic than anything else. It was like watching a car accident in slow motion. And the media just couldn't get enough of it. After I had left office and was living in the United States, the most common question I received when someone learned I was Canadian was, "What's with that mayor of yours?"

Back to John Tory. When he first got the job of leader of the Conservatives, I sometimes got the sense he was acting out the role of a politician rather than being himself. Maybe he was replaying moments from the Davis years. He had been a political insider and observer for so long, I think it took him a while to stop trying to mimic those he admired. And as Tory came into his own, he definitely got stronger. Nothing beats authenticity.

To be fair, Tory also had a tough job as Leader of the Opposition. (I know. I was there.) His added challenge was that his party was not used to acting as the Opposition, having ruled Ontario for forty consecutive years, followed just recently by eight years of power led by Harris and Eves. His colleagues bristled at their new responsibilities and were too impatient to get back into government. Tory also had to preside over a fractious party, split between its Davis and Harris wings.

Tory's undoing, however, was his 2007 campaign platform, specifically the commitment to provide government funding to faith-based schools. His party badly fumbled the development of their policy (they hadn't bothered to get the caucus and rank and file onside) as well as its presentation (their message about fairness for non-Catholic children quickly gave rise to concerns about the ghettoizing of children in faith-based schools).

As the issue developed in the media and in the voters' minds, it became apparent that it was going to create real trouble for the Conservatives. Even some of their own candidates came out against the policy. Clearly, they had not taken the time to consider all the political implications, and they paid a price for that.

The 2007 provincial election was much easier for me than were my two previous campaigns as leader (1999 and 2003). For one thing, the election date was not a surprise to me or to anyone else. In 2005 we passed a law fixing elections for every fourth October. I recall many of my fellow premiers (except for Danny Williams and Gordon Campbell, who had already adopted fixed election dates) looking sideways at me when I told them of my plan. After all, choosing the timing of the election can be of great strategic advantage to the government. But I thought there was something very unfair about a government picking an election date purely to maximize its own advantage. So we made the change in Ontario. Over the ensuing years, I noted with interest that Ottawa and all the other provincial legislatures (save for Nova Scotia) passed fixed-election-date laws.

I was also proud of another feature of the 2007 campaign: we provided an opportunity for Ontarians to revisit the first-past-the-post election system they had inherited and to decide whether they wanted to exchange it for an alternative. In 2006 we established the Ontario Citizens' Assembly on Electoral Reform, made up of 103 randomly chosen Ontarians — one from each riding.

I was then and remain now enthusiastic about this process, one that draws on citizens to help their government grapple with complex issues.

Two policy wonks. With Gerald Butts, returning from a U.K. fact-finding mission (2001).

Working the crowd at the Portugal Day Parade in Toronto with MPP Peter Fonseca.

Meeting former president Bill Clinton.

Generating ideas for a winning campaign platform at our 2001 conference in Niagara-on-the-Lake.

My friend Greg Sorbara (with regional councillor Mario Ferri) wins the 2001 by-election. The wind is in our sails.

In the thick of it — the 2003 campaign.

A real team. With Terri on election night (2003).

With Gerald Butts and Greg Sorbara in the Cabinet room.

Back to school with Gerard Kennedy, Mike "Pinball" Clemons, and Argos linebacker Randy Srochenski (2005).

Addressing the media with B.C. premier Gordon Campbell.

At work in my Queen's Park office.

A typical government meeting in China. Visitors on the left, hosts on the right (2005).

A real star — six-year-old Samantha Bakker, winner of the Ontario Spirit Award for contributions to tsunami relief (2006).

Parked and prepping for a speech.

With Toronto mayor David Miller. We worked together to create the City of Toronto Act.

With Canada's newly appointed governor general Michaëlle Jean on her first official visit to Toronto (2006).

Terri and I honouring a great leader at the Raj Ghat memorial to Mahatma Gandhi during our first visit to India (2007).

Pomp and circumstance in Pakistan (2007).

Governor of California Arnold Schwarzenegger (2007). He said he'd be back, but he made only the one visit.

A visit to Bombardier in Thunder Bay with minister Mike Gravelle (second from left) and MPP Bill Mauro (third from left).

Suiting up. I enjoyed working with Ontario firefighters and I am grateful for their support.

A Canadian moment with Hockey Night in Canada *host Ron MacLean and minister John Wilkinson.*

Terri and I waving to supporters after a campaign stop (2007).

Up close with the media.

With the media near the end of the 2007 campaign. Long campaigns build respect and friendships.

My mom and her second husband, Don McCunn, at Queen's Park for my 2007 swearing-in as premier.

Being sworn in as premier for the second time, with Tony Dean, secretary of the Cabinet (2007).

Assembly members first went through a learning phase; this was then followed by an opportunity to deliberate before making recommendations. On this occasion, the Assembly recommended that Ontarians consider a new way to elect their representatives, an approach called "mixed-member proportional representation." We put this choice to voters in a referendum that coincided with the 2007 election, and 63 percent decided to stick with the voting system they knew. But I became a fan of the citizens' assembly and wish I had found other opportunities to engage Ontarians in shaping government reforms.

As it happened, voter turnout in the 2007 election hit an all-time low, with fewer than 53 percent of eligible Ontarians voting. It would be even worse in 2011, when only 49 percent of eligible voters bothered to cast a ballot. Voter turnout would grow to 52 percent in 2014, but that number is hardly worth celebrating.

Cynicism fostered by a news environment that celebrates all the negatives and routinely gives short shrift to the positives doesn't help with voter turnout. The fact is, there are many more good people in all parties doing good things than there are bad people doing bad things. But you would never know that from your daily dose of news. Almost without exception, Ontarians tell me they are more favourably impressed upon meeting or hearing from a candidate or politician in person than they are based on the profile of that individual created by the media. We politicians need to reconcile ourselves to our reality; the overwhelming majority of people we serve will never get to know us, they will only get to know *of* us. In the world of the seven-second sound bite, it is a constant struggle to convey some sense of who we truly are.

But we politicians must also take our share of blame. When we resort to name-calling, negative advertising, and "narrowcasting" of our message to certain select groups of voters, knowing we need only slivers of the main voting bloc to win, we, too, help perpetuate voter alienation.

Of course, voters themselves can't just claim they are mere pawns in an electoral game between politicians and the media, or that the abuse they have suffered from politicians and government entitles them to stay home on voting day. That doesn't wash. In our personal capacity, we are not mere bystanders in our democracy. We are all driving political and media behaviour.

Every time we click on a news item about one politician calling another names, or about someone's over-the-top, clickbait critique so obviously designed to provoke outrage and cynicism, we become part of the problem we condemn. We have all become news editors, and publishers are eager to give us what we want. The fact is, all of us — politicians, media, the public — have a responsibility to preserve and, indeed, enhance the underpinnings of our democracy. And it doesn't get more basic than voting on election day. Just because you are cynical doesn't give you a pass.

I have no neat and tidy answers, but there are wise people who can help us here. Why not ask Ontarians themselves, through a Citizens' Assembly on Voter Turnout, to consider the issue and provide government with its thoughtful recommendations? As the world gets more complicated, governments will need more help getting things right. We need to "open-source" the development of solutions to our shared challenges. We need to recognize that, truly, nobody is as smart as we all are together. This means closing the door on the antiquated notion that, because we have been elected, we have all the answers, and opening the door to our new understanding of the benefits of calling upon those we serve for their ideas. Glen Murray, one of my most creative ministers, launched Ontario's first open-source policy development plan when he served as the minister of research and innovation. Governments should do more of this.

As the 2007 campaign got underway, I took heart in knowing I had an experienced team — a group that was, by and large, my 2003 campaign team. We had grown, together. As well, everyone in the caucus was running again but for a few exceptions, including Joe Cordiano and Gerard Kennedy. As with Cordiano, I was disappointed to lose Kennedy, who had decided to run for the federal Liberal leadership. Later on, I would lose two other key ministers: George Smitherman to his bid for the Toronto mayoralty and Michael Bryant to his new job with Invest Toronto, an arm of the city government. I never welcomed the departure of a minister. I was intent on keeping my Cabinet intact and working together as a team.

My habit was to try to convince departing ministers to stay on. Only in Michael Bryant's case did he agree to stay a bit longer. I gave him the economic development portfolio to get him re-engaged. But I could tell that his interest had wandered, and I succeeded only in delaying his departure. It was interesting to read stories in the media about how Bryant and I had had a falling out. Interesting but untrue. I was later saddened to learn of Michael's tragic traffic accident with a Toronto cyclist. Criminal charges hung over his head for many months until finally an objective assessment of the facts led to a withdrawal of all charges. Michael later bravely admitted to suffering from alcoholism, something that had escaped my attention while he was in Cabinet.

If I learned anything about losing ministers and caucus members to other pursuits, it is to be respectful of their decision, to say thank you, and to get on with a succession plan. Once they approach you and tell you they want to go, they have already gone. And you owe it to the team to get on with it.

In 2007, for the first time, I had a government record on which to run and for which I would be held accountable. The way I see it, in 2003 voters had given us a pretty simple message: "All right McGuinty, we're going to give you and your team a chance at government. And if you screw it up, that will be the end of you guys." In 2007 I felt we had a strong record of achievement, and I was looking forward to running on it. We certainly didn't have a perfect record, however, and I knew the Opposition would delight in hammering me on my broken promise not to raise taxes. I would be labelled an inveterate liar and promise breaker. None of the progress we had made in education, health care, energy, the economy, and the environment would count in voters' eyes. That's how these things go, but I was ready. I had found my way as a campaigner. This was now my third campaign as leader. I knew how the tour bus worked, what the routine was, and what I needed to do. Thankfully, once again Terri had taken time off from teaching to be with me. And I had more confidence in my team than ever. All this was liberating and made me more relaxed as I interacted with voters and the media. We decided to take the broken-promise issue head on; I owned up to it whenever it was raised. It was part of my record, and I fully expected voters to take it into account along with my reason for raising taxes (the hidden Conservative deficit) and our solid record of progress in education, health care, the environment, and the economy.

I had worked hard to prepare for the 2007 leaders' debate. There were the usual debate rehearsals but my greatest preparation had been my four years of government and my high level of comfort with the decisions I had made along the way. The ninety-minute debate was moderated by TVO's Steve Paikin. A draw had determined that I would occupy centre stage; the NDP's Howard Hampton stood on my left and Conservative John Tory was on my right, mirroring our respective places on the political spectrum.

I began by taking the broken-promise issue head on: "At the time of the last election I told Ontarians that I wouldn't raise their taxes. And I broke that promise. It was a difficult decision. I stand by that decision. It's part of my record. I expect to be judged on that." After that, I spoke about the reasons for my decision before laying out my record of achievement. As I recall, I spent most of the debate under attack from my two colleagues. This was expected. In the end, I felt I had held my own, which had been my objective. I couldn't see a clear winner, which was fine by me. Someone once observed that while in baseball, a tie goes to the runner, in a leaders' debate, it goes to the government.

As I previously related, the most contentious element in the campaign turned out to be the Conservative commitment to fund faith-based schools. A major turning point in the campaign came when veteran Conservative MPP Bill Murdoch publicly split with his leader on the policy and said he would vote against it in the legislature. In response, Tory reversed himself and said he would allow a free vote on faith-based school funding. That stance ended up satisfying neither side in the debate. In the end, while our popular vote dropped four percentage points (at the expense of the NDP and the Greens, not the Conservatives), we still won a strong majority, with 71 of 107 seats.

I felt extremely grateful for the privilege of being able to continue to serve Ontarians in government, and I believed the best way I could express that gratitude was to get back to work. On the morning after the election, when I was tired and bleary-eyed, I proudly announced the creation of a new holiday for Ontarians, Family Day. I said at the time, "This is a small thing but it's an important thing. There is nothing more valuable to families than time together." Later, when I was asked about my motivation for creating Family Day, I said, "I would give anything to have spent a few more days with my dad."

As usual, in spite of our historic win (the first back-to-back victory for Ontario Liberals in seventy years), the McGuinty in me was preoccupied with our next steps and eager to get on with it. I felt stronger, a little chastened, and a little bit wiser in the ways of politics and governing. Things were great on the home front as well. We had all adjusted to the reality of having a premier in the family. In fact, it was no big deal. Happily for all of us, at home my job was no big deal. My foundation was strong, which was important because I was about to be tested by a devastating global recession.

CHAPTER NINE
Best-Laid Plans

My first and usual task following an election win was the formation of a new Cabinet. In 2007 there was a huge vacancy to be filled. Greg Sorbara had decided he no longer wished to be in Cabinet. I replaced him with Dwight Duncan, who had filled in admirably for Sorbara for a brief period in the first term. Dwight remained in the post for the rest of my time as premier and did an exemplary job.

I had tried to talk Greg out of his decision. I played the guilt card; I told him he owed it to his party and his province, but he was not to be swayed. Sorbara loves politics, but he was also aware that it was capable of consuming him. I'm sure the police investigation earlier in his tenure ended up taking its toll too. Although he was completely vindicated, the investigation had been excruciatingly slow and I know it was very hard on him and his family. He wanted to taper off his involvement in politics and spend more time with his family.

He wasn't the only one. At the back of my mind — something I had discussed only with Terri — I had a rough plan to get out of politics roughly two and a half years into my second mandate as premier. By then, I would have served twenty years in politics. That was long enough for me and my family.

Leaving at that point would allow my successor time before the next election to put his or her stamp on the government and our party. Whenever I raised the subject with Terri, she had a stock response: "I'm ready to get out anytime. You don't need to convince me!"

The Great Recession of 2008–2009 hit Ontario just a year after we had won re-election, however, and I thought it would be wrong for me to bail out in the middle of a crisis. The province faced some very difficult challenges. I knew how government worked, and I had established relationships with the other premiers, the prime minister, and the private sector. It would have taken much time for a new premier to get up to speed. My successor would have had to go through that learning process while struggling against the gale-force winds that were blowing through the economy. Plus, the whole idea of a leadership race in the middle of an economic meltdown would have been ridiculous — and for me to have caused it would have been incredibly selfish. Terri understood. Staying was the responsible thing for me to do. She backed my decision 100 percent. And we knew what this meant. It meant I would lead our party in a *fourth* election that was years away, and meant that the political risks would only grow. The longer your voyage, the more barnacles attach themselves to your ship. It's the law of the sea and politics.

Before the recession hit us, however, I had other priorities, notably the exciting expansion of renewable energy (wind, solar, hydroelectric) in Ontario. I was personally very committed to that goal. I had researched the file on my own, and I had had a series of meetings with thoughtful people about it. David Suzuki, the famed environmentalist, arranged a meeting for me with Hermann Scheer, the father of the green energy movement in Germany. Scheer was encouraging. He told me that while Germany's plan was less than perfect and remained a work in progress, that country was definitely moving toward a clean energy future, something in which Germans took great pride. At a caucus retreat at the Benmiller Inn in Goderich, Ontario, I made a presentation on renewable energy to my colleagues and told them that our new initiative would be complementary to our coal shutdown plan;

that it would establish Ontario as a North American leader in the field, giving us a jump on the competition and creating new jobs in a new sector; and that it would allow us to play a leading role in the fight against climate change. I spoke to my colleagues about how, with every passing year, the world invests dramatically more in renewable technology and that I believed Ontario should be a leader and not a follower in this global transformation.

My champion in this was George Smitherman, my newly appointed energy minister. George was results-oriented and had impressed me with his work in the health portfolio. He soon visited Germany to find out what was happening there. The Germans were at the forefront of green energy, but their experience had been mixed. For one thing, they had decided to abandon the nuclear power option, which forced them to import electricity from less-green coal-burning countries. In terms of a commitment to clean and renewable energy policy, that struck me as a bit of a shell game. We decided to maintain our nuclear capability and add up to twenty gas-powered plants, expand our capacity at Niagara Falls, and invest in renewable energy. We introduced the Green Energy and Green Economy Act, 2009, requiring the province to buy more wind and solar power. Suppliers were offered long-term contracts, at a price above what traditional electricity generation sources cost. The quid pro quo was that they had to set up manufacturing operations in Ontario. Samsung, the giant Korean conglomerate, came to us with an offer to invest $7 billion in the province if we would agree to purchase 2,500 megawatts of power from wind farms it would build here. The deal has since been cut by 40 percent, but it is still a huge investment — one that has led to thousands of jobs.

As we pursued the path toward cleaner energy, one of the obstacles we encountered was the failure of world leaders to agree to put a price on carbon. All but the most stubborn climate-change deniers agree that carbon-based fuels ought to be priced in a way that reflects their environmental cost. Even a few industry representatives agree with this argument. Early in my mandate I had a meeting with a representative of Royal Dutch Shell, who told me he favoured a carbon tax. I was surprised. He said the oil industry craves predictability and stability. "We believe a carbon tax is going to happen. We want to help shape it."

Unfortunately, our own political leaders in Ottawa felt differently. Stephen Harper and his government had been completely deaf to the issue of climate change. In my own meetings with Harper, I got the sense that he considered it to be bunk, although he was too shrewd to say so out loud. Rather, he just said and did nothing about it. With no leadership from Ottawa, we tried a workaround in concert with other environmentally progressive premiers, including Manitoba's Gary Doer, Quebec's Jean Charest, and British Columbia's Gordon Campbell. We joined alliances with American states — including California and some on the East Coast — that were interested in a cap-and-trade initiative that would impose penalties on carbon emissions and provide credits for emission reduction. But these alliances were quickly cobbled together and very difficult to sustain. I knew if Ontario moved forward on its own this could unfairly penalize our industries; orders could be shifted to more accommodating plants in Michigan or Ohio. We had good ideas and ambitions, but we knew that to act on our own could cause economic damage, damage we could ill afford in the middle of a recession. We were trapped. In the end, I felt it was too risky to go it alone during a recession or even shortly thereafter, while our economy was struggling to catch up. I longed for some national leadership. We could do a lot as a country to address climate change by working hand-in-hand with our neighbours in the United States and Mexico.

At a meeting in 2010 I told Prime Minister Harper of my plan to keep building up the necessary regulatory architecture to reduce carbon emissions by working with premiers and governors. He showed no interest other than to say, "That's a lot of architecture."

One big reason the proposed Keystone XL Pipeline project (a controversial proposal to carry crude petroleum from Alberta due south almost 1,200 miles to refineries in Texas) kept running into obstacles in the United States (not to mention Canada) is that Canadian energy policy lacks balance. Canadians are thoughtful and pragmatic on the issue of climate change. They want a balanced approach, and they hadn't been getting one from their federal government. They believe climate change is real and that carbon-based fuels contribute to the problem. They also believe we and the rest of the world are not going to wean ourselves off oil and gas for a long time, maybe decades. When the Harper government talked about energy, they talked about oil and gas. They didn't talk about clean energy from renewable sources, at least not with any credibility. Canadians want to feel good about their energy policy. And right now they are troubled by it. We have a hard time looking our children and grandchildren in the eye and telling them that when it comes to our energy plan we are doing what is right for their future.

What Canada needs is a plan to build a bridge to a clean energy future. Canadians want a sensible plan to move us off oil and gas toward renewable energy. We want a plan that allows us to grow our economy and live up to our responsibility as a wealthy, privileged nation that shows leadership on climate change. We all understand that getting to that clean energy future won't happen overnight. It will take decades. We need a serious timetable for carbon energy reductions and renewable energy growth. The plan we need would call for balanced federal investment in energy. For every dollar Canadians have invested over decades in the oil and gas sector, we now need to invest a dollar in our start-up renewable energy industry and in energy conservation. This would represent true balance and it would allow us to get behind our energy policy with pride and purpose. We all know the future is a carbon-constrained world. I have zero patience for those who argue we shouldn't take decisive action because carbon emissions from the developing world will only negate our good efforts. Why should we act?

Because we can. And we all know we should.

The broad plan I propose would lead the world, and the United States in particular, to look at Canada differently. To see us for who we truly are: a nation determined to build a strong, sustainable economy. I am convinced the Obama administration would have seen Canada and the Keystone pipeline in a much more positive light if that proposal had been grounded in a credible plan to build a bridge to a clean energy future. Had I been Barack Obama, who I believe is committed to tackling climate change, I would have welcomed a Canadian ally who sought to prod me into pursuing that agenda. Instead, we have heckled the U.S. president and berated him for refusing our energy entreaties.

When it comes to our energy policy and climate change, Canada lacks moral standing in the eyes of the world. We can change that. And we should. Getting this right will be good for our economy and good for our kids. And we will feel a whole lot better about ourselves. I am proud of the Ontario cap-and-trade initiative being pursued by Premier Wynne. But provincial initiatives cannot make up for national intransigence.

I will admit to feeling some resentment whenever Harper and his government have taken credit for recent reductions in Canada's greenhouse gas emissions, even though the heavy lifting has been done by Ontarians. Closing Ontario's coal-fired plants was the single biggest reduction in carbon emissions in North America, if not the world. But this means we are paying more for power in Ontario, because in part it costs more to make electricity by burning natural gas or by harnessing the power of the wind and sun than by shovelling coal into a furnace and attaching no cost to the carbon emissions. That contribution by Ontario has never been acknowledged by the Harper government. The federal Conservatives were just not prepared to help mitigate our higher energy costs or to invest in Ontario's renewable technology sector. Meanwhile, over decades, the federal government has invested billions in the oil and gas sector in the form of preferential tax treatment or research and development investments.

It was not all smooth sailing for my government's green energy policies. Although farmers welcomed the economic opportunities, many rural Ontarians were opposed to wind turbines. We worked hard to address safety concerns by, for instance, having the toughest setback requirements (the distance between a wind turbine and a home or other building) in North America. Cost was another issue. Clean, renewable energy is today more expensive than other kinds of energy. But as with other technologies, competition and innovation keep driving costs down. Our political opponents prefer to lay the blame for electricity rate hikes entirely on our green-energy policy, while conveniently ignoring the tens of thousands of new green-tech jobs we created for Ontarians. The truth is, the biggest driver by far of rising rates in Ontario has been the more than $35 billion invested since 2003 in rebuilding the failing electricity system *we inherited* from the Conservatives, including the nearly $20 billion Ontario was compelled to spend on transmission lines and distribution.

I am proud that Ontario was the first province or state in North America to pursue green energy in an aggressive and comprehensive way. It was not an easy thing to do. As expected, we took some hits for it. But my preference was to actively lead rather than passively preside.

While fine-tuning our green energy policies will always be necessary, the fact is Ontario has achieved momentum and mass. We now have a solid foothold in a new and rapidly expanding industry with growing global demand. And Ontario can lay claim to having the manufacturing capacity, technical know-how, skills, and resources to help answer the call.

———————

Another second-term initiative that is close to my heart is full-day kindergarten (FDK). I believe that the foundation for our continuing growth, prosperity, and quality of life lies in developing the skills and talents of our people. I also believe the best way to a strong finish at school is a strong start. The jury had been in for a long time on early learning opportunities; they have a strong, positive, and lasting influence on children. Experts like Fraser Mustard, Margaret McCain, Dan Offord, and Charles Pascal were influential for me. Terri's stories about her experience as a kindergarten teacher also helped shape my thinking here. She told me that some children came to her class without ever having been read to, while others could already read at a grade three level. Some children had well-developed social skills, while others struggled to get along in a group setting, a new environment for them. And Terri sometimes spoke of how much more her students could do and learn if they were in the classroom for the full day. (I insisted that our FDK program be optional for parents, believing that parents should have the final say on how much time their four- or five-year-olds should spend at school. Ontario children need not be enrolled in school until the age of six.)

My understanding of how our economy was evolving, and the demands this would place on our future workers if they were to compete successfully in the global economy, brought real urgency to my thinking. We needed to start building a stronger, more innovative, and more entrepreneurial workforce from the ground up. And we needed to begin this work right away. The issue became one of cost. It was apparent that, given our budgetary constraints, we were going to have to phase in FDK over several years. We also opted for one teacher and one early-childhood educator (ECE) per class, instead of two teachers. This was not just a cost-saving measure; it was also good policy, because ECEs have a different skill set from teachers, and the two are complementary. Indeed, I had long been interested in elevating the status of ECEs, who are too often dismissed as mere babysitters.

When we began phasing in full-day kindergarten in September 2010, it soon proved to be one of the most popular things we had ever done as a government. In fact, the most common complaint we got about the program was from parents who wondered why it was taking so long to come to their child's school. (As an ancillary benefit, the program saved parents a lot of money in child-care fees.)

The program's popularity created a new challenge for us: large class sizes with as many as thirty kids in a kindergarten class. Even for two experienced educators, that's a lot. Anybody who has hosted a birthday party with, say, five or six young children knows how difficult they can be to manage. Try dealing with thirty of them! Class sizes are something the government will have to address eventually.

Nonetheless, the early data coming in suggests without a doubt that the program has been a real benefit to our earliest learners. In each of the areas measured for change, including physical health and well-being, social competence, emotional maturity, and language and communication skills, FDK students proved to have accelerated development and a greater readiness for success in grade one in comparison to children in half-day kindergarten.

Of course, we faced some institutional opposition to the program. The Conservatives dismissed it as an example of "nanny statism." The elementary teachers' union fought us on the introduction of ECEs. And some school boards were disgruntled about the capital costs. As we surveyed the critics, it reminded me of what I had heard about a meeting of Pierre Trudeau's Cabinet during which the health minister, Monique Bégin, listed all the opponents to the government's plans to amend the Canada Health Act. Trudeau said, "So, you're telling me the only people in favour of this are the people? Then we must do it." It was the same with full-day kindergarten: institutions opposed it, families loved it.

Today, I feel very proud of the fact that my government expanded educational opportunities for our youngest children. Our FDK program complemented the earlier progress we had made in our schools. It also acted as a bookend in our overall plan to create the best possible opportunities for Ontarians to realize their potential. The other bookend was the massive $6.2 billion investment we had earlier made in post-secondary education, creating spaces for over two hundred thousand more students and doubling student assistance. Later, we also created the 30 % Off Ontario Tuition grant to help more than two hundred thousand students with the cost of their tuition. Ontarians have embraced their new educational opportunities with record enrolment rates. At 65 percent, Ontario has the highest post-secondary attainment rate in the OECD.

People sometimes ask why I drove the education file so hard. I earlier described the tremendous gratitude I feel for the educational opportunities my family enjoyed growing up. But there is more than my personal story behind my belief in the power of education. There is also the liberal philosophy.

Liberalism places its faith in the individual, not in institutions. Liberalism embraces institutions like business, labour, and government, but only insofar as these help individuals achieve their potential and enjoy a good quality of life. This philosophy is well-suited to the information age and its demand for skills and talent. Liberalism is about making individuals stronger to ensure they have everything they need to be the very best they can be. That's why liberals and Liberals champion a strong economy and a caring society that includes quality education for all; these are the foundation upon which individuals can build happy and fulfilling lives.

———————

Another successful but much more politically challenging initiative in my second term was the introduction of the harmonized sales tax (HST) to bring the province's retail sales tax into line with Ottawa's goods and services tax (GST). The dual system, with its administrative burdens, weighed heavily on Ontario's businesses.

Moving to a harmonized system was the business community's number one "ask" of my government. Economists, too, insisted this fundamental tax change was essential to building a stronger, more competitive economy. I agreed. Our businesses, especially our exporters, were at a disadvantage compared with the competition, which benefitted from a value-added tax much like our HST. The federal government was urging us in this direction and offering monetary inducements. So there were plenty of good reasons to adopt the HST. But I also knew there would be some stiff opposition, including from inside my own caucus.

The HST had a reputation as a third rail in Canadian politics: touch it and you're dead. So naturally, the caucus was nervous. As it turned out, the business community itself was far from united. And there were real challenges for us in designing the new tax. We had to make sure middle-class Ontarians did not experience any increase in their overall tax burden. And ideally, I wanted low-income Ontarians to come out ahead by experiencing an overall reduction in the taxes they paid.

I knew I was about to create my own biggest political headache since breaking my promise not to raise taxes. It would have been easy to put this one off to another day and another government. But I hated the thought of merely passively presiding over events. As I saw it, my job as premier was to do what I honestly believed needed doing. And the recession demanded strong medicine. We needed more than economic stimulus for today. We needed a stronger foundation for growth tomorrow. It made it easier that Dwight Duncan, my finance minister, had also come to the conclusion that Ontario needed the HST. I knew I could rely on Dwight's deft political management of this potentially explosive measure.

By this time, I had come to understand how vitally important it was to fully and thoroughly communicate our policies to Ontarians, especially controversial policies. As a lifelong policy wonk, I was inclined to declare victory the second I thought we had got a policy just right. What I hadn't recognized was that getting the policy right only marked the *end of the beginning*.

I am reminded of the story about the effort that goes into moose hunting. First, you enter a lottery for the tag giving you permission to hunt. Assuming you are one of the lucky ones and get a tag, there is the business of collecting all your equipment and driving the long distances it usually takes to get to the moose. Then you have to unload all your equipment and prepare for a long and hot and probably exhausting hike into the woods. Then you have to pray a moose comes your way. And then, if the gods are smiling on you, you come across a moose. Then you have to shoot the moose. And then, and only then, does the real work begin. Getting our HST policy right would be like downing a huge moose. All the heavy lifting would come afterward as we worked to get Ontarians onside.

We began our HST work by cobbling together a plan that included measures to soften the blow for some sectors and for most Ontarians. I deployed John Wilkinson, my eloquent revenue minister as our lead HST spokesperson. He went on a lengthy tour of the province to sell Ontarians on the HST's merits. Just as important, we created an HST information centre inside the caucus to assist Liberal MPPs with any constituent backlash. My feeling was the more Ontarians knew about the reality of the HST the better. To be honest, we had some very bad days in caucus. MPPs would come back from their ridings unsettled by what they were hearing. (The Opposition's job was much easier than ours. They simply shouted, "Tax grab!" We had to explain the workings of a complicated tax change.)

Greg Sorbara turned out to be a major source of discord. He was adamantly opposed to the HST. He felt I was courting disaster and said as much in one of our caucus meetings. "This is possibly the dumbest thing we could do," he declared. "I mean, if we are looking to commit political suicide, then sure, let's go ahead and do it."

From a political perspective, Greg was spot-on. This *was* a hugely risky move. I was fully aware of his feelings and was okay with them. However, my former minister of finance and party president had just gone public with his doubts in front of the caucus. To say the least, this was not helpful. I was not happy. And then there was the opposition outside of caucus.

Many sectors sought to be exempted from the new tax. The housing industry and fast-food restaurants were particularly vociferous in their opposition. Tim Hortons threatened to place an anti-HST brochure on every table in its outlets. We had to pick our spots in response. We ended up granting more exemptions than we had originally intended, but on balance the exemptions made sense. (When the exemptions were finally announced and the newspapers found themselves on the list, I marvelled at how much more favourable the news coverage became.) Eventually, we began to turn the tide of the debate, because we took great pains to explain to Ontarians why the HST was so important to our economy. We reassured them that except for the wealthiest Ontarians, it would not mean a net increase in taxes. I didn't mind the fight because for me it was about conviction, and those are always the best fights.

While the opposition parties were predictably opposed, the Conservatives were in a bind because their federal cousins strongly supported the HST, something we delighted in bringing to their attention in Question Period. It was clear some of the Tory MPPs were uncomfortable with their party's negative position. Tim Hudak, by now the Conservative leader, was visibly irked when his predecessor, John Tory, broke ranks to endorse the HST as sound economic policy. Oddly, the New Democrats also ended up split on the issue, which was something we had not anticipated. Some union leaders, too, spoke up in favour of the HST. And the Canadian Centre for Policy Alternatives, a progressive think tank, produced a report saying our HST plan would be a net benefit for lower-income Ontarians. That made our job a little easier.

In the end, the HST became Ontario law. It was a triumph of sound policy supported by an intelligent and effective communications plan. And I am confident that no future government will undo it. This initiative alone saves Ontario businesses over $5 billion annually.

But we did much more than that to help our enterprises compete. Among other things, over the years we cut corporate taxes and completely eliminated the capital tax. The net result of our tax reforms was to cut *by half* Ontario's tax rate on new business investment. Canadian economist Jack Mintz had this to say about our 2009 (HST) budget:

> Since 1980, when I began modelling the impact of taxes on investment, this is the largest change ever seen in a single budget, leading to the sharpest reduction in the tax burden on capital investment in any one province. Coupled with federal reductions in corporate taxes and Ontario's already legislated elimination of all remaining capital taxes, Ontario will see its effective tax rate on new investments by medium and large businesses plummet from 33.6% in 2009 to 23.7% in 2010 and then to 18.5% by 2018.... The effective tax rate on small business investment will fall by more than half, from 28.6% to 13.3%.

As it turned out, along with freezing public sector pay hikes in 2012, we also deferred further scheduled corporate tax reductions until the budget was balanced.

By the time I left office, my government had reduced taxes for Ontario businesses by over $8 billion a year. On top of that, we invested over $75 billion in infrastructure, stimulating the economy by doing business with Ontario businesses. There is no doubt our government made substantial progress in terms of strengthening the Ontario economy and helping to minimize the damaging effects of the global recession. Government can't and shouldn't try to do everything. Our job was to get the big things right. And that's what we did by strengthening public services and the economy.

Getting the big things right also meant finding a better, more cost effective way to build infrastructure. Instead of the P3 model (public-private partnership) adopted by the Harris government, we created the alternative financing and procurement model (AFP). Unlike the previous government, we insisted that any assets built for us by the private sector would remain publicly owned. Using the AFP model, our newly created Infrastructure Ontario contracted with private-sector builders to finance, build, and maintain important and much-needed new infrastructure, like schools, hospitals, and courthouses. An important safeguard we insisted on in all of our contracts was that responsibility for project delays and cost overruns would rest exclusively with the private sector. This has been an overwhelming success, delivering dozens of construction projects on time and on budget, in stark contrast to what happened in the past. We did more work in concert with the private sector than the Conservatives could ever have dreamed, largely because Liberals were trusted by the public to implement this policy in a balanced way, including our insistence on public ownership. Of course, there was some opposition to our AFPs, mostly based on an ideology that insists construction of public infrastructure must be managed and paid for by government. But governments have proven their inability to deliver these big projects on time and on budget. If ever there was a case where government should steer while the private sector rowed, this was it.

Infrastructure Ontario has been the subject of much international interest, as governments around the world look for ways to partner with the private sector and save money. Much of that success was due to the leadership of David Livingston, a very talented former Bay Street banker who heard the call of the public sector and someone who I later convinced to serve as my chief of staff.

Overshadowing all these achievements was a global economic meltdown dragging Ontario into a recession a year into my second term. Nobody saw it coming and when it hit us, we did not fully appreciate how devastating it was going to be. Unemployment rose to over 9 percent; 250,000 Ontarians would lose their jobs. Our budgetary deficit would climb to more than $19 billion as we fought back with a stimulus plan.

In the initial stages, I was scrambling to get good strategic advice, but it was just not available. Nobody had an answer. I talked to bank presidents and economists. I heard a lot about the impact of the recession, but when I asked for their opinions on how long it would last or their advice on how to get out of it, they were initially less able to help.

Over time though, a consensus emerged. We were going to have to use public dollars to stimulate the economy; otherwise, the recession would grow deeper and last longer.

I got down to work with a small team that included Dwight Duncan, my minister of finance, and Peter Wilkinson, my chief of staff. Peter was a great asset. He brought clear thinking to complex issues and was wise in the ways of the Ministry of Finance, where he had earlier distinguished himself as chief of staff to the minister Greg Sorbara. My energetic new Cabinet secretary, Shelly Jamieson, also played an invaluable role at this time, helping to guide the public service as together we made plans to rise to an extraordinary economic challenge. We all understood that declining revenues and meaningful economic stimulus meant running a deficit. It was not a decision we took lightly. We had worked hard to control our spending and climb out of the deficit hole the Eves government had left us, and we had just balanced our budget three years in a row.

We faced an enormous challenge. And we had to step up.

At a meeting with my fellow premiers, I announced I had decided to run a deficit to stimulate the provincial economy. They were shocked. But as it turned out, a consensus would soon emerge, calling on the provinces, territories, and the federal government to stimulate the economy. The entire country was in an economic hole and local initiatives clearly would not be enough. We were going to have to work together to climb out. Fortunately, all of us, Harper included, were of the same mindset. No one wanted to go back into deficit after we had worked so hard to balance our budgets. But we were even more concerned about what would happen to the Canadian economy if our response to the recession was timid. A big recession called for big stimulus.

A major early test was the rescue of the auto industry. General Motors and Chrysler were facing bankruptcy as a result of the recession. It was clear that without government support these companies would fail. In the United States, President Obama had announced a rescue package. At $80 billion the size of the package was eye-poppingly huge. But it seemed only to underscore the size and seriousness of the threat. Of special interest to me was that Obama had not asked any individual states to contribute to the package.

Unfortunately for Ontarians, Harper saw things differently. He made it clear to me in a telephone conversation that Ottawa was not prepared to support the auto sector on its own. He wanted Ontario to contribute. With four hundred thousand jobs at stake, I didn't hesitate. This was serious. I had a good working relationship with the auto executives and I had seen the fear in their eyes. Even executives from the Japanese automakers were telling us that we had to bail out GM and Chrysler. If Ontario's assembly plants closed their doors, they warned, it would create a domino effect that would sweep through other parts of the industry, like auto-parts suppliers; this, in turn, would harm other areas of the economy. It would be like pulling on a thread and watching the whole sweater unravel. The Canadian auto rescue package ended up costing $13 billion, of which Ontarians contributed $4 billion, most of which has been repaid by the carmakers.

It is worth asking what the long-term future holds for the auto industry in Ontario. There is a continuing consolidation in manufacturing globally and the auto sector has not been spared. U.S. states are more aggressive than ever in the competition for new investments, and Mexican quality and productivity are coming on strong. I believe the question is a very straightforward one. Does Ontario want to compete aggressively to maintain our existing plants and jobs and secure new investments, or are we going to oversee the gradual but inexorable loss of an industry that has been a powerful contributor to our quality of life and economic well-being? I think you can tell by the way I have framed the question where I stand. The auto sector has a promising future. We will still be using cars and trucks long into the future. Furthermore, auto manufacturing is a highly sophisticated production process requiring knowledge workers working with robotics. This is exactly the kind of high-end, high-paying manufacturing we want. I believe that, together with the federal government, we should fight for our fair share of global auto production. During my years as premier, Ontario became the top producer of cars in North America. We can and should reclaim that title. Ontario can and should be at the forefront, building the next generation of clean, smart and, sooner than we think, self-driving cars.

In addition to fighting to preserve our traditional strengths like the auto sector, we need to build new ones. In particular, I believe we must do more to capitalize on the creativity and entrepreneurship of young Ontarians. Every year, nearly two hundred thousand Ontarians graduate from the province's colleges and universities. We need an ever-growing number of those graduates to start asking, "Who am I going to hire?" instead of, "Who is going to hire me?" Driving this agenda means building an ecosystem where entrepreneurship and innovation flourish. It means getting our schools, colleges, universities, business mentors, investors, incubators, and governments aligned to make Ontario richly fertile for start-ups. We need to let a thousand start-up flowers bloom. Properly nurtured, these will blossom into a rich variety of businesses and exciting, new economic growth.

In addition to investing many billions of dollars to stimulate the economy and create short-term jobs, I felt we needed to do more to help workers who had been victimized by the recession. In an effort to better understand the services and programs we were offering, I quietly visited one of our Employment Ontario offices. I asked representatives there to make believe I was a laid-off, forty-two-year-old manufacturing worker with a young family and a mortgage. I asked what support they could give me to get long-term job retraining so I could get a job in a growing sector. I was dismayed to learn our government offered no such program. Armed with this insight, I returned to Queen's Park and sounded the alarm. I charged the hard-working and conscientious John Milloy, my minister of training, colleges, and universities, with developing a new program to provide a real hand-up to older workers who were prepared to commit to going back to school for a year or two and who couldn't afford to do it without government support. That led to the development of our Second Career program, which covers up to $28,000 in tuition, living, and travel costs for middle-aged Ontarians prepared to make the sacrifice to go back to school and start over. I recall meeting Keith, a forty-nine-year-old father of three young children, studying culinary management at Windsor's St. Clair College. He told me, "I've gone from cars to cakes!" He had lost his job after fourteen years at the Ford plant. He was now part of the Second Career program. I could see the pride and hope in his eyes. Second Career has been hugely successful, with 74 percent of students finding a job in their newly chosen field.

As the recession lengthened, it became clear to me that we needed to exercise restraint on provincial spending to prevent the deficit from sky-rocketing out of sight. I had to drive this belt-tightening, along with my finance minister, Dwight Duncan. As a government, we had done what we needed to do to stimulate the economy. But now was the time to restrain spending. It was not going to be easy for us because it pitted us against our partners in the broader public sector — teachers, nurses, police, and others. We had invested heavily in education and in health care at all levels. We had increased the minimum wage and social benefits many times. We had aggressively pursued a poverty reduction plan in the middle of the recession that succeeded in lifting forty-seven thousand children out of poverty. We created the Ontario Child Benefit, paying low-income parents more than $100 per month for each of their children, a support program that had not existed before but was now benefitting over one million children. We had done all this while running the leanest government in Canada (as measured by program spending per capita). And, after eliminating the deficit our government had inherited, we had balanced our budget for three consecutive years. But now it was time to impose greater restraint on our spending. Much of the caucus was very uncomfortable with my determination to address the expenditure side of the ledger. Bob Rae had the same problem when he was premier, and it was his undoing. I was very mindful of that lesson. Much of his caucus was offside, as were virtually all of his traditional allies in the public sector.

We began by making sure we were leading by example, freezing our own pay for five years. Next was a "voluntary freeze" on public-sector wages. This proved to be easier to implement with the three hundred thousand non-unionized workers than the seven hundred thousand unionized ones. In the case of the latter, we asked our public-sector employers, like hospital workers, for instance, to negotiate contracts that froze pay. In many cases, that wasn't happening. In hindsight, it was unrealistic of me to expect our labour partners to voluntarily agree to a wage freeze. I think their concern was the optics of being seen to have surrendered precious real estate before the battle had even started. I certainly got the impression from labour leaders that they preferred to have a wage freeze *imposed* on the rank and file rather than have *consented* to it. It became obvious that, regrettably, we were going to have to resort to legislation.

The toughest opposition came from the teachers. This took me by surprise. I had assumed that our good working relationship and the remarkable results we had achieved together for students would put me in good stead with teachers. After all, we had increased per-pupil funding by 55 percent, hired more than thirteen thousand new teachers, created full-day kindergarten, increased paid prep time for teachers by 50 percent, and hiked teacher pay over nine years by about 25 percent. These negotiated pay hikes didn't take into account the impact of the "grid," which provides for automatic pay hikes for the first eight to ten years of a new teacher's career. Combining the grid and the annual negotiated pay hikes meant, for example, elementary school teachers in the Greater Toronto Area who started teaching in 2003 saw their pay rise from about $40,000 to just over $80,000 nine years later. I don't begrudge teachers their compensation. Hard-working, devoted teachers earn every penny they make. But I had hoped that my demonstrated respect for teachers, indeed my championing of teachers and teaching, would have earned me their support in my quest to constrain public-sector wages for a limited time in the aftermath of a terrible recession. But such was not the case.

Laurel Broten, my determined and resourceful education minister at that time, had the tough job of trying to get the teachers onside. Broten and I both rejected union proposals that we find money for a pay hike by laying off several thousand young teachers and increasing class sizes. It was also suggested by the unions that we shut down full-day kindergarten — or at least slow down its rollout — to fund a pay hike. We said no to this as well. I was determined to constrain pay in a way that did not cost teacher jobs or lower the quality of education for our students. Wage-freeze agreements were reached with two of Ontario's four teachers' federations. The last agreements were imposed by legislation. The wage freeze and elimination of bankable sick days (the practice of compensating teachers for unused sick days) saved us $1.9 billion without the loss of any teaching jobs.

Many teachers were unhappy. My caucus was unhappy too. In an ideal world, we would have found a way to find those savings, preserve those jobs, and reach agreements with all four teacher groups without eroding the goodwill of our teachers, which was so important to me. But we don't live in an ideal world. And there was no deal to be had with the two federations that held out against any deal that didn't include a pay hike. And what we didn't have for our public-sector partners in 2012 was money for a pay hike.

Restraining public-sector compensation is never easy. But you do what you have to do. During my last two years in office, Ontario had the lowest public-sector pay hikes among the provinces and the federal government. We never could have got there in Ontario without hard work, goodwill, and, I must say, the strong and steady hand of my chief of staff, Chris Morley. Morley had grown up in politics, having begun as a press secretary. His quiet determination and unflappable professionalism propelled him steadily up the ladder until he landed in my office as chief of staff. I valued especially the practical rapport he had created between the political and public sectors, two groups that need to work together to get things done. In this work, Chris was building on the strong foundation created by his predecessor, Peter Wilkinson. Restraining pay can always be done with a sledgehammer, but that causes collateral damage to all the important relationships between government and the public service. I preferred the iron fist in a velvet glove approach, one driven less by enthusiasm and more by purpose and responsibility.

Just as in our first mandate, our government had been very active during our second. We had moved forward on a number of new fronts, including the HST, full-day kindergarten, and clean energy. We had also been called upon to confront a terrible recession, which first required massive spending and then imposing fiscal restraint. We had been busy at home. But I also understood that in a global economy, I needed to be busy abroad too.

CHAPTER TEN
With Glowing Heart

As premier, I felt it was important to travel abroad for two reasons. First and foremost, I considered it my job to do what I could to help build a stronger Ontario economy by establishing stronger trade linkages. I wanted more foreign investment at home and more trade opportunities for our businesses abroad. Either way, the objective was more jobs for Ontarians. The other good reason for my foreign travel became more apparent as I began to travel. It broadened my mind. You learn things about another country by being there that you can't possibly learn from a good briefing. And you certainly can't build solid relationships without making personal connections. You have to be there, on the ground. My travels also helped me develop a better understanding both of Ontario's and Canada's place in the world. The more I travelled, the more I grew comfortable interacting with foreign dignitaries and representing my home with pride and purpose. I also learned first-hand just how strong and positive Canada's international brand is. Our home is a bright and shining beacon for many.

Overwhelmingly, people in other parts of the world have a warm feeling for Canada. Canadians are seen as friendly, welcoming, accepting, and caring. We have a free society and a rich economy. And, of course, there is all that land and all those natural resources. At a state dinner in 2008 in

Chongqing, a city of thirty million people in southwest China, Bo Xilai, the city's Communist Party secretary and highest-ranking official, toasted our delegation with these words: "When we Chinese think of Canada, we think of all your mountains, all your lakes, all your forests, all your prairies, all that land, all your riches ... and so few people. No wonder you people believe in God!" I was impressed by our charismatic host, who was then touted to be on the fast track to power in Beijing. Imagine my surprise when, five years later, he was convicted on corruption charges and sentenced to life imprisonment.

It was interesting to see how Canadian artists have found fame and fortune abroad. In 2007 I spoke at a trade symposium in India where the president of Portugal was also in attendance. My staff hastily arranged a brief, informal meeting. I had hardly introduced myself when the president asked, "Do you know Nelly Furtado?" Apparently, he was a big fan of the Canadian musician with Portuguese roots.

On another occasion, when visiting a school in the province of Jiangsu, China, I asked a class of fourteen-year-olds who their favourite musical artist was. Maybe I shouldn't have been surprised by the answer enthusiastically delivered by the group: "Justin Bieber!"

And then there's the ever-affable, Ottawa-born Mark Rowswell, virtually unknown back home but known to over one billion Chinese as "Dashan." Rowswell is a genuine Chinese TV superstar. I know because when I walked with him in 2010 at the Shanghai World Expo, I had to be careful not to get trampled by his adoring fans and well-wishers.

My foreign travels took me to the United States, Great Britain, Austria, Italy, Japan, Israel, the West Bank, Lebanon, Switzerland, Pakistan, Mexico, Denmark, India, and China. It was these last two that received most of my attention (a combined seven trips) — for obvious reasons. They are big and growing economies offering big and growing opportunities.

During my travels to India and China, I would frequently meet trade delegations from other nations. Bumping into these along the way brought home to me just how lucky we are to enjoy our diversity advantage. There are relatively few places in the world that can assemble a large trade mission to China or India, for example, in which so many of the business representatives are of Chinese or Indian descent. It was a joy to travel with

Ontarians who understood our host country's language, culture, and ways of doing business so well. In short, our cultural diversity at home makes us more competitive abroad. I also enjoyed a personal advantage — at least in terms of China, whose true power I had not yet fully come to appreciate.

In 2005 I led my very first trade mission to China. It was, by Ontario trade mission standards, a big one, lasting twelve days, with 125 delegates representing nearly one hundred different organizations. I quickly learned how exhausting and exciting these missions are. As mission leader, I had to be "on" all the time. This meant fighting jet lag (I can't sleep a wink on a plane), encouraging my team to be enthusiastic in their pursuit of new opportunities, and working as hard as I could to cultivate meaningful personal relationships with my Chinese counterparts.

My foreign travel routine was both arduous and stimulating. My days would often consist of a visit to a site of cultural importance (for instance, the Great Wall in China and the Taj Mahal in India), and a visit to a trade assembly where I would deliver a speech and sometimes participate in a signing ceremony. I would schedule visits to a business operation with an Ontario connection, meet with various diplomats and officials, and, of course, there would be a full roster of dinners and lunches, all designed to create new business opportunities. My pace was quickened by adrenalin during my travels and considerably slowed for the first few days after I returned home.

One of my early official meetings in China was in 2005 in Nanjing, the capital of Jiangsu, a province that has been twinned with Ontario for thirty years. I met with Jiangsu's then-party secretary, Li Yuanchao, in an elegant and spacious room inside a government building. The meeting room was laid out in typical Chinese fashion: a horseshoe arrangement of chairs, with members of my mission sitting opposite Chinese officials. Party Secretary Li and I sat at the closed end of the horseshoe and behind us sat our interpreters. Protocol called for me to wait for Li to begin the conversation, which would continue for thirty minutes to an hour.

It was late afternoon and from the start I could tell the Chinese officials were bored, with some struggling to stay awake. I imagined that during their careers my hosts had received countless trade missions from various parts of the world. There wasn't much by way of pleasantries that they had not already heard. When Li finished speaking, I was determined to make an impression. I told him my trade mission was more than just political and professional. It was personal. I reminded the party secretary that, in 1970, Canada had been both one of the first Western nations to officially recognize the People's Republic of China and one of the first to establish an embassy in Beijing. In an effort to enhance relations, China sent nine students to study in Canada in 1973. (By 2015, nearly ninety thousand Chinese students were attending schools in Canada.) Those original nine studied in Ottawa. Three of them moved in with my family and me. My father, a university professor, had volunteered to give the young Chinese students a real Canadian family experience. Our guests were a little timid at first and understandably so. But soon we got along famously. We learned much from each other and about each other.

As I told my story, my hosts sat upright with rapt attention. They were enthralled by the notion that long before self-interest dictated that the world make its way to China, the McGuinty family had welcomed their youth as a genuine gesture of friendship. When I stopped talking, Li, who had until then spoken to me only through his interpreter, began to speak to me in near flawless English. (He had attended Harvard University.)

From then on, wherever I went in China, I told my story. In 2012, during my fourth and final trip to China as premier, I spoke to a group of retired ambassadors in Beijing. To my delight, my hosts had arranged for my 1973 house guests to attend.

As a footnote, and as evidence of the importance of investing time and effort in developing personal relationships, every time I led a trade mission to China I met with Li Yuanchao. And every time I met with Li, he held a position of greater authority. At the time of my last official visit in 2013, Li was vice-president of China.

Travel in foreign lands can be tricky when it comes to food. With my busy schedule and an entire business delegation counting on me, I couldn't afford to get sick. All went well for me, with the exception of one brief misadventure in New Delhi, when I attended an elegant dinner in a government minister's stately residence. I was seated at a table along with seven others, including the minister and several influential Indians. The meal was served and I ate with confidence, my staff having assured me the food was safe for me to eat. And it was, save for one small green bean. Not knowing any better, I put the bean in my mouth and bit into it. I instantly felt an explosion of heat in my mouth. I later learned the bean was a hot pepper, inserted for flavouring only, not for eating. I thought the best thing I could do to avoid making a scene would be to quickly swallow the pepper. Bad idea. My body went into minor convulsions and I had dark thoughts of never making it back to Canada. Fortunately, I quickly recovered and chalked the experience up to a learning opportunity.

————————

Some of my most vivid travel memories were created during my 2007 mission to India and Pakistan. I had worked hard to get my "stump speech" for India right. It was the speech I used to kick off all our events there. As it turned out, it was very well received by Indian audiences. It began with these words:

> I want to thank India for the welcome it has provided us, of course, but for the wisdom it has shared with us, most of all. Every citizen of the world owes your country a profound debt of gratitude. And my personal debt to India is as large as any other. I have the privilege of speaking to you today on behalf of the thirteen million Canadians who live in our greatest province, Ontario, because I am their elected leader. So I thank India for the vibrant example set by the world's largest democracy. I have formed a government of men and women dedicated to public service. And we thank India for the example set by the great Mahatma Gandhi, who taught that politics without principle is a sin.
>
> I am a politician, so words are my shield, my sword, and my source of inspiration. So I must, again, thank India, for Sanskrit, the mother of Europe's languages. Before I sought public office, I practised law. So I thank your country for its respect for the rule of law. My four children live in a world of microprocessors, instant messaging, and the World Wide

Web. So, on their behalf, I thank India, for giving us the zero, which made all technological advances possible. My family is fortunate enough to live in one of the most diverse places on the planet. Ontario speaks every language, embraces every culture, and practises every religion. And it was India that taught us that diversity is a source not of division, but of strength. I am enormously proud of my daughter, Carleen, who left her comfortable life in Canada to spend the past year as a volunteer in Sri Lanka, helping its people recover from the tsunami. So, as a father, I thank India for yet another lesson from Gandhi: that privilege, like pleasure, must be accompanied by conscience.

With so much to thank India for, is it any wonder that the American historian Will Durant once said, "In many ways, Mother India is the mother of us all." Imagine our excitement, then, when we see what is happening in India today! Suddenly, Mother India has added to the wisdom of the ages the vitality of a teenager. It is outracing its younger competitors and outperforming the world's strongest economies.

Terri and I were transfixed by the sights, sounds, and smells of India. On a car trip near Agra, where we had visited the spectacular Taj Mahal, we saw the most remarkable things. We saw cars, of course, but we also saw some of the world's most expensive cars travelling alongside motorcycles, which were obviously a mode of family transportation, with Mom, Dad, and two children on board. We also saw motorized rickshaws — comfortable transportation for possibly six, sometimes accommodating what seemed closer to twelve. In addition, there were bicycles, tractors, trucks, pushcarts, buses, horses, cows, camels, and an elephant. And pedestrians. There were traffic lanes but they were of little interest to drivers. Virtually all the cars bore scrape marks on their sides and holes where the mirrors once were. There was an endless cacophony of horns. One of the locals told me that driving in India is summed up with the expression, "Good horn. Good brakes. Good luck."

I visited a number of cities and officials in India but one of the most fun connections I made there was with Bollywood, India's Mumbai-based movie industry. I had not understood just how big this industry was in India, producing some one thousand films a year (about double Hollywood's output). When I learned that the prestigious International Indian Film Academy (IIFA) was looking for its first North American awards venue, I jumped at the chance to compete for the rights to host an event that draws the world's biggest television audience, with an estimated five-hundred-million-plus viewers. I sensed this was a great opportunity to market Ontario to the world. I knew there was a strong Bollywood fan base in Ontario, especially in the Greater Toronto Area, and I felt we could fill a huge venue and generate the energy and excitement these events require to succeed. I was delighted when we won the 2011 IIFA, leading to a very successful sold-out event at Toronto's Rogers Centre. I was pleased to hand out the best movie award. The Bollywood star with whom I worked most closely in this venture was Anil Kapoor, who later honoured me by appearing at a campaign event with me in Brampton in 2011.

After completing a successful mission to India in 2007, which included a visit to Amritsar to visit the marvel that is the Golden Temple, we crossed into Pakistan at the Wagah border crossing. We knew we were breaking new ground because this was the first-ever Canadian premier–led trade mission to Pakistan. We just didn't know it was going to be that big a deal.

We crossed the border on foot, as required. To our amazement, Terri and I were greeted by a military band, children performing traditional dances, and bleachers filled with hundreds more children in traditional costume. All of this was adjacent to a large tent with rugs underfoot, where we were served tea and an assortment of foods. Later, we drove to the city of Lahore, a half-hour's drive. Light standards along the road were used to hang thirty-foot-high posters of my face. I leaned over to my assistant and said, "Make a note. I want those hanging in Toronto to greet me on my return."

Overshadowing our trip to Pakistan was the heavy presence of military security. I never felt threatened, but our hosts were visibly nervous and went so far as to post armed guards outside our hotel room. Hindsight helped me better understand their nervousness. On the day we left Islamabad for Canada, a nearby hotel frequented by Westerners was bombed. We also lost a new friend to violence. Zil-e-Huma Usman, a young and dynamic female minister in the Punjab provincial government, had befriended Terri during our visit. When I was meeting with state officials, the minister led Terri on her own tour, including a visit to a school. To our horror, two weeks after our return home the minister was murdered by a religious extremist opposed to women holding political office.

———————

While most of my trips were planned out many months in advance, on a few occasions I had to hop on a plane on relatively short notice. One of those times was in 2009, when I was invited to travel to Mexico City to meet with Mario Vázquez Raña. Now deceased, he was at the time a powerful Mexican media magnate and, more important, president of the Pan American Sports Organization. I had met Vázquez Raña in Beijing, where I had been lobbying him for the 2015 Pan Am Games. I had been told he could sway ten of the fifty-two votes up for grabs. I didn't know if any of my competitors had been similarly summoned by Vázquez Raña, but I wasn't about to tip them off. I instructed my staff to keep the twenty-four-hour trip quiet. I saw our meeting as an incredible opportunity to restate my case for Toronto to win the Games. My host said very little about Toronto's chances, but I certainly felt he had been impressed, and I returned feeling I had left nothing on the table in my personal efforts to land the 2015 Games. (Earlier, I had made short jaunts to Beijing and Copenhagen.) Of course, I was later delighted when Toronto won the bid.

In 2008 Fiat, the Italian automobile company, announced plans to build a new assembly plant in North America. Our competitors in states like Georgia and Kentucky had already made direct overtures to Fiat officials in the United States, so we had to act fast. This was going to be a real fight. Encouraged by my energetic minister of economic development, Sandra Pupatello, we decided to get the jump on the competition by travelling to Italy and meeting directly with the head of Fiat, Sergio Marchionne, someone who had grown up and attended university in Ontario.

Marchionne was well known for being a tough, somewhat inscrutable, and highly successful businessman. I was told I would get a private thirty minutes with him. I made my pitch, but it soon became apparent he was interested in a bigger conversation — one about the future of the North American auto sector and how Ontario would fit in to that.

About an hour later, Marchionne asked if I would like to see his "toys." I had heard about his personal collection of high-performance cars stored in the basement of the Fiat headquarters, and I jumped at the chance. Marchionne warmed to the subject of his cars as he removed their cloth coverings and described them to me. Afterward, he sent a driver around to pick me up in a Maserati and take me to a restaurant he had recommended for my team. The two OPP officers accompanying me were visibly nervous when I climbed into the car with an Italian driver and no room for them. Once at the restaurant, we were escorted to our own room and served champagne. I was worried about the cost of our meal until the waiter explained to us that Mr. Marchionne was picking up the tab.

Fiat never did build a new plant in North America. Instead, it bought out Chrysler, one of the manufacturers our government had assisted during the 2008–2009 recession.

———————————

I would have enjoyed travelling with the prime minister on the sort of "Team Canada" trade missions that Jean Chrétien led during his tenure in office, but there were none under Stephen Harper. From time to time some of the premiers would organize a trip together, as I did once with premiers Robert Ghiz of Prince Edward Island, Shawn Graham of New Brunswick, Gary Doer of Manitoba, and former premier Pierre-Marc Johnson of Quebec when we visited China. We all did our best travelling abroad on our own and, sometimes, together. But the truth is that no single province or collection of provinces has the same clout as a Team Canada delegation. In terms of recognition, the world knows Canada far better than its individual provinces. In fact, as I learned in my travels, Toronto, Montreal, and Vancouver are all better known than our provinces. That's just the way it is.

Harper's refusal to work together abroad was one thing. But for the federal government to throw up obstacles in our way as we worked hard to build constructive relationships was another. China is an excellent example of how Harper's actions got in the way of our attempts to establish relationships with foreign governments.

Freshly minted as prime minister in 2006, Harper was critical of China for its human rights policies. He said he wouldn't sell out Canadian values "to the almighty dollar." He then took pains to avoid Chinese leaders and refused to attend the Beijing Olympics in 2008. This may have played well to his supporters in Canada, but it was naive to think it was going to influence a superpower like China. All it succeeded in doing was cooling off our trade relationship for a few years while diminishing our influence on human rights. Harper's approach struck me as completely out of keeping with Canada's tradition of effectively wielding soft power and pursuing a policy of constructive engagement. (My mother's advice on my wedding day comes to mind: "Whatever happens, keep talking.") Fortunately for Canada, Harper has since revised his thinking and visited China to promote trade and human rights.

There is nothing wrong and everything right with raising human rights concerns. It's just a question of how you raise them. I'm not a fan of bullhorn diplomacy. It doesn't work for us, it's not who we are, and we don't have the military might to back up our bombast. We are a small country and we should definitely be seeking to exercise influence in a big world, but instead of puffing ourselves up, we should play to our strength. Few countries are as well positioned to punch above their weight as Canada. We can exercise real influence but only so long as we play to our strength, soft power. Canadian culture, values, and ideals can be powerful influencers because of their inherent attractiveness. They are why millions around the world would jump at the chance to become Canadian. And because of who we are and what we have built at home, we are well-suited to playing a meaningful role in today's world of growing anxieties and tensions. Former prime minister Joe Clark put it well in his very thoughtful book, *How We Lead: Canada in a Century of Change*: "In such a world, the ability to bridge conflicting identities and hostile groups, and patiently seek common ground to build trust and collaboration, is critically needed. At home and abroad, no one is better at this than Canada."

Not long ago, when I was a fellow at Harvard, I was approached by a former European diplomat who wanted to talk to me about Canada. "It used to be," he said, that "whenever we Europeans were struggling with some difficult international issue, sooner or later someone would ask, 'Well, what are the Canadians doing?' We no longer ask that question." We are slowly but surely losing our moral standing in the world. This is what happens when our international policies are driven by domestic politics.

In my last speech delivered in China as premier, I made the following remarks before the Chinese People's Institute for Foreign Affairs in Beijing:

> I understand that many of you served your country as dip-lomats. I consider you to be bridge-builders, and for all the bridges of goodwill and understanding you have built, I thank you. People-to-people diplomacy is inspired by a noble, deep-seated conviction shared by people everywhere. Something that tells us it is right to look beyond ourselves and to reach out to each other. It is right to try to understand each other. It is right to support each other. Human nature often leads us to focus on our differences. But it is our higher nature that leads us to understand how much we have in common; that we all share the same home, this planet; that we all seek happiness; that we are all mortal; and that we can lead fuller, happier lives by building together....
>
> What is truly remarkable are not our differences but what we have in common. We both have hopes for ourselves and dreams for our children. We both work hard and we are prepared to do what it takes to build a bright future for our families. We both value good schools, quality health care, a safe and clean environ-ment, and a strong economy that creates jobs and opportunity. It seems to me the bedrock of successful diplomacy, whether between nations or people-to-people, is a profound understand-ing of the lesson offered by all the great faiths and the world's wisest people since time immemorial. And that lesson is this: what matters most when it comes to people everywhere is not the colour of our skin. It's not the language we speak. It's not the culture we inherit. It's not the traditions we cherish. It's not the faith we practise. It's not the wealth we accumulate. And it's not the power we wield. What matters most for people

everywhere are not our differences; it's what we have in common — our humanity.… This is about more than being nice to each other. It's about rising in the strongest possible way to meet the great challenges confronting humanity. Challenges like global conflict, terrorism, climate change, disease, and a growing disparity of income and opportunity. Conquering these challenges demands our very best. And that means working and building a bright future together.

Being premier also allowed me to welcome distinguished guests to Ontario. Along the way, I met presidents George W. Bush, Bill Clinton, and Barack Obama, as well as Prime Minister Tony Blair. But the two guests I got to know best were Queen Elizabeth and California governor Arnold Schwarzenegger.

I admit to having secretly questioned the value of the monarchy to Canada and Canadians. But having the opportunity to spend much of three days with her made me a huge fan of the queen. For one thing, I was impressed with the queen's intellectual curiosity. She was genuinely intrigued by the making of a 3-D movie on a Toronto movie lot, and in conversation she asked me about everything from the prevalence of iPods in Canada to the security features of the BlackBerry. The commitment of politicians to their responsibilities pales in comparison to the queen's. She is a public figure for life, never having chosen the job. I had the luxury of choosing public office and the duration of my temporary commitment. I was impressed by the queen's stamina and seemingly limitless patience, as well as the kindess shown to the thousands who came to see her.

She also proved to have a sense of humour. My protocol office had warned me off jokes, telling me these would not be appreciated by the royals. Nonetheless, at my last event with the queen, I addressed our audience by saying, "I have spent the past three days with Her Majesty and I cannot get over the size of the crowds I have been drawing."

I was a bit disappointed when the queen failed to react to my humour. But later, when we were walking together, she quietly acknowledged my effort: "That was a good joke."

Actor and California governor Arnold Schwarzenegger was, as they say, a horse of a different colour. I hosted him for three days in 2007 when we entered into agreements committing Ontario and California to curb emissions that contribute to climate change, and to boost stem cell research. (The latter commitment led to renewed calls by the Catholic pro-life movement for my excommunication.)

Unlike any other politician I had met, this was a guy with star power. And he knew it. The crowds he drew in Toronto were unlike those that had assembled for the queen. Hers were reserved and respectful. His were excited and energetic. Schwarzenegger's remarkable career had seen him transform himself from world-class bodybuilder to Hollywood movie star to governor of the most populous American state.

I welcomed Schwarzenegger at the airport. He arrived on a private jet and was greeted by a group of cheering schoolchildren who had been assembled at his office's request. The governor was very much at ease and interacted well with the children, cracking jokes and shaking hands. The welcome ceremony concluded with the children singing our two countries' national anthems, again at the request of the governor's office. Schwarzenegger then climbed into his SUV and drove into Toronto accompanied by a four-car police escort. The governor was also accompanied by a large contingent of staff and support people, including a makeup artist. I squeezed into the back seat of a Ford Escape hybrid (I had insisted the OPP purchase some environmentally friendly vehicles) and quietly made my way back to Queen's Park.

It wouldn't be the first time I was reminded of how accessible (and relatively inexpensive) Canadian premiers are. I think this is a really good part of politics in Canada.

Save for Quebec, premiers don't have jets or official residences, and our security details are modest. Whether at public events or just grocery shopping with Terri, I have frequently met new Canadians who openly marvelled at how easy it was for them to approach me and speak to me. They told me how in their native countries they would never have been allowed to get close to a political leader. One man told me, "The closest we would have come to a leader would be to see a bunch of cars drive by on a road that had been closed to the rest of us." To this day, when I hop in the back seat of a taxi, it is not at all unusual for my driver to do a double take when he sees me in the mirror and to ask me why I'm not being driven around by security officials.

I have always enjoyed the opportunity to meet people up close. In my early days as premier, Terri and I were shopping at a Loblaws market on St. Clair Avenue in Toronto when an elderly woman hunched over her grocery cart called out to me, "Mr. McGuinty, I need you to do something for me."

I had been making my way down her aisle and she remained perfectly stationary as I approached her. She had obviously recognized me and was now lying in wait. As I pulled my grocery cart alongside hers, I wondered what she had to say to me. She wasn't smiling, so I figured it would be a complaint about health care or electricity rates or maybe public transit or something like that. Instead, she surprised me.

"Yes, ma'am, how can I help you?" I said.

"Get me the cookies on the top shelf, would you?"

I happily handed her the package, all the while laughing to myself that public service had a *much* broader definition than I originally understood.

CHAPTER ELEVEN
In Hindsight

I worked hard as premier to try to set a high standard in everything I did. Growing up at home, I had learned about the power of good example from observing my parents. I tried to emulate that example in my own efforts to influence my younger siblings. People can be indifferent to words, while on the other hand, as Shakespeare put it, "action is eloquence." I was determined not to contribute to the cynicism that has robbed so many of their faith in our political institutions — a cynicism that is, in effect, a loss of faith in our capacity to come together and do great things for each other.

I was very cognizant of the nature of the broader environment in which politicians act and the fact that it can be very hostile to idealism and, perversely, welcoming to missteps that contribute to cynicism. Our political opponents were genuinely hopeful that we might stumble and get into trouble. Partisanship, as it too often manifests itself today, does not seek so much to bubble up better public policy as it seeks to dredge up and even concoct embarrassing mistakes in order to ridicule the other guys. Sadly, many of us in politics subscribe to the view that if you have nothing bad to say about your opponent, don't say anything at all. Many in the media also warmly welcome genuine political missteps as well as the fabricated outrage of opposing politicians. Given the choice between covering policy progress and a fabulous food fight, guess which is deemed more worthy of airtime? As I previously observed, the media are simply producing what consumers want.

The media's tendency to highlight political mistakes has been accentuated by the demands of that new phenomenon: the digitally enabled conversation, a.k.a. social media. While it had been claimed that the Internet would help us broaden our thinking and facilitate constructive debate, I'm not so sure it has entirely succeeded. I believe it has also led to the creation of partisan echo chambers where the like-minded gather to reinforce their views, right or wrong. As well, the Internet has become a comfortable refuge for the many voices, often anonymous, who luxuriate in negativity, including the worst species, "trolls" and "haters," who deliberately seek to poison online conversation with rabidly partisan and often personal attacks.

There is one more aspect of political reality worth mentioning here. We all make mistakes. Although all organizations and the people within make mistakes, government is one of the very few where those mistakes are published on the front page of the newspaper. What's more, ministers and the premier are politically accountable for the missteps of hundreds of thousands of direct and indirect employees.

All this constituted the broader political environment in which I was acting. And it reinforced the need in my mind to strive to be beyond reproach.

I expected a high standard of myself and everyone around me, including my caucus, my staff, and the senior civil servants with whom I interacted. And by and large we walked the line. I certainly didn't provide perfect leadership, nor did I lead a perfect government; there were occasional transgressions. I was leading an enterprise made up exclusively of people, with all their noble strengths and human frailties.

When there were failings, I tried to acknowledge them and take steps to ensure they were not repeated. Under a glass on my desk I kept some of my favourite quotations, including one from Sophocles: "All men make mistakes, but a good man yields when he knows his course is wrong, and repairs the evil. The only crime is pride."

There are two kinds of mistakes in politics: when you do the wrong thing and when somebody else does the wrong thing and you are, rightly, accountable for it. I learned that the former is a lot easier to prevent and manage than the latter.

Two good examples of mistakes that were entirely caused by me (there were certainly many more) are those I earlier described from my 1999 campaign: when I called Harris a "thug," and when I unintentionally offended an Alberta family that had lost a son in a school shooting. In both cases, I crossed the line. The good news about these kinds of mistakes is that they were generated by me alone and I learned from them.

The more challenging mistakes were those that arose without my knowledge, but for which, as head of the government, I was rightly accountable. In the simplest cases, I apologized. For example, I apologized for a Cabinet Office civil servant who referred in an email to a black job applicant as a "ghetto dude." Another time, a Crown attorney's office failed to inform a resident of St. Catharines that a charge of criminal harassment against her neighbour had been dropped. I also apologized to victims of sexual abuse at provincial reform schools, a clear case of a grievous, historic wrong.

There were many more demands for apologies from me (likely hundreds, because this was a standard Question Period refrain). There were also complaints made by some that I was apologizing *too much* instead of firing ministers. The Opposition was always happy when they got a political head. In this regard, I was usually happy to keep them unhappy.

I always knew that, sooner or later, something was bound to go off the rails. History bears this out. In my own time, after all, I had witnessed this in the Peterson, Rae, Harris, and Eves governments. And there were many examples in Ottawa as well. Political stripe is no indicator here. In politics, misfortune favours the many. The question was not whether "stuff" would happen on my watch, but when it would happen and how I would respond. I certainly understood that by postponing my departure from politics from 2009 to 2013 I was tempting the fates. There is no doubt that in my case the biggest controversies involved the gas plants, eHealth, and Ornge. I wish none of these had arisen, but they did. They are now part of my record and I accept responsibility for these failings. It is worth examining each of them. I'd like to start by discussing what happened with the gas plants.

My government's energy plan called for a massive, multi-billion dollar investment in new transmission lines and power generation. This was principally motivated by the need to repair an aging system, one that was barely keeping up with Ontario's energy demands; it was also necessitated by the need to replace power from the dirty, coal-fired plants we were shutting down. Our coal plants were significant contributors not only to climate change but also to asthma in children and respiratory ailments in seniors. At their peak, coal plants were producing 28 percent of Ontario electricity. An important element of our energy retrofit plan was the construction of new gas-powered plants, which are better for the environment and our health.

I did not get involved in the decision about where to locate the gas plants but I did get involved in the decision to relocate two. When this became controversial and I had to get up to speed on the issue generally, I was surprised to learn eighteen new gas-fired power plants had already been located on my watch, in communities like Brampton, Windsor, and Toronto. These generated little or no controversy because they were properly sited. The problem with the Mississauga and Oakville gas plants is that they were not. These plants were eventually relocated to "willing host" communities, proving that, like the other eighteen, there is a right way and a wrong way to locate a gas plant.

I learned the hard way that the wrong way to locate a gas plant is to leave it to the experts to decide. This is not an indictment of the experts. The experts followed the rules for locating gas plants. It is an admission that my government and I failed to bring the necessary oversight to ensure the rules were sensible and that, even if the rules were being followed to the letter, the outcome was sensible.

I recall clearly making the point at an early Cabinet meeting back in 2004 that we politicians should keep our hands off issues like electricity rates and new power generation. Did I ever get that one wrong! Almost no one knows the names of the heads of the Ontario Power Authority (OPA), Ontario Power Generation (OPG), the Independent Electricity System Operator (IESO), and Hydro One — the various agencies established to run Ontario's complex energy network. But people knew my name. This was normal. Ontarians don't elect the heads of government agencies. They elect their government. And they have a legitimate expectation their government will oversee agencies under their ultimate control. The buck doesn't stop with the agency. It stops with the premier and the government.

That meant, of course, that I found myself being drawn into the energy morass.

My government began to intervene, and rightly so, in the development of a long-term energy plan, in the establishment of electricity rates, and the development of renewable energy, most notably through our Green Energy and Green Economy Act. While I had eagerly followed the closure of our coal-fired plants and I had been involved in wrestling with the future of our nuclear sector, an area that had escaped my personal attention was the construction of gas plants.

In 2004 inspired in part by my naive desire to give greater control of the energy file to experts, we created the Ontario Power Authority, an arm's-length agency to decide when and where power was needed and to contract with the private sector to provide it. In 2009 the OPA made the decision to locate a gas plant in Oakville, beside the Ford auto assembly plant there. As a government, we stayed out of the decision; the matter did not come to Cabinet for approval.

The Oakville gas plant escaped my attention until my government began to get some serious blowback from the local Liberal MPP (Kevin Flynn), the mayor of Oakville (Rob Burton), a citizens group, and local health officials, who argued the Oakville airshed was already overtaxed by industrial emissions.

The opposition parties jumped on the issue as a chance to embarrass the government. Both the Conservatives and the New Democrats called for outright cancellation of the plant. It became obvious that we had to rethink the OPA's decision.

I met with Flynn a couple of times on this issue. I also met with the mayor. The most compelling argument Flynn made to me was that, under our own newly created rules for locating wind turbines, we would not be allowed to place a single wind turbine on the Oakville site. Indeed, our new Ontario law, one of the toughest in the world, prohibited the location of a wind turbine within 550 metres of a home. And yet what had been decided for Oakville was to locate a new gas plant — at nine hundred megawatts, it would be one of the biggest in North America — four hundred metres from the nearest home, 320 metres from the nearest school, and sixty-five metres from the closest offices. Talk about getting it wrong!

I felt terrible about what we were about to foist onto the people of Oakville. Yes, the OPA made the decision, but the buck stopped with me. After some hard reflection on my part, I decided there was no way we could let this plant proceed. So, in 2010, one year before the next election, I decided to relocate the plant. The opposition parties did not complain. They saw my decision as a win for them and as a capitulation by me — a "flip-flop." I didn't care what they called it. What mattered to me was that I had made the correct call. Moving the plant was the right thing to do.

Where I came up short at the time was in not immediately demanding to know with some precision what the costs of relocation would be. By failing then to pressure the Ministry of Energy and OPA for these numbers and failing to understand early on just how limited our capacity was to project these costs, this later led to my government coming under intense pressure to release "the number." What unfolded was the embarrassing spectacle of us releasing a succession of different numbers, starting at $40 million and culminating with the auditor's projection of a cost that could be as high as $650 million spread out over twenty years.

The Opposition predictably accused us of hiding the real numbers. That served their purposes, but it did not serve the truth. The truth is that neither my office nor, as it turned out, the Ministry of Energy, had the capacity to determine the complicated projected costs of relocating the plant to a new site, and transmitting the electricity to where we needed it. We relied on the OPA for the cost projections, and, to our chagrin, the experts there kept changing them, always doing so upward. I felt for Premier Wynne when she later expressed frustration after receiving four different numbers from the OPA for the Oakville plant costs. In my case, before doing a media scrum where I was to confirm the relocation costs to be $40 million, I cross-examined my staff to make sure we had it right. "Are we absolutely sure this is the right number? I don't want to go back out there tomorrow or next week with a different number!" I was assured the number the experts had given us was rock solid. It wasn't, and we looked stupid for months as a result.

This was bad enough, but it wasn't the only gas plant my government took steps (rightly, in my opinion) to relocate. A year after we had made the decision to relocate the Oakville gas plant, we also started to take some heat for the proposed Mississauga gas plant in the months leading up to the 2011 election. Community opposition grew slowly, but then it boiled over just before the campaign. Indeed, in a local information session hosted by the plant's private-sector proponent a few weeks before the campaign, the discussion grew so heated the police had to be called in and the meeting shut down.

As I was to learn, seven years earlier — in 2004 — the Ministry of Energy (this was before the OPA was fully up and running) had decided we needed a gas plant in the Mississauga area. In 2005 the city granted approval for a plant to be located on the site in question. About a year later, Mayor Hazel McCallion and her council changed their minds about it, and, for the next few years, the matter was caught up in legal wrangling. The project appeared to energy officials to have finally died on the vine because the builder could not secure the necessary project financing. But then, a few months before the 2011 election, events changed and it became clear the plant was going ahead. The community reacted strongly in opposition. This was when the matter came to my attention. Mayor McCallion came to see me and, in her own inimitable way, made a no-nonsense argument, concluding, "Mr. Premier, I'm telling you your energy experts have got this one wrong and you are going to have to fix it."

If there were savvier politicians in Ontario than Hazel McCallion, I never met them. I should have listened sooner to the advice and urgings of Her Worship.

(I must admit I later enjoyed the tongue lashing she gave Opposition committee members when she appeared before the gas plant committee: "I don't know why you are wasting a lot of time.... The people of Mississauga are fed up of hearing all this controversy at Queen's Park over something they wanted cancelled. The government agreed to cancel it and you folks are making a big fuss about it. C'mon. Let's get on with the business of the province, folks.")

Besides criticism from the opposition parties, government caucus members representing ridings in Mississauga and neighbouring Etobicoke, such as Charles Sousa, Bob Delaney, Donna Cansfield, and Laurel Broten, expressed their opposition to the project. As I began to wrestle in earnest with the issue, I found it hard to distinguish *this* gas plant from the Oakville gas plant. In Mississauga, the gas plant was again to be built on a site where not one wind turbine could have been lawfully located. The new plant was to be built in a residential community adjacent to two condominium towers, a hospital, and backing onto a conservation area.

A few weeks before the election, I hinted at the decision I would make to relocate the plant. When a reporter asked me what I intended to do about the brewing controversy, I said, "It's never too late to do the right thing." The whole matter didn't sit right with me. My gut was telling me this plant was to be located in the wrong place and, like before, I was going to have to make things right for the community.

Of course, the issue was hardly going to go to sleep during the campaign. It was understandably going to become the subject of debate. That's exactly what campaigns are for: raising issues, generating debate, and taking positions. The community wanted to know where the parties stood on the issue, and the Opposition had made it clear they were opposed to the plant. Voters expected a response and I believed they were entitled to one. My brother Brendan and my chief of staff, Chris Morley, briefed me on the campaign bus about how the issue could not be sidestepped and we needed to take a position. My advisors did not advise me to decide one way or the other. They left the decision to me because they knew me well. They knew I could be at my best as a campaigner only if I ran on policies and positions I truly believed in. I decided the right thing to do was to make a commitment to relocate the Mississauga gas plant. Ironically, the Conservatives reacted by saying I could not be trusted to deliver on my promise, and only a vote for them would ensure that both the Mississauga and Oakville plants would remain dead.

Later, the opposition parties would label the Mississauga plant relocation a politically motivated decision designed to win seats. While I can't speak to the Opposition's motivation to put a stop to the gas plant, I can speak to mine.

I made the decision to relocate the Mississauga gas plant for the same reason I had chosen to relocate Oakville's one year earlier. This was yet another case of a gas plant being wrongly located by the experts, and my job was to make it right. I relocated both plants because it was the right thing to do. And I would have done it for any Ontario community. I was pleased to later see both plants relocated to communities that embraced them. Napanee and Sarnia welcomed the plants and the economic benefits, including jobs, that came with them.

After the election, the whole embarrassing and frustrating exercise regarding the ever-changing cost of this second gas plant relocation was now repeated. Again, we looked like fools as we put out numbers one day only to have them changed by the experts on the next. The Opposition went to town, accusing us of an elaborate conspiracy to hide costs.

I had seen much by way of personal attacks in the Ontario legislature during my more than two decades there, but the Opposition struck a new low with their vicious attacks against my minister of energy, Chris Bentley. Bentley was one of the most thoughtful, intelligent, and hard-working people I have had the pleasure to work with in government. He took his responsibilities in Cabinet very seriously, demonstrating integrity every step of the way. Ironically, given the extreme nature of the partisan attacks he suffered, Bentley was one of the least partisan politicians I knew. He was genuinely interested in hearing the other side. None of this counted for anything as the Opposition launched a malicious contempt motion against Bentley for refusing to disclose the details of the confidential negotiations (over the costs of relocation) between the OPA and the gas plant companies. Later on, in committee hearings convened to answer questions about our handling of the gas plant decisions, every single witness who commented on this — senior bureaucrats, energy officials, and the auditor general included — testified it would have been entirely inappropriate for Bentley to make this information public. But the Opposition would have none of this. They were uninterested in facts. Clearly, partisanship had overtaken reason in the Opposition benches at Queen's Park. It was poisoning the well of trust between government and Opposition, trust that is very much in the public interest.

Sensing an opening to pursue this on a longer-term basis, the Conservatives and New Democrats colluded to hand the matter to the legislature's justice committee, purportedly to find the truth about the gas plants. That was never the purpose of the committee's hearings. Dominated as the

Getting briefed by my chief of staff, Peter Wilkinson, and principal secretary, Jamison Steeve.

Walking and talking with Cabinet colleagues (left to right) Gerry Phillips, George Smitherman, and David Caplan.

Celebrating our Second Career program. It allowed thousands of Ontarians to get new skills during the recession (2009).

Cabinet meeting with one of my hardest working ministers and future premier, Kathleen Wynne (2008).

Standing up for the auto sector with ministers Sandra Pupatello and Dwight Duncan.

Politics was always a family affair. In 2006, I celebrated my brother David's re-election as a member of Parliament.

It was always a privilege to meet with our veterans.

Five premiers in China, 2008 trade mission. (Left to right): Robert Ghiz (P.E.I.), Gary Doer (Manitoba), me, Pierre-Marc Johnson (Quebec), and Shawn Graham (New Brunswick).

The team I was proud to lead on a China trade mission. (Left to right): Paul Lehmann, Fareed Amin, minister Michael Chan, Karman Wong, Lloyd Rang, Tracey Sobers, me, Dave Gene, Laura Miller, and Peter Wilkinson.

Congratulating Finance Minister Dwight Duncan on the 2009 HST budget.

Down to business — a weekly Cabinet meeting.

Ontario-Quebec Cabinet meeting with Quebec premier Jean Charest (2009).

Boy from Alta Vista opens for Elton John!

With Prime Minister Stephen Harper in Toronto announcing transit improvements (2009).

The McGuinty clan celebrates my father's contribution to the University of Ottawa (2010).

My favourite kind of event as premier — in a school, speaking to students.

Welcoming president of China, Hu Jintao, to Ontario with minister Michael Chan on the right (2010).

Taking in the Sea of Galilee and its rich history, Israel (2010).

The family of fallen police officer Vu Pham. The boys and their mom (far right) inspired me with their strength and courage (2010).

Building up Ontario's clean energy industry with former MP Joe Jordan (left) and Ontario Liberal candidate Stephen Mazurek (right).

Friends of different political stripes — John Tory, a true "progressive" conservative (2011).

With Her Majesty Queen Elizabeth II and Research In Motion CEO Mike Lazaridis in Waterloo (2010).

My home on wheels during the campaign (2011).

On the bus and getting ready for the next campaign stop with chief of staff Chris Morley (left) and assistant Chike Agbasi (centre).

Two chiefs and a brother — the best political minds in the business. (Left to right): Chris Morley, Don Guy, me, and Brendan McGuinty.

Always fun having one of the kids onboard the campaign bus. Dalton Jr. happily distracts me from my work (2011).

Strategizing in mid-air with Don Guy, Chris Morley, and Brendan (2011).

Counting down the days on the campaign bus (with Tracey Sobers, director and executive assistant) (2011).

Lucky for me, Terri has always had my back (2011).

On the edge of our seats. Family TV time on election night (2011).

Entering the victory party in 2011.

Celebrating our "major minority" in 2011. It was the first time an Ontario Liberal leader had won three successive elections in over a century.

The celebration continues with the extended McGuinty family on election night.

Our great 2011 Liberal campaign team.

In politics you are always on the go and being led from one event to another with the help of great staff (left to right): Jennifer Beckermann, Nabil Shash, and Beckie Codd-Downey.

Welcoming U.S. president Barack Obama to Ontario, with Foreign Affairs Minister John Baird (2012).

With pictures of family behind me and Dad's watch on my wrist, I prepare to announce my resignation (2012).

Announcing my resignation to my Liberal caucus colleagues (2012).

A great team. Looking forward to life after politics.

Congratulating Kathleen Wynne — a new Ontario Liberal era begins.

After the adrenalin of politics came reflection at Harvard (2013).

Carleen's wedding (2012).

Loving my new responsibility as granddad — Ellis and me (2015).

committee was by the opposition parties, its hearings were a purely partisan exercise. The *Oxford Dictionary* defines "partisan" as "prejudiced in favour of a particular cause." The committee was prejudiced in favour of the defeat of the government and that coloured everything it did. Opposition members were happy their efforts were getting them into the news. With every passing day, their allegations grew more outlandish.

Had I been advising the opposition parties, and understanding they were intent on setting the table for the next election, I would have urged a little caution. After all, this was the same Opposition that had urged us to close the plants and, later, to relocate them to their ridings. (I had often been accused of failing to keep a promise, but this was the first time I came under Opposition fire for keeping a promise they had urged me to make.) This was also the same Opposition that asserted the government was impeding their work by refusing to co-operate. And yet, when the committee passed dozens of motions demanding government documents, each of those demands was complied with. In the end, the committee was provided with over three hundred thousand pages of documents, including thirty thousand from my office alone. I was asked to appear before the committee on two separate occasions, a request unprecedented in the history of Ontario provincial politics. I willingly appeared at the earliest possible opportunity. The minister of energy also appeared twice, as did Premier Wynne. All told, the Opposition-led committee sat for two years, heard from ninety-one witnesses, and received more than 140 hours of testimony.

Finding no evidence of a smoking gun, the Opposition grew ever more frustrated and ramped up the rhetoric and innuendo. They grew most excited by their claim that emails had been deleted by my staff during the transition period from my premiership to the Wynne administration. Not finding anything incriminating in the three hundred thousand–plus pages of government records, they insisted the smoking gun had been destroyed.

In making this attention-seeking assertion the Opposition deliberately chose to ignore two facts. First, the rules regarding the preservation of government documents explicitly do not require that personal or political documents be preserved. This accords with common practice (and common sense) in virtually all workplaces, where personal information is removed from a computer to protect privacy and give the next computer user a fresh start.

As for the various government rules and guidelines authorizing the destruction of political records, this too is part of parliamentary practice virtually everywhere (caucus and Cabinet confidentiality stand out), a practice I fully support. It is absolutely essential that politicians be free to kick around political ideas — good ones and bad ones, wise ones and foolish ones. They must be free to think through their decisions out loud before they make them. There was a shredding truck outside the outgoing premier's office after my party won the 2003 election. This did not strike me as untoward. I knew the civil service had a record of all the decisions made and related Cabinet minutes.

The second fact the Opposition chose to ignore in the matter of government emails is that while these can be removed from a government computer's hard drive, they continue to exist on the government's central server. In his testimony before the gas plant committee, David Nicholl, the government's corporate chief information officer, was asked about the impact of "wiping" a government computer. He answered, "But don't forget, the wiping of the hard drives would not affect the email and the email accounts. The email accounts are on a server...."

But none of this — the official rules authorizing the destruction of political records and the continuing existence of emails on the government's central server — was of interest to the Opposition. It was not in accord with the public tale they were weaving.

I do not regret doing the right thing for the people of Oakville and Mississauga. I would do it for any community. Among those who have been critical of my decisions, no one has ever told me they would welcome a gas plant the size of a hospital beside their own community hospital. In the end, I did my job, which in this case was to right a wrong. But it never should have got that far. I should have been on top of these issues much sooner. It was a mistake for me to delegate decisions to locate gas plants to the energy experts. While it's true the experts got eighteen out of twenty right, those last two more than establish why I should have kept this responsibility inside my government. I take full responsibility for this failing and I deeply regret this.

I also regret that my successor, Premier Kathleen Wynne, and her government had to spend so much time on this issue. I am incredibly grateful to Ontarians for electing the Wynne government and demonstrating their capacity to look beyond the Opposition's hyper-partisan agenda — something that, for an extended period of time, dominated the news coming out of Queen's Park. In the end, Ontarians chose progressive policy over partisan games. They chose a party and a government that focused on priorities they shared, like education, health care, and the economy.

In addition to the costs of relocating the plants (estimated at nearly one billion dollars spread over twenty years), what bothered me most was the breach of faith this represented in the eyes of many Ontarians. I had worked so hard for twenty-three years in politics to always do the right thing and to be seen as having done that. And while I believed I had done the right thing in the end, I felt I had let Ontarians down.

As for my family, I know they were hurt, offended, and angered by the headlines. The media were unrestrained in reporting the outrageous allegations being made by the Opposition.

From time to time during my political career, Terri would grow angry at how I, and by extension our family, had become the subject of gratuitous attacks by those unhappy with me, whether politicians or pundits. I would respond by saying it was the modest price one paid to serve as leader in a strong democracy. But that was a tough argument for her to accept as the gas plant feeding frenzy grew unabated. The nightly news or a spiteful column could cause her tears, anger, or both. I was alleged to be corrupt, to have ordered the destruction of emails, to have fabricated the cost of relocating the gas plants, to have subverted the committee's work by withholding information, and to be the subject of a criminal investigation.

None of these allegations were true, but they suited the Opposition's narrative. And they served the media's purposes in an age where outrage is all the rage. Terri said, "This is terrible for our family! Why can't they be fair? They don't have to like you but at least they can try to be fair!"

I had never put too much stock in the ups and downs of how the media presented me. But there sure seemed to be a lot more downs at the time.

Before the controversy over the gas plants there was eHealth. The eHealth controversy had many similarities to the one involving the gas plants. As with the gas plants, we did not get on top of it quickly enough. But eHealth had its own peculiarities.

Long before I became premier, the Conservatives had rightly recognized there were compelling reasons for everyone in the province to have an electronic health record. They assigned the task of digitization to the bureaucrats in the Ministry of Health. One of the greatest challenges facing any government is how to keep up with evolving information technology. The private sector seems to find a way, but I discovered the government bureaucracy could not handle the demands, especially in the health field.

By the time we got to office, a lot of money had been spent without much being accomplished. So we brought in experts from the private sector, who told us to do this and do that. And they kept coming back to us and saying they needed more time and more money. Accordingly, in my second term, we set up eHealth as an arm's-length agency to do the job. I installed Alan Hudson, who had done a superb job on wait-time reduction, as chair of the agency. I needed a guy who would get me results and I expected him to bang heads together to make this happen. I felt assured he would get the job done.

While I knew digitized health records were important, I never had the same passion for this as I did for other issues, like health care wait times or graduation rates. I wasn't regularly asking what was going on at eHealth, how much we were spending, and what we had to show for it, and my office did not discern that we had a problem in this area.

So it came as a surprise to me when it finally exploded in the press, thanks to some untendered eHealth contracts and silly expense claims. (An eHealth consultant who was being paid $2,700 a day had billed taxpayers $1.65 for a Tim Hortons tea and $3.99 for Choco Bites. This was delicious fodder for the Opposition and media.)

The auditor general added fuel to the fire with a report saying that $1 billion had been spent by the province on electronic records. Much of that spending was attributable to the Conservatives when they were still in power, but the opposition parties and the media ignored that detail and accused us of wasting $1 billion with nothing to show for it. However, that is not what the auditor general (Jim McCarter at the time) said. Rather, he said we had built the highways but had yet to put the cars on them. In other words, he said, although we had a lot of the necessary infrastructure, since the health system is so big and the institutions (hospitals, doctors) so entrenched, it was not yet being fully utilized.

It is fair to say that eHealth had run out from under us as a government and it had most certainly escaped my personal attention. I had not followed what was happening there, in terms of the investments being made and the results we were getting, or not getting. In the end, senior staff at eHealth, including Alan Hudson, offered to resign. I was sorry to see Hudson go. I will be forever grateful for his leadership in lowering Ontario wait times.

Another victim of the controversy was the health minister, David Caplan, whom I had named to replace George Smitherman at the beginning of my second term. We were under daily assault in the legislature and in the media. It became clear to me that the only way we could bring an end to it was with the resignation of the minister. I came to that conclusion reluctantly, given that most of the problems had occurred before Caplan became health minister. But nothing else was going to satisfy either the media or the Opposition. They wanted a head — namely, Caplan's.

Caplan was smart, hard-working, and had great political instincts. I hated to see him go. (Two years earlier I had been equally reluctant to accept Mike Colle's resignation from Cabinet because of concerns over grants to cultural groups. Colle was then my minister of citizenship and immigration.) But in our parliamentary system there is a principle of ministerial accountability for the misbehaviour of others under the minister's sway. And it soon became apparent that the only way to defuse the situation and move on was for the minister to step down.

Caplan was understandably unhappy about that. Even though it was commonly understood that eHealth troubles had happened on his predecessor's watch and that no real blame attached to him, that didn't make it easier for Caplan. I could tell he took his demotion personally and I couldn't really blame him.

Politics is a contact sport and he had been dealt a hard blow. That's a side of politics I have never liked, even when I was in Opposition and a government minister was forced to resign. It may be the rule, but it doesn't make it fair to ministers and their families who must live with the public embarrassment of a forced dismissal.

As for electronic health records, the uproar unfortunately slowed down the pace of change. We eventually put a solid group of people in charge, and we haven't heard too much about eHealth since. Today, there's a broad understanding that the digitization of health records is a long, complicated process that needs patience and oversight.

———————————

Finally, there is the strange case of Ornge, the air ambulance service. (The name is not an acronym; it refers to the colour of the aircraft. It's also not a typo. The letter "a" was dropped because of trademark issues.)

When the Ornge headlines first hit in 2011, I didn't fully understand how this organization worked or what the government's relationship to it was. I had a faint recollection of Ornge coming before the Cabinet earlier (it was in 2005). George Smitherman, then minister of health, brought forward a proposal to improve air ambulance coverage across the province, a laudable objective and certainly not then considered to be controversial. I'm certain Smitherman would have made a strong case for this reform — creating a new private, non-profit entity. I had huge confidence in his ability to see problems and fix them.

From the time the first story broke in the *Toronto Star*, the whole affair grew and grew, and we were caught totally by surprise. The CEO of Ornge, Chris Mazza, was making an annual salary of $1.4 million, about double what the CEOs of our largest hospitals were being paid. (The Opposition was desperately trying to establish some personal connection between me and Mazza. There was none apart from a chance meeting six years earlier as he toured me through a field hospital in Sudbury.) The not-for-profit company had a for-profit spinoff that had made a dubious deal with an Anglo-Italian helicopter manufacturer. There was a questionable payment to a Brazilian law firm. And so on. Opposition accusations kept piling up in Question Period. And the auditor general again chimed in with a report slamming our oversight of the agency and declaring, "The ministry didn't do its job in protecting taxpayers' money."

We fired Mazza and his senior management team, but that wasn't enough for the opposition parties, who were calling for the new health minister, Deb Matthews, to resign.

The Opposition deployed a tactic common to Question Period: for days and weeks on end they targeted the minister with an incessant barrage of questions. The purpose of the onslaught is twofold: to elicit what the Opposition hopes will be incriminating information and to make the minister crack under pressure. "Cracking" can range from being overly defensive in response to the accusations, to responding in kind with outlandish accusations of your own, to being reduced to tears.

The capable Matthews personified grace under pressure as she fended off Opposition attacks at the same time as she struggled to obtain information from the unhelpful administrators at Ornge. I sat beside Matthews in the legislature, offering regular words of encouragement. I would remind her that her audience was not the boisterous and partisan Opposition but calm and thoughtful Ontarians. I repeatedly said to Matthews, "Pretend you are speaking to my mother."

I often invoked my mother in caucus as a representative of typical no-nonsense Ontarians who were uninterested in political games but very much interested in the progress (or lack thereof) we were making in government on their behalf.

While the Opposition has the right — and indeed the responsibility — to hammer away at the government's perceived shortcomings, when their attacks are over the top they can cause serious collateral damage beyond the government. In the case of Ornge, the repeated attacks on the organization and the ensuing media reports had a devastating impact on the morale of the men and women who devote themselves to Canada's biggest air ambulance service, one that safely transports over eighteen thousand Ontario patients every year. Fortunately, morale there is now much improved.

Ornge was yet another example of an arm's-length entity with a quasi-independent management team, out there just beyond our sight, acting in a way that was contrary to the public interest and for which my government was accountable. Ultimately, Matthews introduced a bill giving the minister the authority to rein in the managers at Ornge, who had basically run away from us.

In establishing Ornge, our thinking was that we needed a central agency to coordinate all the independent air ambulance operations across the province and provide better service to Ontarians. Who could argue with that?

But the framework we put in place obviously led to some problems. Too much power was delegated to the agency. There was a board of directors, but given that Ornge was the recipient of public money, my government should have been more diligent in our oversight.

———————————

What are the lessons here?

For myself, I learned that while creating new entities, like Ornge, eHealth, or the OPA, was a fairly straightforward matter for my government, staying on top of these new organizations was something else altogether. I learned through painful experience about the dangers of failing to keep a close watch on the operations and decision-making of our new creatures. I placed too much confidence in the agencies themselves and in this I did not live up to my responsibility owed to Ontarians. With some 560 distinct agencies, boards, and commissions reporting to the government, I believe it's time to consider more effective ways to hold these entities to account. While I am a firm supporter of the principle of accountability for the premier and the ministers — the buck must stop with our elected representatives — we need to reflect on the implications of this as we continue to create an ever-greater number of arm's-length agencies, each with its own governing body. In an age of heightened transparency and accountability, I also worry about the legislature becoming so easily distracted that for a few (or many) days, all other business is effectively halted by the news that someone among the several hundreds of thousands of persons for whom the government is accountable, including those who work in arm's-length agencies, has expensed a doughnut. The principle of accountability is sound. I'm just not sure we are today honouring that principle in a way that serves the public interest.

I have no doubt some will remember me as premier only for the ways I came up short; others will see the big picture and judge my record accordingly. I do not know how history will judge me nor does this preoccupy me. What counts is what we do every day, and how we do it. I struggled always to do what I believed to be right. I gave my very best to my party and my province.

CHAPTER TWELVE
A Successful Succession

The question of my record was something that occupied my mind a great deal in 2011, as I understood very well that it would come under close scrutiny in the upcoming October election. I would be seeking a third mandate, knowing conventional wisdom dictated that I should have left on a high note after two wins. But as I've mentioned, I didn't feel right about bailing out in the middle of the global economic meltdown that was ravaging Ontario. Dwight Duncan, my minister of finance, had quietly raised the subject of retirement with me. "I just want you to know I will be here as long as you are. But when you go, I'm going too." Knowing Duncan, that was his way of saying, "I hope you are giving some serious thought to retiring sooner rather than later." Brendan had also broached the topic with me. "You know, you don't have to do the job forever."

Apart from Terri and my mother, I can't recall anyone else raising the subject of my retirement with me. Maybe that's not surprising. Everyone could see I took the job very seriously, and I never showed any signs of being less than enthusiastic about my responsibilities. I knew that there had to be some among my caucus who saw themselves as my successor. There may even have been some very quiet efforts made to begin to organize candidate teams for an eventual leadership bid. And had there been any that had been brought to my attention, I would not have discouraged such efforts — just so long as they were discreet. I considered it an important part of my job to ensure that whenever I left, I was leaving behind strong candidates who would compete in a hotly contested race. But I never felt any pressure to leave. Even at home, Terri had supported me in running once more, given the state of the economy. We had essentially made this decision together two years earlier. At that point, the window had closed on both a leadership race and on any hope that a new premier would have time to get up to speed to put his or her own stamp on the government. As my mother always said, "Remember, Mick, you don't have to stay if you're not having fun." I was still having fun. I was fully committed.

By 2011, I had been premier for eight years. In a 24-7 news environment, juiced up by social media and starved for content, political leaders are in the electorate's face much more today than they were in the old days. It has become impossible to follow the sage advice of the Chinese philosopher Lao Tzu, who said, "Leaders are best when people barely know they exist." Inevitably, over time and with lots of exposure, you begin to wear on people. You can mitigate this by just *presiding* instead of *leading*. Presiding will surely limit your missteps. But I had chosen to lead. I had led real change. And change is bound to make some people unhappy.

I was excited to begin my fourth campaign as leader of the Ontario Liberals. Our caucus and party were in good shape. While we had earlier lost the very capable Jim Watson to the mayoralty in Ottawa, in a 2010 by-election we picked up Bob Chiarelli, another hard-working and experienced Ottawa politician. It was Chiarelli whom my father and I had consulted back in 1987 when my dad was considering running for office. Chiarelli was then part of the Peterson government and he had impressed me with his political savvy and energy. It felt good to have him back on the Liberal team.

As before, we assembled a strong team of candidates to run in our unheld ridings. These men and women never failed to inspire me with their energy and commitment to our party, their community, and the democratic process. I was especially impressed by those candidates who contested an election in a riding that was a long-time Opposition stronghold. Now that was dedication!

We went into the campaign a dozen points behind the Conservatives. I didn't see that as insurmountable. To state the obvious, I knew very well it wasn't how you went in to the campaign that counted; it was how you came out. I was by now an experienced campaigner working with an experienced campaign team. The other two party leaders, the PC's Tim Hudak and the NDP's Andrea Horwath, were each heading up their first provincial campaign. I knew how tough that was. It meant a lot of learning on the job. But I didn't underestimate them. Unlike the other leaders, I had a track record in government and I fully expected attacks.

The PCs launched their media campaign in June with an opening round of ads attacking me as the "Tax Man." They ran their ads on CBC's *Hockey Night in Canada* during the playoffs. They followed up with a round of radio ads hammering away on the same theme. Our caucus had differing views on the effectiveness of the ads, but I well remember Dwight Duncan's story about how he had visited an elementary school and asked the students there if they knew who Dalton McGuinty was. "He's the tax man!" was their cheerful reply.

The PCs had also earlier launched another kind of attack, one where I wasn't the only target. In November 2010, I had made a trip to China, where I announced that, as part of our strategy to build a globally competitive economy, we were going to create a high-end ($40,000) scholarship to attract the best and brightest Ph.D. students from around the world to study and then stay and work in Ontario. We already had thirty-eight thousand international students studying in Ontario, contributing over one billion dollars annually to our economy. I called our new scholarship a "brain gain" strategy to add to our growing intellectual prowess.

The Conservatives jumped on this announcement and accused us of giving money to foreign students at the expense of support for our own kids. This was demonstrably false. We had been putting a lot of money (over $6 billion more) into post-secondary education and had created over two hundred thousand new spaces in our colleges and universities. We were also running on a plan to create a 30 percent–off tuition grant (now benefitting over 230,000 students every year). So, it was pretty hard for Hudak to argue that we were shutting out Ontario's youth. Nevertheless, he found his argument was getting some traction. The notion that Ontario tax dollars would support the education of foreign students angered some Ontarians, and Hudak decided he would exploit this.

In a similar theme, during the campaign Hudak jumped on a relatively innocuous plank in our campaign platform proposing a $10,000 tax credit for businesses to offset training costs for new Canadians with professional degrees in areas such as architecture, accounting, and engineering. My thinking was that we should get these Canadians launched on career paths in their areas of expertise rather than remaining underemployed because they lacked domestic job experience. This would be good for those workers and their families as well as for our economy. However, Hudak and the Conservatives attacked the idea for allegedly giving preference to "foreign workers" over native Canadians. As for the Conservatives' own platform, they called for implementing "chain gangs" for prisoners and publishing the home addresses of sex offenders (an idea immediately discredited by the OPP).

Hudak's strategy was clear. He was practising the politics of division. He was inviting some Ontarians to join him against others, whether these others were international students, "foreign workers," or convicts. He was appealing to baser instincts rather than promoting positive ideas enhancing opportunities for all Ontarians.

I'm a fan of Abraham Lincoln. I, too, believe in appealing to "the better angels of our nature." I have always thought that while voters may display a veneer of cynicism, they actually want to be inspired. And while they can appear to be selfish, deep down they want to be part of something bigger than themselves. They want to make a difference beyond their own lives.

Maybe it was because I had studied biology in university that I sometimes thought of the human head, heart, and gut as areas politicians can target. I think it's wrong for politicians to target the gut in an effort to elicit a visceral reaction. It's not hard to evoke anger, outrage, envy, and resentment, and to use those dark emotions to turn one group of people against another. But that's a betrayal of progressive leadership. Instead, politicians should target the head and the heart — that is, we should appeal to voters' intellect and compassion.

Today's Ontario is a place where people from a rich variety of backgrounds live together in remarkable harmony. In large part, this is due to our unusual history. Most societies have been founded on sameness: people with the same language, same religion, same culture, and same traditions. In Canada, we took a different approach. The English kept their language, their faith, and their legal system, and the French retained theirs. It is only recently, however, that we have come to start appreciating the immense significance of the rich history of our Aboriginal peoples, who were here from time immemorial. The Canadian ideal led us to find strength in our differences. It taught us to be accepting and respectful of one another. This distinctive feature of our home is something we cannot truly appreciate until we leave Ontario and Canada. When I left politics, I spent a year as a fellow at Harvard University in an international program. My colleagues marvelled at how a city like Toronto, the most diverse city in the world, could be so peaceful. As I earlier observed, our diversity was also a real advantage when I travelled abroad as premier, because I was accompanied by Chinese-Canadians in China, by Indo-Canadians in India, by Pakistani-Canadians in Pakistan, and so on.

Later in the campaign, Hudak tried to back away from his divisive approach, but he had caused himself serious damage. I knew the leaders' debate was going to be very challenging for me given that I was going in with an eight-year record as premier. I was pleased when the result was labelled "inconclusive," and I worked as hard as I could during the final week of the campaign to convince Ontarians we were worthy of a third mandate.

As the campaign was winding down, I would find ways to occupy myself between stops on the bus. This included calling into riding campaign offices to urge on the local team. Another activity was to take a poll by just looking out the bus window. The bus "wrap" prevented people from seeing in but we could see out. Once in a while someone in a passing car would drive by, look at our bus, and be inspired to signal how they felt about me. We would tally up the number of thumbs-up and middle fingers to see how we were doing.

On election night, as usual, my team and extended family gathered in Ottawa's Chateau Laurier hotel. Don Guy, fresh from directing my fourth campaign, whispered, "Premier, not sure we'll have a majority or minority. It's going to be close." As usual, he was right. When all the ballots had been counted, we were one seat shy of a majority. I could see the disappointment in my team but I felt very grateful for the privilege of a third mandate, something that had not been won by an Ontario Liberal premier in nearly 120 years.

When I spoke to the media the following morning, I labelled my new government a "major minority." I was very hopeful. I did not fully understand that night how fundamentally the situation had changed at Queen's Park in terms of my ability to get things done. I was about to discover the Opposition had no interest in making the legislature work for Ontarians. It would be frustrating for my government and my successor, but the Opposition would pay the price in the next election.

Ever the optimist, I quickly got back to work, hoping we could build some bridges with the other parties. I was sorely disappointed. I recall one particular post-election meeting with Hudak. I started out by asking him how his family was doing. I was trying to make a human connection. He immediately brushed that pleasantry aside and demanded that I fire Dwight Duncan, my finance minister, for incompetence. This was laughable, but I kept my cool and told Hudak his demand was a non-starter, but he didn't back down. I never got the sense from him that he had any sincere intention of making the minority legislature work effectively. Indeed, he was quite clear publicly that he did not want it to work.

NDP leader Andrea Horwath was more open to talking to me about initiatives that would allow her party to continue to support the government. This was soon put to the test when, in a meeting with Horwath, I agreed to meet her demands and we struck a deal that would allow the NDP to support the 2012 budget. Those demands included a more comprehensive freeze on public-sector executive compensation (basically freezing incentive pay for executives at hospitals and universities, in addition to their salaries) and a new tax on the rich. I was personally very much opposed to the latter. I know it was a popular move — even within my own caucus — but I didn't like the motivation or the effect of the policy. While the motivation was said to be a desire for fairness, I believe it was a case of envy and anger, neither of which are a basis for sound public policy. And as for the effect, these kinds of "tax the rich" schemes never bring in as much money as projected; the wealthy just take steps to move their money elsewhere. I also worried about the signal we were sending to the international community as we competed for top-notch professionals to live and work in Ontario. In any event, I agreed to swallow this pill to secure passage of our budget and ensure the survival of my government.

Then, in a surprise move I never saw coming, Horwath went back on her word and began issuing new demands for changes in the budget bills as they wound their way through the legislature. I was disappointed. I suspected Horwath couldn't sell her caucus on the agreement we had struck.

I felt caught between a rock and a hard place. Hudak made it clear he had no interest in working together. Horwath was more pleasant but she had proven that she couldn't deliver on her commitments.

I think it's also fair to say that by 2011 the opposition parties had had more than their fill of me. I was supposed to lose in 2003 because I lacked experience. I was supposed to lose in 2007 because I had raised taxes when I said I wouldn't. And I was supposed to lose in 2011 because of Ornge, eHealth, the HST … take your pick. But I kept on winning. So they were fed up. Neither party had any real intention of making the government work for Ontarians. It was now all about badly bruising the government and bringing it down. Nothing else mattered. This was the political environment at Queen's Park in the aftermath of the 2011 election.

And it wasn't as if I was trying to coast after the election. After balancing our budget three years in a row, the recession had struck Ontario in 2008. This caused our revenues to plummet, but at the same time we needed to invest in economic stimulus. This led to a big deficit and I had decided it was time to execute our aggressive plan to get back to a balanced budget. It's difficult even for a majority government to pursue a restraint agenda. And, as I quickly discovered, in the highly combative atmosphere in which my minority government was working, it was next to impossible. In the 2012 budget "lockup" (the term for the period on budget day when the media is given a sneak peak at the documents), TVO's Steve Paikin expressed surprise at how aggressive our cost reductions were.

"How are you going to get this passed?" he asked. "Or do you *want* an election?"

I didn't want an election. What I wanted was a partner to get the budget passed. In the end, Horwath came through, but not before she had poisoned the well of trust between us by failing to honour the original agreement the two of us had struck.

——————————

Governing in the wake of the 2011 election, then, was all about struggling to find a way forward under those circumstances and confronting challenges as they arose. One such challenge — a crisis, in fact — was the collapse of the roof of a shopping mall in Elliot Lake on June 23, 2012.

I first learned of the collapse early that evening while driving to the airport after attending a Liberal Party meeting in Sudbury. During my time as premier, I had been called upon to respond to a number of emergencies, including a flood in Peterborough and a tornado in Goderich. I got in touch with the Elliot Lake mayor and followed the rescue operation very closely over the next few days. When I was told the rescue effort had been called off with two victims still possibly alive in the rubble, I reacted immediately.

"Don't we owe the community another look at it?" I asked my staff.

We set up a conference call for me to speak with the rescue officials. I made it clear to them.

"If that were my mother or my wife in there, I would want us to do everything we could to try to save her."

The officials explained there was too great a risk for rescuers to attempt a rescue from inside the collapsed building. I asked why a rescue couldn't be attempted from the outside even if that meant the structure might collapse. Better to try a rescue than give up. The rescue effort was back on and the rescuers were pleased to get the go-ahead from their team leaders.

As it turned out, the bodies of two women who had tragically lost their lives were recovered from the wreckage. No one was rescued alive. In his report of the public inquiry held into the mall collapse, Mr. Justice Paul Bélanger commented on the intervention I had made to restart the rescue after it had been prematurely concluded:

I find that Premier McGuinty's actions and those of his staff were appropriate, responsible, humanly genuine, and warranted in the circumstances....Their intervention led to a renewed sense of urgency and determination.... It also provided much-needed reassurance to the public and to the families that they had the whole-hearted support of senior officials in the provincial government. In short, it gave renewed hope.

I am very proud of the role my team played in lending whatever support we could to the people of Elliott Lake in their time of crisis, and I am especially grateful for the role played by the ever-diligent and thoughtful John O'Leary, the manager of legislative issues in my office.

———————

While crisis-management is still possible in a minority government, dealing with longer-term issues was proving to be much more difficult.

Legislative progress had come to a standstill at Queen's Park. Partisanship reigned supreme. Rancour was at an all-time high.

George Stamou, the long-time Queen's Park cameraman for CTV, told me, "I have been here for twenty-seven years and I have never seen it this bad."

The opposition parties had become drunk on the power they wielded over our minority government. Their abuse of their newly acquired power was never more apparent than in their malicious attack on Chris Bentley, waged through a spurious contempt motion, and the unseemly and reprehensible conduct of their gas plant committee. It will forever be mind-boggling to me to ponder how opposition parties that had committed themselves to putting a stop to gas plants and urged my government to do the same could concoct the phony outrage that powered their gas plant committee mischief for two years. Of course, all this theatre in which the Opposition was starring was welcomed by the media. It made for easy stories, spoon-fed with a daily dose of artificial fury and indignation.

———————

This change in atmosphere occurred at the same time as my daughter Carleen's wedding in the fall of 2012. Just as my heart had led me into politics, now it was telling me it was time to go. There are three ways to leave office: die; lose an election; or by choice. I picked the last of those. It was a time for renewal for me and my party.

Two things happened as soon as I had made the announcement of my retirement to caucus on October 15. First, I immediately triggered a leadership race and second, I had transformed myself into the proverbial lame duck leader, with no recognized mandate beyond that of caretaker. Maybe I was reading too much into things, but I thought people were already looking over my shoulder as I chatted with them after my announcement. I still held the office of premier, but my influence and authority had been instantly, and greatly, diminished. I understood and accepted this. This was in the natural order of things. This is how politics works. I knew our party would move quickly to host a leadership convention. I had already planted that seed with our party president, Yasir Naqvi, when we met earlier that day.

Given the unprecedented toxicity that had poisoned the workings of the legislature, I decided to prorogue. Predictably, the Opposition criticized my decision to prorogue as an affront to democracy. They insisted I was unduly curtailing legislative sittings. The truth is, in 2012 the Ontario legislature sat longer (seventy-eight days) than any other Canadian provincial or territorial legislature. In fact, the Ontario government sat longer than any other legislature in Canada during seven of the nine full years I served as premier.

The 1996 and 2013 Ontario Liberal leadership contests bear some interesting similarities and differences. The 2013 race would be a fast three months, so the House could quickly resume sittings. Mine (1996) lasted over a year. In both cases, the races were hotly contested, with seven candidates in the field. One thing was certain: the prize for the 2013 race was much bigger. The winner would be premier.

The candidates vying for this prize were: Kathleen Wynne, Sandra Pupatello, Gerard Kennedy, Harinder Takhar, Charles Sousa, Glen Murray, and Eric Hoskins. I was proud of the candidates, and pleased they had all had the opportunity to mature as aspiring leaders in my Cabinet.

I had been personally involved in the recruitment into our party of several of these fine people. Over the years I came to see my responsibility as leader as more than building a party that won while I was there. It also had to win after I was gone. That meant taking years to help develop a stable of well-qualified potential successors. And it meant handing over a party that was united, well funded, and built to win. While I knew my successor would face an Opposition that would be especially vindictive and acrimonious, I was confident I had done much to build a strong foundation for their success. Certainly, as I considered the state of our party and compared it to how it was in 1996 when I became leader — a party lacking in money, self-confidence, and the capacity to win; a party that bore no resemblance to the powerful political machine I was turning over to my successor — I felt very optimistic about our future. And on a personal note, believing as I did that we would win the next election, I was glad that my successor would not have to spend, as I had, seven years as Leader of the Opposition before becoming premier. Happily for Ontarians, my successor would have the advantage of years of experience in government.

While I did not express a preference and, indeed, stayed away from any involvement in the campaign, I could see that it would come down to a contest between Kathleen Wynne and Sandra Pupatello in the end, and I felt either would be a good choice. Both were capable, experienced, and determined, with proven leadership skills. On the political spectrum, Wynne was centre-left and Pupatello was centre-right. Wynne won over Pupatello on the third ballot, with the backing of Kennedy, Hoskins, Sousa, and Murray. After the leadership vote, I was determined to arrange a smooth exchange of power.

I met Premier-Elect Wynne early after her victory, welcomed her, and asked what I could do for her. I had always admired Kathleen because she is a person of conviction and integrity, as well as very competent and hard-working. Of all the ministers who sat at the Cabinet table with me, she was one of the best briefed, especially on measures that rubbed her the wrong way. She is philosophically to the left of me, but I always heard her out, and I was often influenced by her cogent arguments.

I can think of two occasions in particular where we saw things differently. Kathleen was decidedly uncomfortable with my handling of the teachers' negotiations leading up to a legislated pay freeze. She felt that, whatever the outcome, we needed a negotiated settlement. I wasn't prepared to settle for a pay hike, even a "net zero" pay hike, if it was paid out of savings generated by laying off young teachers or anything else that compromised education quality. We had given the teachers seven successive raises, but now, in the aftermath of a terrible recession that left us with a big deficit, we needed to temporarily freeze public-sector pay in a way that created savings without touching the classroom experience for students.

Kathleen disagreed also with my decision to put our sex-education reforms on hold. She felt we were caving to right-wing ideologues. I felt we were being prudent and believed it was necessary to get Ontario parents onside, especially since, from their perspective, our reforms had come out of nowhere. I was happy to later see Premier Wynne launch an extensive consultation with parents, taking a full two years before rightly moving ahead with these reforms.

To Kathleen's credit, she accepted the outcome whenever I disagreed with her. She was a team player. I had brought her into Cabinet to serve as education minister, a post she much enjoyed. But over the years I moved her around, assigning her to other portfolios, including transportation, municipal affairs, and Aboriginal affairs. The first move, to transportation, was a very deliberate one on my part. I wanted Kathleen to develop a feel for an economic portfolio. I felt I needed to round out her thinking. She had the social issues nailed down. They came to her naturally. I wanted to develop her economic side. Regardless of the responsibilities I assigned her, Kathleen shone. She quickly got on top of her files and developed a good working relationship with ministry staff and stakeholders. She was a model minister. She was also a role model for young women and, indeed, gay youth generally, who I feel certain are inspired by her resilience, courage, and success.

———————

I had hoped that, following an efficient and orderly transition process that included the choice of a new premier and the creation of a new Cabinet, the legislature could turn over a new leaf and the parties could strike a more conciliatory tone when sittings resumed. Again, I was sorely disappointed.

Sadly, the new premier was met with the same obduracy and intransigence with which the Opposition had confronted me. It became obvious a fresh start would require more than a leadership change. It would take an election. In the year leading up to the 2014 election, the Opposition made life for Kathleen Wynne and her minority Liberal government a living hell. Scant progress was made for Ontarians on the many issues needing attention as the Opposition luxuriated in an orgy of fabricated outrage.

It is said that every dog has its day. In the year prior to the election, the opposition parties had their day. But on election day, Ontarians had their say. And Ontarians won. By voting in the Wynne government, voters chose to refocus Queen's Park away from political games, back to policy gains. They said no to the tiresome antics and childish name-calling that had so characterized the two opposition parties and yes to a government and a leader pledged to build up Ontario by building up education, health care, and the economy. In the campaign, as in life, Wynne had stood tall as a model of civility and responsibility. Hudak and Horwath were mistaken in believing they could change their spots in the campaign. They had been revealed in opposition, where they had set an exceedingly low standard. Ontarians would not be fooled into thinking they had somehow been transformed. I know Opposition is a tough job. I was leader there for seven years. But I also know that if you can't evince some elements of statesmanship while in Opposition, you're not going to get the top job. People don't want a pit bull as the top dog.

Soon after the transition, I resigned my seat in the legislature and accepted a fellowship at Harvard University, where my father had studied earlier. Going back to school was something I had wanted to do for over thirty years.

When I had nearly completed my law studies in 1983, I came home one day and told Terri that I wanted to go to medical school. Terri's response was direct and unequivocal: "We have two kids. Get a job."

I countered with a request to go to the London School of Economics for a master's degree in law. "It's only one year," I pleaded.

"Get a job."

As usual, Terri was right. It was time for me to get on with my career. And as it turned out, my desire to go back to school was merely delayed, not denied.

Terri and I thoroughly enjoyed our later-in-life university experience at Harvard. We had no car, so we walked and used public transit. We lived in an apartment above an antique furniture store across from a pizzeria and next to a place that sold good beer. Apart from missing our kids, we were in heaven. For one thing, we were now enjoying university in a way we hadn't when we were young. Back then, we were in a rush and very serious about making something of ourselves. But now, we were at a different stage in our lives and happy to be in a place where we could slow down and reflect. We also very much enjoyed being anonymous for the first time in a long time. Being well known as a political leader means being "on" all the time. While I got used to that, it still took a lot of energy — a lot more than I had actually understood.

In addition to enjoying the academic environment, my time out of the country allowed me to go through the requisite withdrawal from politics. I came to understand that, as premier, I had become an adrenalin junkie. I had been running at one hundred miles per hour and had suddenly come to a dead stop. It was a shock. I stared into a huge, gaping hole that had been filled by my political responsibilities. The void in my life was like being in one of those flotation tanks used for sensory deprivation. For the first time in a long, long time, my mind wasn't consumed by the demands of a relentless agenda and public life. It was time to get to know myself again.

I began to think of what I might do next which led me to think of where my natural interests lay. Terri was her usual, patient self as she dealt with her middle-aged husband trying to find himself. When I told her I was interested in things like education, innovation, renewable energy, and global affairs, she said, "That's a government agenda!" I found I actually took comfort in Terri's astute observation. Not only was I fortunate to have served as premier, I had pursued an agenda in which I had truly believed.

I left Queen's Park and politics with a tremendous sense of accomplishment, but also with one chief regret. I had been unable to arrest the descent of politics in the legislature into extreme partisanship. Queen's Park is no exception in this unfortunate devolution. Our descent is characteristic of what is happening in so many vibrant democracies, including the United States and the United Kingdom.

Partisanship has its purpose. It can and should serve as the basis of a vital democracy, defined by an environment that engenders a vigorous competition of ideas. But when partisanship becomes an end unto itself, when it leads to a fundamental disrespect for the other side and their ideas, we have a problem. The truth is, the others are not always wrong and we are not always right. What's best for the people we serve is found in the collective wisdom of their representatives — all of them. Easy to say. Hard to do.

People sometimes ask me about the reasons behind my political achievements. There are only two: luck and hard work. The last one is easy to understand. The first one may be less obvious.

I was lucky to be born in Canada, a place where, if you work hard, you can achieve your potential. There are countless boys and girls around the world who will never enjoy my advantage.

I was lucky to be born into a loving and supportive family, to parents whose unconditional love and sacrifice for me and my brothers and sisters was nothing short of astonishing. It was my parents' example that taught me the joy of service and the responsibility I had to make a difference. It was my siblings who helped sustain me as we each sought to live up to that example.

I was lucky to meet Terri and fall hopelessly in love with her, and she with me. It is because of Terri that we so successfully navigated our demanding political voyage while completing our life's most important work — raising our four children, who inspire us every day, as does my grandson, Ellis.

I was lucky to be embraced by my political family, the Ontario Liberal Party. Anything good I have been able to do as leader of our party and premier of our province, I have done while standing on the shoulders of Liberal caucus and party members.

I was lucky to be blessed with political staff whose devotion to me, our cause, and to the people of Ontario I can never repay.

I was lucky to have the support of so many Ontarians, especially in my hometown of Ottawa, who, through the years, guided and encouraged me in my work.

The other question people sometimes ask me is: Why? Why did you go into politics? The simple answer is I wanted to make a difference. I think we all do. I think we all want to do something meaningful for our family, our friends, our community, our world. There are so many ways we can make our contribution. I chose politics. And I encourage others of whatever political stripe to do the same.

To all those who were part of my adventure, I say thank you. Because of you, I served as premier of Ontario, the greatest province in the best country in the world.

EPILOGUE
Lessons in Leadership

On many occasions, people, young people especially, have asked me for advice about politics. If I have one political mission left in life, it is to encourage young people from all backgrounds and whatever political leanings to consider making a difference through politics. Indeed, I believe that any society that fails to harness the energy and idealism of its youth does itself a tremendous disservice.

It only makes sense for me to begin by answering the question: Why should you get involved in politics? Why should you choose to set foot in the arena and give up the comfort, convenience, and anonymity of the stands? Life has always been challenging for those who choose the political arena, but it has been made even more so today. We live in an age of heightened transparency and accountability, something that tests our public representatives but, by and large, serves the public interest. Much more ominously, politics today is frequently characterized by a self-destructive partisanship in which our elected representatives, aided and abetted by new and old media who welcome misbehaviour, devote themselves to attacking each other at the expense of the public interest.

While the downsides of politics are surely there, my own experience has taught me these are more than outweighed by the upsides. For me, politics remains a noble calling. It is a richly rewarding endeavour, giving us the opportunity to make a positive difference.

Despite an all-too-easy cynicism professed by many, I believe we all long to make a difference. We all want to look beyond our own immediate wants to the needs of others. We want to build something on the strong foundation we have inherited, something enduring, something that flows from our deep understanding that we are all in this together, that we touch one another, and that it is right for us to help each other. Politics is a great preserve for those kinds of builders — builders who first began their work in a democracy in ancient Greece. Pericles's observation regarding the basis for the superiority of the Athenian state is as relevant today as it was when he made it two and a half millennia ago: "We do not allow absorption in our own affairs to interfere with participation in the city's. We differ from other states in regarding [persons] who hold aloof from public life as useless."

In my maiden speech in the Ontario legislature in 1990, I said there can be no doubt that politics has its problems, but these are problems inherent in the players, not in the play. Or, as Immanuel Kant put it: "Out of the crooked timber of humanity, no straight thing was ever made." Politics is a very human enterprise with ample opportunity for us to express both our noble strengths and our contemptible weaknesses. Every one of us comes up short. But what counts is the struggle. What counts are the ideals that inspire our efforts, and the integrity of those efforts.

Getting involved in politics is one thing; knowing how to govern yourself as a political leader in your community is another. With this chapter, I hope to provide you with a compass to help inform your leadership and guide your actions. When I go on canoe trips with my sons, we always take a compass with us so we can be sure we are headed in the right direction. From time to time, in the face of obstacles — a portage route that has become impenetrable, or rapids that are too dangerous — we may have to find an alternate path, a path that allows us to move forward even if it also takes us off course. We use the compass to get back on course. Having a compass doesn't guarantee that we will always be headed in the right direction, but it does guarantee that we will know the difference between the right and the wrong one. So it is with leaders. We need to have a compass, a set of guiding principles, to which we can refer. That way, we know whether we are still on course and, if we have wandered off course, how to correct ourselves.

My observation, study, and practice have led me to develop my own leadership compass. My best teacher has been experience, and as I have described in this book, I have on many occasions wandered off course. With the hope that they might be of interest and, better still, of real value to aspiring leaders at the starting line of careers in politics and public service, I offer the following ten lessons in leadership I learned along the way.

ONE: Leadership is about service

Leaders seek to serve. Leadership is not about exalting ourselves. It's about lifting others up. It's not about us. It's about others. It's about those we serve. In caucus, I would regularly remind my team, "We're here for them. It's about their schools, their health care, their jobs, their environment, their future, their hopes, their dreams."

Leaders understand that the reward of service is found in service itself. The great Indian writer and philosopher Rabindranath Tagore put it this way: "I slept and dreamt that life was joy. I awoke and saw that life was service. I acted, and behold, service was joy."

Growing up as the oldest boy in a big family was good training for me in the practice of service to others. Getting into politics allowed me to keep asking that all-important question: How can I help?

TWO: Leaders have a vision

Leaders see beyond the here and now to the *what could be*. We have a clear vision of what we want to do and where we need to go. We can see it in our mind's eye. Inspired by our vision, we are not consumed by today at the expense of tomorrow.

Think of old wooden sailing ships. The leader's place is not below deck, ignorant of the conditions in which we are sailing. Neither is our place on the lower deck of the ship, where we can see no further than the next big wave. Leaders are on the upper deck, studying the major currents and tides affecting our people, developing a solid understanding of where the world is going today, and charting a course that will assure our people's success tomorrow. As leaders, we make sure we can see the big picture in order to make informed decisions that lead to the realization of our vision.

As leaders we take risks to achieve our vision, and when it is not reckless to do so, we will place the public interest ahead of our political interest. My wisest advisors warned me that adopting the HST would be fatal to my political career. I moved forward with this initiative because I believed it was in the best interests of Ontarians.

Of course, our vision need not be developed by us alone. It can be developed by a group of people working together. It need not spring from the mind of any one individual. A collective vision is a powerful thing. But, in the end, a specific leadership is needed to drive change.

THREE: Leaders are persuasive

It takes more than a vision to lead. As leaders, we need people to join us in the realization of our vision. We need to persuade them. And the best way for us to do that is to make our causes the causes of our followers. The art of leadership involves getting people to move from point A to point B, not by using our authority and requiring people to do so, but by inviting them to do so and making the journey a journey of their choosing.

My decision to shut down the coal plants is a good example. While there was initially no widespread demand for my government to shut down any coal plants, as Ontarians became aware of my commitment, it accorded with their expectations. They understood our coal plants were spewing pollution and contributing to climate change, and they expected me to find cleaner alternatives for their energy supply.

To be persuasive, a leader must be a good communicator, but, in my opinion, the best communicators are simply the most authentic. I discovered that the very best kind of communications training I received just encouraged me to be myself. I also learned that persuading people involves more than getting them to believe you, it involves getting them to believe *in* you.

And we can make that happen only if we are persons of integrity. It takes a long time for people to develop confidence in our integrity, so we must jealously guard it. It can be lost in an instant through an action that greatly offends people of goodwill.

It is only the estimation of the people that is important. Leaders don't worry about the standards applied to us by the rabidly partisan or by extremists. We can never live up to their standards … nor should we try.

FOUR: Leaders are incomplete and they know it

As leaders, we need to have the good sense and the humility to acknowledge our shortcomings. The idea of an all-seeing, all-knowing leader is a myth. And if we try to live up to that myth, we will exhaust ourselves and render a great disservice to those we serve. This means we need to work hard to fill in our personal gaps, and we can do so in a number of ways.

For one thing, leaders must be diligent students. We can never stop learning, and that includes learning from our mistakes. Leaders actively seek new information and advice from a broad network of people we can rely on to be honest. As leaders, we must weigh all advice carefully, and we must not substitute our advisors' judgment for our own. We can't delegate our leadership to our advisors, whoever they might be. Advisors enjoy the luxury of moving on to new advice. Leaders are stuck with the decision!

Having said that, it is crucial that we have a team that will make us stronger as a leader. We must fill in the gaps in our skills and knowledge by surrounding ourselves with people who have strengths that complement our weaknesses. It's important that we are aware of our weaknesses. If I kept getting the same criticism over and over again from my own team and I didn't agree with that criticism, I learned that it didn't matter what I thought. How I was perceived was what was important, and I needed to take action to strengthen my leadership.

Leaders can't be insecure about having smart, capable people around them. When I did feel insecure, it was for the opposite reason: I was trying to grapple with a big challenge on my own. I felt a whole lot better framing problems and developing solutions in concert with my team, which included my caucus and staff. The moral of the story is a simple one: the stronger your team, the stronger your leadership. It was this thinking that led me to bring my leadership competitors into my Cabinet. Their strengths were different from mine and my job was to turn those strengths to the advantage of Ontarians.

As leaders, it is also vitally important that we take time to reflect. It has been said that we live in a time when we are drowning in information and thirsting for wisdom. Well, our job as leaders is to struggle to be wise. And we cannot achieve anything approaching wisdom unless we take time to reflect. Among other things, this means we mustn't allow our connectivity to steal our thinking time. I banned smart phones from our Cabinet meetings because I wanted us to be better able to think.

FIVE: Leaders take the high road

As leaders, we must always try to take the high road and represent people at their best. The truth is that we human beings can be small. We can be selfish, shallow, short-sighted, and mean-spirited. But at our best, we are kind, caring, thoughtful, determined, resourceful, resilient, courageous, and wise. In short, at our best, we are not small. We are bigger than ourselves. Our responsibility as principled leaders is to appeal to the better angels of human nature.

Living up to this responsibility can be challenging. It is easy to get caught up in a negative moment. During my early days as Leader of the Opposition, egged on by my caucus colleagues and eager to get on TV, I was sometimes over the top or personal in my attacks during Question Period. I later learned not to allow the roar of the crowd to drown out the quiet voice of my conscience. Over time, my understanding of human nature and its higher aspirations would grow, making me ever more determined to stay on the high road. In the words of former Canadian governor general Sir John Buchan, "The task of leadership is not to put greatness into humanity, but to elicit it, because the greatness is already there."

SIX: Leaders value their character more than their reputation

Our reputation is who people think we are. Our character is who we truly are. As principled leaders we want a good reputation but understand that a good character is more important.

As leaders intent on driving change, we need to understand a basic fact of politics: when we make tough decisions on issues where the people are divided, our reputation *will* suffer. Some *will* think less of us. And I'm not just talking about our opponents — they will be against us from the beginning of our leadership. If you do something you believe to be right but another believes is wrong, your reputation will suffer in the eyes of that other. My government's initiatives to reduce smoking among Ontario youth, which I thought would be universally supported, raised the ire of many in the tobacco-farming community as well as those who operate convenience stores. I lost those votes doing something I believed was right.

What's more, people will also judge their leaders based on misinformation or disinformation. I was regularly criticized for things I never planned to do or never did. I was also attacked for things that would never happen — a favourite of mine being the attacks I received for my "big fat government pension." Ontario MPPs do not receive a pension.

As leaders, we have no control over the number or nature of such groundless attacks, and it would be an abdication of our leadership to become unduly preoccupied with our reputation. If we make preserving our reputation our highest priority, we will then have no choice but to run away from tough issues. And that's a failure of leadership. In short, even if we are leaders of impeccable character, we will suffer a loss of reputation in the eyes of some. This is the price of leadership.

And we can't feel sorry for ourselves. We freely decided to step into the arena, surrounded by an audience of critics. It would have been more comfortable, of course, to remain a member of the audience, but we chose a leading role. And with that privilege come the knocks against our reputation. We need to accept this reality and get on with our leadership.

I tried to take a poll every night. I stood in front of the mirror and asked myself if I was doing what I thought was right. Not easy. Not expedient.

But *right*. Right for Ontarians. If we do what we honestly believe to be right, we protect our character. And in the end, our character is more important than our reputation. My decisions to raise taxes in 2004, to adopt the HST in 2010, and to intervene to relocate two badly located gas plants are good examples here. In each case, I did what I knew to be right.

Unpopular decisions are not necessarily fatal to our leadership. I discovered that when I did unpopular things, so long as I was motivated by principle and I took the time to communicate my reasons, I could go a long way to rebuilding my popularity. People respect decisions of conviction more than those of convenience.

SEVEN: Leaders compromise

Compromise is not a dirty word for principled leaders. As leaders, we often compromise in order to get closer to our goals. We do this to make progress. We should never compromise our principles and our values. We should never compromise our integrity and our character. But we should compromise when it serves the interests of those we serve. We should accept half a loaf instead of no loaf. We should go slower, or not as far, if the alternative is to make no progress at all. Leaders seek progress, not perfection.

Sailors know it's just not possible to sail straight into the wind. Progress requires sometimes tacking to the left and at other times to the right. Most every initiative I pursued in government, whether it was a budget, a bill, or a regulation of some kind, was the subject of compromise. And not infrequently, compromise led to better public policy.

Just as leaders shouldn't avoid compromise when it serves the public interest, neither should we be afraid to change our mind when it is called for. Yes, our opponents will accuse us of flip-flopping, a charge the media will happily parrot, but our responsibility is to remain true to ourselves. If we honestly believe that changing our mind would better serve the interests of those we serve, then we owe it to them to do so. Better to admit we were wrong than to pursue the wrong policy. Circumstances can change. When I discovered the former PC government had hidden a $6 billion deficit, it was no longer possible for me to honour my commitments to both hold the line on taxes and invest in smaller classes and shorter wait times. I chose to raise taxes.

At other times, it won't be circumstances that will have changed. It will be us. Hopefully, over the course of our leadership, we will grow in wisdom and perhaps see things differently than we did originally. My position regarding gay rights changed dramatically as I grew in my leadership. Better to be right than consistent. Be mindful of Emerson's dictum: "A foolish consistency is the hobgoblin of little minds."

EIGHT: Leaders lead!

This should be an obvious point, but sometimes, for some leaders, it isn't. For me, leadership isn't about passively presiding over the evolution of events. It's about leading change.

The fundamental responsibility of leaders is to lead. It is to decide. To choose. After we have been informed of the facts, listened to advice and wrestled with our choices, being sure to be true to ourselves and placing the interests of those we serve ahead of all others, we *must* lead. We *must* choose a path.

I hated indecision so, as a rule, I was eager to decide. My decision-making motto was: "Nos" are good. "Yeses" are better. "Maybes" will kill us. So I tried to avoid "maybes." Being stuck in maybe mode is unfair to everyone who is waiting on a decision. Better to decide and move on.

This isn't a call for rushed decisions. It is important for leaders and their team to be as comfortable as they can be with a decision. But don't expect absolute comfort once we have made a difficult choice. If a choice is really difficult, it almost certainly is true that there was some merit in making an alternative choice. In an ideal world, we would not have to choose. But we live in the real world. So we must make our choice and work hard to communicate our reasons.

Too many leaders wrestle in earnest with a difficult decision, forgetting that the people affected by our decision may be oblivious to the careful consideration we have given the matter. We will have to put at least as much and probably more effort into communicating the reasons for our decisions than we put into making the decisions.

If a choice is difficult, it is certain that some people will be unhappy with that choice. From time to time, we will have to spend some of our popularity. That's the way it is. To hoard our popularity is to follow. Our job is to lead. Being true to myself and what I believed was right for Ontarians led me to make a number of decisions that gave rise to significant opposition, including my decisions related to pursuing renewable energy and wind turbines, freezing teachers' pay, reducing generic drug costs, et cetera. Robert Kennedy said that a life without criticism is not worth living. A principled leader committed to change can count on leading a very full life!

NINE: Leaders are idealists

Leadership demands much from us as leaders. We need to be aware of those demands and the impact they will have on us. Left unchecked, they can make for an exhausting and demoralizing leadership experience. Expectations will be high, criticisms plentiful, and the choices before us often painful. Leadership can be lonely. Sure, there are lots of people working closely with us but if we take our job seriously, no one feels the weight of responsibility more than the leader. More than anything else, it is this weight that isolates us from the rest of our team. What's more, our work environment and politics can oftentimes be corrosive. They can wear us down. Our antidote to this toxicity, the life-sustaining oxygen for our leadership, must be our idealism. Idealism is not optional for a leader. A leader without idealism is vulnerable to cynicism. And nobody wants to be led by a cynic.

Leaders never give in to cynicism. We can never allow the corrosive effects of our work environment or life's inevitable disappointments to rob us of our guiding belief that, working together, we can not only do good things, we can do great things. Young leaders especially should be mindful of Tennyson's note of caution:

> What should I be at fifty
> Should nature keep me alive,
> If I find the world so bitter
> When I am but twenty-five?

As leaders, we must reject cynicism and arm ourselves with a rich and sustaining idealism. Leaders who have lost their idealism have lost their right to lead. Of course, idealism is no substitute for a pragmatic plan for progress, but in the tough world of leadership, idealism is an indispensable, shining beacon that draws us forward and illuminates our way.

TEN: Leaders know when to leave

One of the most difficult decisions a leader must make is deciding when to leave. Many of the forces that act on us would have us stay on in our leadership indefinitely. After all, to leave would be disruptive to our team and to the broad network of people and institutions that have grown comfortable or at least familiar with our leadership. Giving up the reins is also very disruptive to our personal lives, which, notwithstanding the demands of our responsibilities, have grown comfortable with the routine and privilege of our leadership. And then there are the more personal questions that haunt us when we consider stepping down: Is anybody good enough to replace me? Will my successor champion my policies and defend my legacy? What will I do with myself? Who will I be if I am no longer the leader? How will people see me? How will I see myself? (This last one is, as I learned, surprisingly perplexing. During my many years as leader of the government, I told myself being premier was just a job — an important job, but just a job nonetheless. But when I left the job I discovered I had wrapped up much of my identity in that job, making it hard to, as Terri would say, "go normal.")

There are always reasons to hang on to our leadership forever, but to do so would be to betray our responsibility to leave at the right time. There are no hard and fast rules telling us when the right time is, but here are a few questions, which, if answered in the affirmative, should tip the scales in favour of our departure: Have we ensured that our political organization (our riding association or party) is well funded and competitive? Have we made it attractive for strong potential candidates to enter the race to succeed us? Have we laid a foundation of political achievement upon which our successor could reasonably build and win an election? Do we believe a change in leadership is in the interests of our political organization and the people we serve in office? And, on a more personal level, do we feel we have completed the work we set out to do?

I was able to answer yes to all of the questions. This led me to conclude it was time for leadership renewal in my circumstances.

People will comment on our decision to leave. Some will say we left too early. Others will say we left too late. Many won't even notice. My son Liam was at the gym when the televisions there reported on my decision to step down as premier. He overheard a brief conversation between two men.

"Hey, McGuinty is resigning!"

"Who?"

"McGuinty."

"Resigning from what?"

This was a good reminder for me that the true reward of leadership is not to be found in the recognition of our efforts but in the service we give and the satisfaction that comes from knowing we gave our best.

If I had to sum up in one word how I felt about all my years in politics, that word would be "grateful." I will forever be grateful for the opportunity I had to serve and make a difference.

After seventeen years as leader of my party, I was leaving behind a political organization that had grown into a powerful, well-funded and experienced champion that had learned how to win. I took great pride in leading my party to three successive victories, just as I did in having personally helped groom a strong stable of potential successors, with all of the eventual leadership candidates having served in my Cabinet.

After nearly ten years as premier, I was leaving behind a record of real achievement in areas of great importance to me. Ontario education was stronger than ever, with our schools ranked among the top five in the world. Families were getting better, faster health care, with the shortest wait times in Canada. Shutting down our coal plants cleaned up our air, preserving massive green space had enhanced our quality of life, and launching Ontario on an exciting renewable energy trajectory created tens of thousands of jobs while readying us for success in a carbon-constrained world. Working together with Ontarians, our government laid a strong foundation for continuing growth and prosperity — we invested unprecedented billions in infrastructure, dramatically reduced business taxes, adopted the HST, and supported our auto sector specifically and innovation generally, all while fighting off a terrible recession. Subsequent to the recession, I made difficult decisions to constrain our costs and set us on a path to balancing our budget, as we had been doing before the recession struck.

Looking back on my time in politics, I am proud to say I was part of that grand human endeavour that brings people together to build on the rich foundation we inherited. I was able to make a difference and nothing could be more rewarding. My wish for you and your leadership is that you, too, make a difference and experience the joy of service.

SAYING GOODBYE

I have described the events of the evening of my resignation, but something else, something very memorable for me, occurred after the formal part of the day was done. After my announcement to caucus, I made my way back to my office to discover it was filled with staff members — active and former — who had quickly gathered when they heard the news. No one had asked them to come. They just showed up on their own.

Gathered among the dozens there were my former chiefs of staff, Don Guy, Peter Wilkinson, and Chris Morley, my former press secretary, the warm-hearted Jane Almeida, and her husband and tour whiz, John Zerucelli (a.k.a. Johnny Zee) — the two had met at Queen's Park. Also present were Gerald Butts, Jamison Steeve, and John Brodhead — brilliant policy wonks all — as well as the passionate and incredibly hard-working Laura Miller. Matt Maychak, my savvy former head of communications, and Lloyd Rang, my talented former lead speech writer were present and trading zingers. Also joining in the celebration were current staff David Livingston, Wendy McCann, Chike Agbasi, Jennifer Beckermann, Paul Lehmann, Patricia Favre, and Neala Barton. Tracey Sobers and Beckie Codd-Downey who, happily for me, exercised executive authority over the premier's office and me, were beaming to see so many of our friends appear spontaneously. From somewhere the always resourceful Dave Gene, the best grassroots organizer I ever met, produced a bottle of Scotch.

As I looked around the room, it struck me that this, too, was a family. And that they were united not only in their support for me, but in their respect and caring for each other. In my time as premier, I was fortunate to have had the support of some of the best political minds in Canada — and they also happened to be wonderful people. I won't forget them.

ACKNOWLEDGEMENTS

Writing a book was a new journey for me and I could never have arrived at my intended destination without the help, encouragement, and inspiration of some very special people. I am especially grateful to Ian Urquhart for getting me started. He interviewed me over the course of many days and created the foundation upon which I then built my story. I must also acknowledge the diligent work of my reviewers, Lloyd Rang, Tracey Sobers, Carleen McGuinty, Connor McGuinty, and the editorial staff at Dundurn, particularly Dominic Farrell. Jenna Muirhead, Dave Bailey, and Ross Lamont kindly helped me locate and organize the many, many photos I use in this book.

I thank the McGuinty family — my mother and all my brothers and sisters and their families — for being so supportive over the many years I was in politics working to make a difference. My story is our story. In particular, I thank my mother, Elizabeth McGuinty; my sister Joyce Page and her children, James, Annalise, and Matthew; my sister Liseanne and her husband, Don McKee, and their children, Michael, Thomas, and Daniel; my brother Dylan and his wife, Maria, and their children, Caroline, Matthew, Nikki, and Patrick; my brother Patrick and his wife, Cathy, and their children, Gordon, Julia, and Duncan; my brother David and his wife, Brigitte Bélanger, and their children, Stéphanie, Eamonn, Joseph, and Fiona; my brother Michael and his wife, Maria Angeles, and their children, Gabriela and Claudia; my sister Anne-Marie and her husband, Michael Schreider, and their children, James and Elizabeth; my brother Brendan and his wife, Catherine James McGuinty, and their children, Mairin, Ellen, and Bobby; and my sister Noralyn and her partner, Janet Hall.

My political family, the Ontario Liberal family, also deserves my sincere thanks. To all those on whose shoulders I have stood in the caucus and in the party, thank you for your support and your dedication to our cause. You continue to inspire me.

To the people of Ottawa South who shaped my youth and made a home for my own family, and who made it possible for me to serve all Ontarians as their premier, thank you.

To Ontario's dedicated public service, who was there before I came and will be there long after, thank you for your hard work and commitment to our great province and the people who live here.

To all those everywhere who are committed to the noble enterprise of politics and seek to make a difference for those they serve, thank you. You are building a better world.

I am profoundly grateful for the assistance and friendship of Tracey Sobers who, more than anyone else, helped me complete this book.

Finally, I wish to thank Terri and our children and their families for their love, support, patience, and guidance as I gave myself to my political calling and then to the task of writing and rewriting our story. I am forever grateful to Carleen, Eric Mysak, and their son, Ellis; Dalton Jr. and Joanne Ghiz; Liam and Erin Hall; and Connor and Bianca Ricci. I apologize to baby Ellis for spending more time on this book and less time doting on him than a grandfather should.

PHOTO CREDITS

---

10. Office of the Premier (top); Jenna Muirhead (bottom)
11. Office of the Premier
12. Jenna Muirhead
13. Jenna Muirhead
14. Jenna Muirhead (top); Personal collecion (bottom)
15. Ontario Liberal Party (top); Jenna Muirhead (bottom)
16. Jenna Muirhead

INSERT 3
Page

1. Jenna Muirhead
2. Jenna Muirhead
3. Jenna Muirhead (top); Bruno Schlumberger/*Ottawa Citizen*. Reprinted by permission. (bottom)
4. Jenna Muirhead (top); Office of the Premier (bottom)
5. Personal collection (top); Jenna Muirhead (bottom)
6. Jenna Muirhead
7. Jenna Muirhead
8. McGuinty family collection (top); Jenna Muirhead (bottom)
9. Jenna Muirhead (top); McGuinty family collection
10. Jenna Muirhead
11. Jenna Muirhead
12. Jenna Muirhead
13. Jenna Muirhead
14. Jenna Muirhead
15. Rob Ferguson (top); Jenna Muirhead (bottom)
16. Jenna Muirhead
17. Jenna Muirhead
18. Office of the Premier
19. Office of the Premier
20. Office of the Premier
21. Office of the Premier (top); David Chan, Ontario Liberal Party (bottom)
22. McGuinty family collection
23. Andrew Geddes
24. McGuinty family collection

INDEX